# Murder in Mayberry

## Greed, Death and Mayhem in a Small Town

**NEW**
**HORIZON**
**PRESS**

Dear Reader,

We proudly present the newest addition to our internationally acclaimed true crime series of *Real People/Incredible Stories*. These riveting thrillers spotlight men and women who perform extraordinary deeds against tremendous odds: to fight for justice, track down elusive killers, protect the innocent or exonerate the wrongly accused. Their stories, told in their own voices, reveal the untold drama and anguish behind the headlines of those who face horrific realities and find the resiliency to fight back...

In *Murder in Mayberry: Greed, Death and Mayhem in a Small Town*, federal agent Jack Branson has never worked a murder investigation – until his multimillionaire aunt is found bludgeoned to death in a small Kentucky town where everyone knows everyone. With no witnesses, no DNA and few clues, the list of suspects continues to grow. Will Jack find out the identity of the killer before this shocking crime turns into a cold case?

The next time you want to read a crackling, suspenseful page-turner, which is also a true account of a real-life hero illustrating the resiliency of the human spirit – look for the New Horizon Press logo.

Sincerely,

Dr. Joan S. Dunphy
Publisher & Editor-in-Chief


*Real People/Incredible Stories*

# Murder in Mayberry

## Greed, Death and Mayhem in a Small Town

By Mary Kinney Branson
and Jack Branson,
Special Agent, U.S. Dept. of the Treasury (Ret.)

New Horizon Press
Far Hills, NJ

New Horizon Press
P.O. Box 669
Far Hills, NJ 07931
Kinney Branson, Mary and Branson, Jack
Murder in Mayberry: *Greed, Death and Mayhem in a Small Town*

Cover design: Wendy Bass
Interior Design: Susan Sanderson

Library of Congress Control Number: 2007936335
ISBN 13: 978-0-88282-325-6
ISBN 10: 0-88282-325-6

New Horizon Press books may be purchased in bulk quantities for
educational, business or sales promotional use.
For more information please write to:
New Horizon Press
Special Sales Department
PO Box 669
Far Hills, NJ 07931
1-800-533-7978
Email: nhp@newhorizonpressbooks.com

www.newhorizonpressbooks.com
Manufactured in the USA

2012  2011  2010  2009  2008  /  5  4  3  2  1

# Dedication

To Jack—

You were Ann's constant voice during the four-and-a-half-year ordeal to bring her killer to justice.

You made that justice possible by your relentless dedication to the truth, regardless of the cost to you personally.

No son could have done more.

# Author's Note

This book is based on the experiences of the authors and reflects their perception of the past, present and future. The personalities, events, actions and conversations portrayed within this story have been taken from interviews, research, court documents, letters, personal papers, press accounts and the memories of some participants.

In an effort to safeguard the privacy of certain people, some individuals' names and identifying characteristics have been changed. Events involving the characters happened as described. Only minor details may have been altered.

# Table of Contents

# Introduction

Note to self: Never die mysteriously in a small town.

Many murders go unsolved. Both large and small cities often lack sufficient staff for lengthy investigations. But in addition to work overload, small towns can face inexperience and insecurity.

Small-town officers spend their days serving as crossing guards for elementary schools and ticketing drivers with expired tags. The only dead bodies most encounter are traffic accident victims and old people who died in their sleep. Small-town police are well-trained in what they do everyday. Yet because of understaffing and strained budgets, they're seldom taught to handle complicated murder investigations. Police chiefs must play the odds, hoping their officers won't need the extra training.

When such inexperienced officers come upon a murder scene where the victim is a prominent multimillionaire with massive blows to the head and nearly one hundred stab wounds, they're in unfamiliar territory. But their desire to be the ones to apprehend the killer can keep them from seeking help from those more experienced. And when state and national agencies are forced to step in, small-town law enforcement sometimes shows its insecurity.

Add all these dynamics and you may have a crime scene waiting to be swept under a small-town rug.

That's the beginning of this story.

Add that the crime took place in the Bible belt, where church involvement is a way-of-life—even for killers.

Add that those closest to the victim are honest believers who respond to the tragedy in often unique ways.

Add international extradition struggles.

Add family secrets, lies lived and told to neighbors, addiction and greed.

Add that one of the people closest to the victim is a federal agent and you have a true crime story with an unusual perspective, accurate inside details and emotional insights not usually available.

*Murder in Mayberry* is not a clinically researched crime story. It's the emotional journey of my family, as we moved from normal to changed forever.

I've shared Ann's story as honestly as I know how. And I realize that in doing so, I've broken many of the ties to the small town where I grew up, where I married my high school sweetheart and where our children attended public schools.

For many years, the newspaper in the town where Ann died included a quote from Lord Byron as part of its masthead: "With, or without offence to friends and foes, I sketch your world exactly as it goes." That's the honesty with which I've tried to write.

To understand it all, you need the entire story. Impressions, perspectives, exact quotes, real actions and reactions. The lovely and the not-so-lovely. What I've written is my reality of Ann's murder.

Ann deserves an accurate account of the motives, investigation and greed that surrounded her murder. By telling her story accurately, I feel that I've brought dignity to her death.

*Mary Kinney Branson*

# Prologue

Ann Branson grew up in Madisonville, Kentucky. Her daddy was the well-to-do owner of one of the local coal mines. She fell in love with a poor farm boy named Carroll Branson, and they were married. They were dirt poor during their early years, but they worked shoulder-to-shoulder and eventually became multimillionaires.

They made their fortune in, of all things, a Dairy Queen. It was one of the first chain restaurants in the little town and year after year, generation after generation, it was the teenage hang-out.

Ann was an icon in Madisonville. "Prominent businesswoman" was how the newspapers described her.

Ann and Carroll had no children. But eight years after their marriage, Carroll's brother married Ann's sister. This couple's only child, a tow-headed blue-eyed boy, became the focus of Ann's maternal instincts. He was like her own son and she was like a second mother to him. That boy was Jack, my husband.

Jack and I grew up in Madisonville, too. We were high school sweethearts and as soon as we were old enough, we married. I knew of Ann before I knew Jack. Everyone knew Ann, Carroll and the Dairy Queen. For all of us growing up in the small western Kentucky town, the greatest amusement on Saturday night was "circling the Queen" to wave at friends and maybe pull in and give a carhop your order for a cone.

Growing up in the midst of small-town Americana, Jack and I had goals and borders that reflected our surroundings. When a high school newspaper reporter asked senior Jack his long-range plans, he reached for the hand of his steady girl and replied, "To own the Dairy Queen and raise little Dillies." It was my hand he was holding.

But Jack and I soon dreamed dreams that couldn't come true in Madisonville. His career as a federal agent caused us to move several times, each time to a larger city. And eventually, Ann and Carroll retired, selling the Dairy Queen and erasing the Branson DQ icon for future generations.

Carroll spent most of his retirement creating intense and moving works of art that you'd never imagine coming from the hands of the once farm boy. Ann had more difficulty weaning herself away from business. She occupied herself buying, fixing up and renting a good chunk of Madisonville's real estate. She busied herself further with church work, bridge clubs and an occasional cruise.

In 1994, Carroll died of cancer and Ann became a rich widow. She was still the envy of most women in the town. She possessed that combination of qualities most of us long for. She was rich, successful, smart and beautiful.

Ann had a closet full of furs and no less than twelve carats of diamonds in the rings she wore with her everyday wardrobe. She lived alone in a stately 1923 Dutch Colonial home, where every piece of antique furniture and every accessory was unique and carefully chosen.

She eventually tired of the old home and the antiques and was planning to build a new home in an exclusive area, on a lot overlooking a lake. She'd purchased the lot but builders had not yet broken ground.

Ann certainly had not given up on life or the future. She now was engaged to an eye surgeon, but she wasn't sure she was ready to settle down, at least not yet. He was working diligently to persuade her to marry him, but she had decided to wait until her younger sister, Grace, died.

Grace had been diagnosed with small cell lung cancer—oat-cell carcinoma—more than two years earlier. It had spread quickly, and she had long ago outlived her doctor's expectations. Ann figured she had less than a year left. She alternated Grace's care with other relatives, but as the oldest of five siblings, she felt the strongest responsibility for her unmarried sister.

Ann would have been beautiful without the furs and jewels. Heads turned when she entered a room, admiring her slim body, chiseled face and graceful demeanor. She dressed tastefully but flamboyantly. She had a certain presence that no money could buy, though if there'd been a price tag attached, she could have paid it.

Ann was a bridesmaid at our daughter's wedding. Penny decided she wanted only family members in the wedding party—people who still would be dear to her years later—and I was privileged to be both matron of honor and mother of the bride. Penny's three "grandmothers" were her attendants—my mom, Jack's mom and Ann.

She loved being in the wedding, from the pedicures that resulted in periwinkle-hued toenails to the bridesmaids' luncheon at a quaint German restaurant. In the photo of her walking down the aisle, Ann's face is animated, her eyes are sparkling and the smile inching across her face looks just seconds away from a joyful laugh. All eyes were on her that day (something she was comfortably acquainted with) and she loved it.

Ten months after the wedding, Ann was murdered.

A few weeks before the murder, Ann spent Christmas with us, as she had done each year since Carroll's death. She and her sister Iva Ray—Jack's mother—drove from Kentucky to Georgia in Ann's crimson pearl Cadillac Seville. We stayed up late playing Rook, laughing and good-naturedly accusing each other of cheating.

"You Winstead sisters can't be trusted," joked Jack to Ann, referring as he often did to the sisters' maiden name. "Before you know it, we'll see your picture plastered all over television."

Before we knew it, we did.

The last time I saw Ann alive was the day after Christmas. She was wearing one of the gifts we gave her the day before, a black cape with a leopard skin collar. I often thought, *I hope I look that good when I get to be her age.* Then I'd remind myself: *Too late. I don't look that good now, and I'm decades younger.*

Jack walked to the car with Ann and his mom, carrying their luggage.

"Thanks for the Christmas money," Jack told Ann.

"I'm sorry it wasn't more," Ann replied. "Next year, it will be."

Jack remembered that being an unusual comment. Ann strapped for money? Not likely.

I stood at the door with our grandson, Taylor, and waved good-bye.

"Good-bye, Winstead sisters," called ten-year-old Taylor. Ann pulled her head from the car's trunk, smiled and waved. Her chestnut hair was perfectly styled, her makeup flawless, her smiling face framed in leopard skin.

# Part 1

# Ann's Murder

# Chapter 1

# Blood Ties

Saturday, January 11, 2003. I packed for a short trip to Alabama the next day. Jack phoned his mother, then Ann. Ever since Ann was widowed nine years earlier, Jack had made it a habit to call her once a week.

Jack came into the bedroom as I finished packing.

"Did your mom have anything to say?" I asked.

"No, not really," Jack said matter-of-factly. "Her leukemia's flared up again. She said it's not serious, but I can't help worrying about her."

I nodded. "What about Anna Mae?" Only close family called Ann by her full name. In fact, Jack and I were about the last hold-outs.

"No big news." Jack paused, then added, "I told her she needs to kick that crazy renter out."

"He's still bothering her?"

"Yeah. He calls her in the middle of the night, begging her to come over and chase the ghosts out of his attic. She said she's not afraid of him, but he makes her uneasy. I told her to have Earl evict him if she didn't want to."

Earl was Ann's younger brother. All five siblings lived within a few miles of each other—two brothers and three sisters. Earl was a widower with grown children, so he was the self-appointed protector who repaired broken locks, helped the sisters find a good plumber and chased away scary renters.

"Anything else?" I asked Jack.

Jack laughed. "She said she doubts she'll ever get back the money she loaned Russell."

"I can't believe she loaned him that much money in the first place," I responded. "I don't think she would have done that for us and you're her favorite. He must know how to charm older women."

Ann had been mentioning the money for a couple of years, but never with much intensity. Russell, a mining engineer, was Earl's son. He'd borrowed $10,000 to buy a piece of mining equipment, thinking he could resell it for a profit. He'd had trouble locating a buyer, and now Ann was finally impatient.

Ten thousand dollars was nothing to Ann. She was a millionaire in rental property alone. But she also was a serious businesswoman, and she kept a journal of every rent receipt, every loan and every payment. She'd often let renters who were down on their luck delay payments, sometimes letting them catch up when they received their tax refunds, but she eventually collected her money.

It wasn't like Ann to let a loan drag on for years. When a young man in town borrowed a couple of thousand from her, she had him sign a promissory note. When he didn't pay her back in a timely manner, she threatened to put a lien on the house he'd bought for his mother.

But Russell was kin, and Ann believed in the blood connection. Just a few weeks earlier, over the Christmas holiday, I'd been reminded of that. Earl's other child had married a man with a daughter the same age as her daughter. The two girls had grown up like twins. I asked Ann what had happened to her niece's now grown stepdaughter.

Ann began talking about her and casually commented, "I always got her a Christmas gift—of course, not as nice as I got my own niece." I couldn't imagine the two little girls, raised as sisters, receiving Christmas gifts of different value simply because one was a blood relative.

However, the blood thing was a family trait, probably part of their Kentucky roots. Not being a Kentucky native, I found it a little disconcerting. Jack said Ann and Carroll had, at one time, considered adopting a child, and I was grateful—for the child's sake—that they hadn't. I doubt an adopted child could have been fully welcomed into their lives. Jack's great aunt had raised a neighbor's child—from a poor family with too many kids—and when his great aunt died, she left little or nothing to this woman who had shared her home. Instead, this wealthy woman left stock and money to distant blood relatives, including Jack.

The blood connection was so strong that Russell could take his time paying Ann back, but eventually she'd want her money. Ann discussed all her business ventures with Jack in their weekly calls, but family loans were rarely mentioned. The fact that she'd brought up Russell's loan showed she'd reached her limit, even for a family member.

"What's the latest on Ann's fiancé?" I asked. We'd only met him once when we'd come to Kentucky a few months earlier. We'd joined Ann, her fiancé Bob, Jack's mom and another older couple for supper at a local restaurant. Bob was a dignified older man, attentive to Ann, and eager to make a positive impression on her favorite nephew.

"She told me she wasn't sure she was ready to get married again, at least not right now," Jack responded. "She wants to wait until Grace dies."

The conversation turned to the conference I was attending the next day. Soon our grandsons, Taylor and Elliott, would be dropped off to spend Saturday with us, as they did each week. So we stopped thinking of the conversation with Ann, the conversation we would replay hundreds of times in the weeks and months that followed.

# Chapter 2

# Something Terrible

Sunday afternoon, January 12. My administrative assistant, Nancy, drove with me from North Georgia to a wooded retreat center east of Birmingham. As marketing director for a national mission agency, I was attending the conference of a sister agency primarily as a goodwill gesture. Nancy and I set up a small display about our agency and lured people to visit by announcing a drawing Monday afternoon.

After the first afternoon conference session on Monday, I slipped into the restroom to comb my hair before standing in front of several hundred ladies to do the drawing.

It was a women's conference, so the ladies restroom was packed. My cell phone rang and I pulled the small Nokia from the clip on my belt. My mother-in-law's name flashed across the screen.

All around me, women laughed, talked and primped. The buzz of my surroundings grew louder as an uneasy feeling gripped me. Iva Ray had never called my cell. She would have been concerned about interrupting me during a meeting. I knew the call had to be important, and I didn't want to answer in front of this crowd of scurrying strangers.

I let the phone ring until it went to voicemail, then immediately retrieved the message. Uneasiness changed to panic when I heard Iva Ray's voice. Her usually calm, controlled voice was quiet but urgent.

"Mary, call me back as soon as you get this message. Please, call me back."

I knew something terrible had happened. I sensed it in every part of my being. I hurried out of the restroom, my mind racing wildly and irrationally. Had something happened to Jack? Or our children, Penny and Dave? Or our grandsons? I knew that it was unlikely that my mother-in-law would receive such news before me, but that didn't ease the panic.

It was unusually cold for southern Alabama, ten degrees at best. I rushed outside in just khakis and a long-sleeved oxford shirt. Gripping my cell phone, I walked as far from the conference center as I could to hear the news alone.

I called Iva Ray, and she answered immediately. If you've ever been in a car accident and felt as though time went into slow motion as you waited for the impact, you'll understand the seconds between making my phone call and hearing my mother-in-law's words.

"Mary, it's Ann. Someone broke into her house, and she's gone."

I felt an immediate relief that Jack, our children and our grandchildren were safe. Then the gravity of Iva Ray's words hit me.

Gone? Was Ann kidnapped? Was she dead? I couldn't tell, and I couldn't ask. I could tell from the tone of her voice the words had been too agonizing for Iva Ray to say. I couldn't press her for more.

Then I recalled that, years ago, when Jack's dad had died in his sleep, Iva Ray had called early one morning and told Jack, "Your daddy's gone."

Sleepy and confused, Jack had asked, "Where is he?"

"In heaven" was his mother's answer.

Ann was dead. There was no use forcing Iva Ray to say the words. Sobbing, I responded to the reality of her message. "I'm so sorry. I'm so, so sorry."

Finally, the words of confirmation: "Earl found her lying at the bottom of her basement stairs. At first, he thought she'd had a stroke. Then … will you tell Jack … and Penny and Dave?"

I wanted to know more, but again, I knew she'd told me all she could. "I'll tell them," I promised her. "And we'll be there as soon as we can."

I closed my cell phone and sank to the ground. Putting my face in my hands I sobbed until I felt someone's hand on my shoulder.

"Are you okay?"

I looked up to see one of the hundreds of strangers from the conference. In an almost trance-like voice, I began telling her what had happened. And through the numbness, I could think of only one way she could help me. She could get word to the conference leader that I couldn't do the drawing.

She turned back toward the conference center, and I sat on a low rock wall. In the quiet chill of the afternoon, with tall pine trees shading the sun, I felt the most amazing presence of God. As surely as if I'd heard an audible voice, God assured me that Ann had simply walked down her basement stairs and into His presence. I tried to hold on to that vision in the awful months which followed.

# Chapter 3

# A Promise

I stumbled blindly back to my room at the nearby lodge. Unable to deal with the immensity of what had happened, I forced myself to focus on the practical. Call Jack, call the kids. Cancel the cleaning service for Thursday. Pack my suitcase. Cancel my room for the rest of the week and see if I can get a refund for my company.

I sat on the edge of the bed, wondering how I would tell Jack. Ann was his second mother. He was her only son.

She spent Thanksgiving and Christmas with us each year. Years after her husband Carroll died, she came to Jack when she began dating, seeking his approval. She ran business deals by him. He had been the executor of her will until a year or so ago when she decided that, since we lived so far away, it would be stressful for Jack to handle the details of her large estate. She had an insurance policy with Jack as the beneficiary—he was her son every way but biologically.

Our children and grandchildren treated Ann like a grandmother. She was part of our immediate family. How could I tell my family that someone had broken into Ann's home and killed her?

I sat on the bed until I thought Jack would be home from work. This wasn't the type of news I wanted him to hear at his office or while driving through traffic.

I called our home phone. Busy. Jack was probably on the Internet. But I knew he was home and it was safe to call.

"Honey?" I said when he answered his cell.

"Hey, babe. What's up?"

My pause communicated the seriousness of the call.

"Is everything okay?" Jack asked cautiously.

"It's Anna Mae." Not as skilled with phrasing as Iva Ray, I blurted out, "She's been murdered. That's all I know right now."

Jack listened in shocked silence, so I continued. I often jokingly described Jack as "edgy and sometimes volatile," but in times of extreme stress, he reverted to his family's quiet, stoic and emotionless demeanor.

"Honey, I'm so sorry. I'm sorry I'm not there with you, but I'll get home as fast as I can. And I'll call the kids and tell them."

We said we loved each other, and hung up.

I called our daughter Penny's cell and got her voicemail. She's probably still at work, I thought. So I forced the panic from my voice as I said brightly: "Hi, Pen. It's me. Give me a call as soon as you get home. It's NOT an emergency. The boys are fine. Dave's fine. Dad and I are fine. Granny Ive and Mom Mom are fine. I just need to talk to you."

I hoped Penny wouldn't notice that I'd omitted Aunt Ann from the list of safe family members. I hoped she'd just hear the message of assurance and wait till she was home to call.

I left a similar message on Dave's cell.

Still at work, Penny picked up a land line and called her dad as she sometimes does, wanting to tell him some bit of trivia—something she'd heard on the news, something the boys said or did.

When Jack heard Penny's upbeat conversation, he realized she didn't know about Ann. Summoning all his remaining emotional strength he said, "I have some bad news. Aunt Ann's been murdered."

Penny screamed hysterically. The sound of his daughter in such anguish was more than Jack could bear. He quietly hung up the phone. Co-workers had to drive Penny home. In the midst of her own grief, she had to explain to her seven and ten-year-old boys that their beloved aunt was dead.

I was able to tell our son Dave the news myself. At that time, a young bachelor, Dave lived alone, and I hated that he had no one to share his grief. I knew Jack was alone, too, and I wanted so much to be there for all of them.

My administrative assistant, Nancy, came to my room just as I was finishing the call to the cleaning service. She took over just when I had expended my last particle of energy. She loaded the rental car and led me to it.

All the way home, I talked about Ann. Nancy listened and asked questions, keeping my mind off the immediate issues. We laughed at the outlandish Ann stories that bounced in and out of my mind. Ann still wore false eyelashes and leg makeup. She had a closet filled with mink and chinchilla coats, relishing their elegance and ignoring the anti-fur protest-ers. For years, she drank a daily tonic, made with honey and an array of lesser ingredients, and claimed it kept her young. She had an extensive collection of antique dolls and she happily mixed them with the inexpensive ones Dave occasionally gave her for Christmas.

Finally, Nancy pulled into the parking lot of our company, where Jack had agreed to meet us. I immediately saw Jack's bright blue Corvette, purchased just months earlier to feed his penchant for fast cars. As a Special Agent for the Department of the Treasury, he'd driven a lot of amazing cars seized from dopers, but his favorite government car was an emerald green Firebird. Soon after being assigned the Firebird, he surprised me with a gold Trans Am, which I told him was like Elliott buying me a Lego set for Christmas.

As soon as Jack recognized the rental car, he was out of the 'Vette and moving toward us. He was wearing his federal "uniform"—khakis and a tan many-pocketed vest similar to those worn by photographers. Agents often wear them to cover their weapons when not wearing suits. Since Jack always, without fail, carries his SIG 229, I was used to seeing him in these vests.

A high-school-trim six footer, with thick blond hair just graying at the temple, Jack still made my heart race after thirty-five years of marriage. Tonight, he looked even more appealing than usual.

Seeing Jack made the evening more bearable. We drove the thirty minutes home, cliché-ing the quiet with "I can't believe this has happened" and "I hope this is a nightmare and pretty soon we'll wake up."

Typical of Jack, he'd spent the past hours investigating the case. Like most men, he had a strong desire to fix a problem by taking concrete steps. But unlike most men, Jack had the ability to fix this type of problem. Though he'd never worked a murder case, nineteen years as a federal agent made investigating crimes second nature for him.

After calling Iva Ray and Earl and getting as much information from them as possible, he called Marc Boggs, a friend who worked for the Madisonville Police Department. We'd lived in Madisonville years ago, before Jack became an agent, and he still knew a couple of officers.

"Marc said Anna Mae was stabbed," Jack told me. "He said there'd been a struggle. Her hands were cut up pretty bad, and that usually means the victim tried to protect herself from the knife."

"I don't know why her hands were cut," I told Jack. "But I know this: There was no struggle. She was dead instantly."

I shared with Jack my confidence that Ann had not suffered. And no matter what evidence we heard to the contrary, I encouraged him to have that same trust.

In the weeks, months and years that followed, I've thought about that January 12 night more times than I can count. Though I shudder at the incredible violence of the crime, I know that the damage was done to a shell, because Ann's spirit had already gone to be with the Father.

Jack and I couldn't sleep that night, so we talked a long time. We talked about Ann, about how he'd always felt as though he'd grown up with two sets of parents, how she was a part of nearly all his childhood memories.

Wishing I could have told Jack the awful news in person, I wondered how he had handled it alone. "What's the first thing you did when you hung up the phone after we talked, the first thing you did after learning that Ann had been murdered?" I asked.

"I made a promise to Ann that I'd find her killer," Jack said quietly.

# Chapter 4

# Searching for a Killer

Driving to Kentucky early the next morning, with a snowstorm hours behind us, we spent the six hours going over every possible suspect. Jack's years as an investigator had taught him not to rule anyone out.

Earl had told Jack that Ann's security system wasn't activated, so we concentrated first on people Ann knew. If she had known her killer, she would have turned off the security system to let them into her home.

We pieced together what we knew of Ann's last hours. She'd walked across the street to attend the evening worship service at her church. The service ended at 7:00, and sometime after that, the killer entered Ann's house and murdered her.

The next day, Monday, Ann was scheduled to have lunch with her fiancé, Bob. When she didn't answer the door or her phone, Bob became alarmed. He could see her car in the garage and was concerned that she was inside and hurt.

Bob walked across the street to the church and called the police. Since Ann had told him Earl had a key to her house, Bob suggested that they also call Earl.

The police and Bob were waiting outside when Earl arrived. Earl knew that Ann hid a spare key on the first holly bush near the back door. The key was missing. They eventually found it hanging on a different bush.

They entered the house together, the officers going from room to room, calling for Ann.

Earl started down the basement stairs. He saw the lower half of Ann's body lying in the shadows at the base of the stairs. He stopped in mid step when he saw her bloodied hands. Calling for the police, Earl backed up the stairs.

As the miles passed, Jack and I made a mental list of possible suspects.

Joseph Knight, "the crazy renter," was first on our list. He could have become enraged if she told him she was evicting him.

"Actually, any renter could be a suspect," observed Jack. "She had a lock box outside where they dropped off their rent. I guess one of them could have forced their way inside. And someone was always behind in their rent."

As we moved down the mental list of suspects, Jack paused.

"It's hard to imagine a family member could have done it, but we have to consider the possibility," he said softly.

"I just can't believe that," I said.

"There's one thing I've learned as an investigator. Never rule out anyone." Jack shook his head and continued. "And the first suspects are always family."

We drove for a while in silence, mentally digesting our conversation thus far. I looked over at Jack's profile. His jaw was set so slightly that only someone who had known and loved him for thirty-five years could detect the stress.

Jack was wearing a short-sleeved dress shirt—he said it was easier to draw his weapon in short sleeves. My gaze traced the taut muscles in his arms and moved to his knuckles, white from gripping the steering wheel too tightly. Jack could be intense, but not with the loud, fast-talking, hand-waving demeanor often associated with intenseness. "Still waters run deep" could have been written to describe Jack.

"Speaking of family members," Jack said slowly. "I don't think we can eliminate Grace."

"You're kidding."

"On Saturday, Anna Mae said Grace's cancer had spread to her spleen and possibly her brain. She's gotten so hateful no one can stand to be around her for long," said Jack. "She's never gotten past the anger stage of dying. She's angry because she's the youngest sibling and she's dying first."

"Not anymore."

Jack nodded. "She actually told Anna Mae a couple of weeks ago that she should be the one dying, and not her."

The thought of a family member hurting Ann was more than I was ready to consider.

Several exits blurred by. I closed my eyes and listened to the hum of the Goodyear Eagle F-1s, built for speeds up to 175 miles an hour. I knew they were being tested today. I could smell Brut, Jack's familiar aftershave, the same one he'd worn since high school. Jack didn't trust change, and if something worked, then good enough. I smiled slightly as I remembered when Jack's public corruption task force moved from a dingy undercover hole-in-the-wall to a brighter office. The old office was rundown, but it was familiar. So Jack drew a detailed diagram of his old office and placed everything in his new work area in exactly the same place.

Even good change was hard for Jack. What must today and its nightmares be doing to him.

Jack's voice interrupted my musings. "Ann had two employees, a handyman and a housekeeper. I don't know much about either of them, but they'd have access to the house and she'd have opened the door for them."

"Is there anyone we're ruling out?" I asked.

"Honestly? Only the family members who live out of town. And Mother. Everyone else is a possibility."

# Chapter 5

# A Bloody Scenario

Madisonville is a coal-mining town of about 15,000 people. To a passing motorist, its welcoming sign might seem like an oxymoron of the run-down buildings and closed shops that pepper its main thoroughfare: "Welcome to Madisonville, Kentucky—Best Town on Earth." But we'd lived there once and we knew it was a good town.

Dirty snow and gray slush blanketed the town as we drove in on that mid January morning. We stopped first at the police station, cautiously maneuvering the icy parking lot and stepping out of the car. I abruptly remembered how long we'd lived in the South as my open-toed shoes disappeared into the snow. We pulled our lightweight coats tightly around our necks and walked gingerly through the inches-deep snow to the police station.

Before a word or glance was exchanged, we sized up the receptionist as one of those people who served her time at work, arriving in a sour mood and leaving in a worse one. As we approached her desk she seemed oblivious to our presence.

"Is Captain Randy Hargis here?" asked Jack. "I'm Ann Branson's nephew from Georgia."

Still staring at her computer screen, she replied, "Captain Hargis is in a meeting."

Jack is even-tempered and calm until someone presses his buttons. Arrogance and laziness are two of his buttons, and the receptionist pushed them both. I was surprised that she didn't feel the current in the air. I did, and I wanted to shout to her, "*Duck!*"

Jack drew his federal badge as quickly as he would have drawn the gun he wore under his trench coat. He slammed his badge case on the receptionist's desk. She tried not to ruin her aloof image, but I saw her flinch.

"Then tell him there was a federal agent here to see him."

Moving like syrup on a winter day, the receptionist got up and—still not looking at her opponent—adjusted a stack of papers near her computer, then inched her way out of the room.

"Let's go," Jack told me, and we were out the door before the receptionist returned. As Jack helped me across the snow, he made a prophetic observation.

"This case will drag on as slowly as that MPD receptionist moved. A town this size is going to have trouble solving a complicated murder case."

As we pulled from the parking lot, a young uniformed officer trotted through the snow toward us.

"Mr. Branson?" he called through the rolled-up window. "Captain Hargis would like to see you if you're still available to talk."

Inside Captain Hargis' office, Jack's prophecy began to unfold. Within minutes we realized that Ann's murder was the most complicated case the MPD had investigated in a long time.

Early on I sensed a strain between Captain Hargis and Jack. Jack already used his federal badge to lay the first bricks of the wall between them, but now he was letting down his guard. He was the nephew of a murder victim, and *wanted* and *needed* information. Hargis had the information, and therefore, the upper hand. The two professionals sparred around each other, with Hargis cautiously selecting what he told us.

"First of all, Mr. and Mrs. Branson," said Hargis formally. "Let me offer my condolences. Ms. Branson was well thought of in Madisonville. She was a pillar in the community. The whole town's shaken by her murder."

Jack nodded. "Any leads?"

"Not yet."

"Have you checked out her renters? There was one she was concerned about. He was always calling her to chase the ghosts out of his house."

"Yeah." Hargis placed his folded hands across his stomach. "We brought him in for questioning. Seems harmless. Just a little crazy."

"Did he have an alibi?"

Hargis nodded vaguely and changed the subject. "We're trying to determine if anything was stolen. Do you know of any valuables Ms. Branson kept in her house?"

"She had several large diamond rings."

"We've accounted for all but one of those," said Hargis. "And we've accounted for all but one of her furs. The housekeeper said she thinks there's a mink coat missing. Did she keep any weapons in the house?"

"She had a factory engraved Smith & Wesson .22 caliber revolver," Jack offered. "It was my Uncle Carroll's. She used to keep it in the kitchen cabinet, but I'm not sure where she's kept it recently.

"She told me at Christmas that she and Bob, her fiancé, had tried to see if it was loaded. They looked down the barrel to try to see the bullets. That scared me—neither of them knew anything about guns. I told her to put it away and let me look at it next time I was there.

"Call Bob. He'll know where she's been keeping it." Jack paused, then: "Do you think robbery was the motive?"

The captain's eyes apologized for what he was about to say.

"This was no robbery, even if a few things are missing," Hargis struggled to find the right words. "This was a crime of rage. Whoever killed her wanted her more than dead.

The captain's demeanor softened, and it seemed as though his shoulders sagged slightly from the weight of what he was about to say. Jack and I braced ourselves for his next words.

"Ms. Branson was such a dignified lady," said Hargis. "It was like..."

He paused, then: "It was like the killer wanted to take away her dignity. Her body was pretty messed up."

"She was stabbed?" Jack's voice was even, but I knew the words were painful.

"Hit with a blunt object—maybe a hammer. Then stabbed," answered Hargis. "They took her body to the state police crime laboratory in Louisville. We don't have a forensics lab here. You'll have to delay the funeral until after the autopsy."

Silence hung heavy in the air.

"Did you find DNA or fingerprints?" asked Jack.

Hargis shook his head. "We're not sure yet about the DNA, but not a single print. We took the paint off the handrails trying to get even a partial print—nothing."

"That basement's dark. It would be hard to wipe away every fingerprint," Jack observed. "I took a shower down there when we spent the night back in August, and you could hardly—-"

Hargis interrupted. "You took a shower in Ms. Branson's basement?"

I could see that Jack was grasping something I had not yet grasped. "Yeah," he said slowly. "No one used that shower after my uncle died. We were running late, so I used the basement shower while my wife got ready upstairs. I'm sure I would have been the last person to use it."

I was overcome by nausea as I realized the scenario the men were suggesting. The killer had wiped the crime scene free of fingerprints, then taken a shower in Ann's basement. With Ann's body lying a few feet away.

"So you're not looking at anybody in particular?" Jack's voice jolted me back from the image, and I knew he'd pulled himself away from it as well.

"Nobody yet. I hope it's not like the Granstaff murder. It took us nine years to solve that one."

Ann Granstaff was murdered twenty years ago, and it was the last high-profile murder in Madisonville. Granstaff was a speech therapist. Earl was one of her clients. She'd bought a greyhound dog that had been used for racing and trained not to bark. Because of her speech training, she challenged herself to teach the dog to bark. Soon his hearty barks could be heard by neighbors on the crowded street.

When Granstaff didn't show up for work one morning, co-workers went to her house and discovered her body. She'd been choked with an electrical cord. Her dog had not barked, so everyone assumed that she and her dog knew the killer.

The case went unsolved until a suspect was picked up five years later in Chicago and convicted of murder, rape and burglary. But some people still doubted the convicted man was the killer, since Granstaff's dog hadn't barked.

"Who's assigned to the case?" Jack asked.

"I've put all three detectives on it," replied Hargis.

"How much homicide experience do they have?" Hargis' almost-imperceptible pause spoke clearly before his reply: "None of them have worked a homicide. It's been a long time since I have."

"Captain, if there's anything I can do, please let me know. I have investigative experience, and I'll do whatever's necessary to solve this case."

# Chapter 6

# Stress Grows

Jack's family can best be described as stoic. We arrived at Iva Ray's to find no tears over her sister's death. No quivering voice. No outward grieving. But I'd known the Winsteads for thirty-five years, and I understood that she was hurting.

"Start locking your doors," Jack warned his mother as he carefully hugged her fragile five-foot-three body against his six-foot frame. She nodded, but we both knew she wouldn't change her small-town pattern.

Earl lived a half block from Iva Ray, so we walked across the snow to his one-story yellow brick house, upper class thirty years earlier but now solidly middle class.

His son, Russell, answered. We only came to Madisonville for funerals, and I was surprised at how much Russell had changed since Carroll's funeral nine years earlier. He'd shaved his mustache, maybe because he now had more gray hair at thirty-seven than Jack had at fifty-four. He looked much thinner than I remembered him, probably 175-180 on his six-foot-one frame.

Russell looked exhausted as he hugged me and shook Jack's hand. We were all tired, and our ordeal had just begun.

Earl was sitting in an overstuffed chair in his den. The utilitarian room was void of a woman's touch. Earl's wife, Sue, had died fourteen years earlier, and he'd sold the house they shared and eventually moved to this one. The only touches of warmth in the house were family photos, and I was certain Earl's son and daughter had supplied them.

I glanced around, imagining the touches Sue would have added to the house. Her home was always neat but cozy and welcoming. One day, she woke up with a fever and went to see her doctor for medication. The next day, she felt well enough to mow the yard, using a riding lawn mower.

But halfway through mowing, her fever rose again. It was Saturday and her doctor was unavailable, so she drove herself to the emergency room. Moments after being admitted, most of her major organs shut down and she was dead. Her body swelled and darkened, and it was necessary to have a closed coffin at the funeral. Iva Ray later told us doctors suspected a rare blood disease but that she never felt the cause of death was clearly identified.

Earl had a girlfriend, Betty, for the past several years, but obviously she had not helped decorate his house. She had, however, helped keep Earl trim and youthful. He'd begun running, and we often teased that his exercise regiment was an effort to stay lean for a lady friend ten years his junior. Today, in spite of his weariness, Earl looked boyish and young. With graying blond hair and a height and build similar to Jack's, he looked more like Jack's brother than his uncle.

Jack and I sat on the nondescript couch opposite Earl. Russell sat on the arm of the couch.

"How're you holding up?" Jack posed the question to Earl.

Earl responded with a cracked voice that skipped back and forth between octaves, much like a boy in early puberty. Jack's mom once told us Earl was afflicted with spasmodia dysphonia, a disease that affected his vocal cords and intensified under stress.

Earl just referred to his condition as "bruised vocal cords caused by a virus." Whatever it was, that day it was difficult to understand him.

"Okay, I guess. I'd be better off if I could cry. But you know our family. We don't show no emotion..." Earl's voice faded.

"You found her?" Jack asked.

"Yeah, but I didn't go down the stairs. Once I seen she had blood on her, I let the police handle it."

Jack's usually smooth neckline began to swell with purple veins, and I could see the veins pulsing as he imagined Ann covered with blood. He chose each of his next words carefully, and he said them one at a time.

"That's...one...execution...I...want...to...see. I want to watch... the lights...go out in the eyes...of whoever did this."

"You'll have to get in line with the rest of us," said Russell. Rising from the edge of the sofa, he walked over to Earl and placed a hand on his shoulder.

"Dad, since you've got company, I'd better get home to Terri and the kids."

Earl placed his hand awkwardly over Russell's. "You go. I'll be fine. Thanks for stopping by, son."

As the door latched behind Russell, Earl began talking business. A few years earlier, when Ann finally accepted that Jack and I had no plans to return to Madisonville, she appointed Earl as executor of her estate. He had helped Ann with a lot of business details in the past years and was probably best-suited to handle her affairs.

"Her rent houses are valued at a million two. We may have to sell them off one at a time. I might give *her* house to the church since it's right across the street. They could use it for visiting missionaries and pastors.

"She had insurance policies for all the siblings," Earl continued. "And she had a nice one for you, too...Ya know you were her favorite."

Jack nodded solemnly, but I knew how much that assurance meant to him right now. Still, he was more interested in solving the murder than disbursing the estate.

"Do you think the handyman or housekeeper could have done it?"

asked Jack.

Earl shrugged his shoulders. "Don't know about the handyman. Heard he's got a temper. He does work for Iva Ray, too, and he's been working for them both for a long time.

"Judy, the housekeeper, she's a good woman. Besides, she's got a bad back and probably couldn't have done that kind of damage."

"What about Knight, the crazy renter?" asked Jack.

"Nah, I know him. He's a little off, but he couldn't do nothing like that."

"We're all capable of worse than we think," observed Jack. Jack rose from the couch and walked to the chair where Russell had laid our coats.

"Is anyone behind in their rent?" Jack continued to run through possibilities.

"Yeah," said Earl. "A couple. One hasn't paid since July."

Earl paused, then said with finality: "I imagine it was a drifter that killed her. That railroad behind her house and all."

I could tell by the way Jack refocused the conversation that he already felt strongly that the killer was no drifter: "There hasn't been a violent murder here since Ann Granstaff. Except for that jogger who was stabbed in the park—just a mile or so from here."

"That woman stabbed in the park was my daughter's mother-in-law," said Earl. "Actually, ex-mother-in-law."

Jack was silent for a moment, and then to me, "Come on, hon. We'd better see what we can do to help Mother."

Earl rose slowly from the chair and stretched out his hand to Jack. "Thanks for coming by," he said in his signature cracked voice. "Guess I'll be stopping by Iva Ray's later tonight. I'll see you if you're gonna be there."

Iva Ray's house was beginning to fill with food from friends and church members. She insisted we eat something from the enormous spread. Perched on the edge of a stool and herself eating like a bird, Iva Ray periodically pushed large bowls of salads and vegetables our way.

She talked brightly of all the people who had been by, the flowers, the food, the cards. I wanted to scream, "Your sister's been murdered!" Instead, I took another helping of fruit salad, smiled and nodded. I knew Iva Ray was dealing with the nightmare in the only way she knew. Stoically.

After supper, I approached Jack with an idea I'd been thinking about all day. I'd once asked him if the police cleaned up the blood after a murder so the family didn't have to see the crime scene. He said that, unfortunately in most instances, that was left to the family.

"Honey?" The next words to Jack were some of the most difficult I've ever uttered. "I'd like to volunteer to clean up the crime scene. Until the housekeeper's cleared as a suspect, I wouldn't want her to do it. And I don't want any of the immediate family to go through that."

Jack objected, but I could see from his face that he was relieved. He knew what a crime scene was like, and he knew what it would do to Ann's sisters and brothers—and to him—to clean it. After I assured him that I could handle the job, he wrapped his arms around me and said softly in my ear, "I'll call Hargis."

Jack placed the call. I listened as he told Hargis about my offer. Then, as he listened to Hargis' response, his expression changed from solemn to baffled.

"Really?" asked Jack. After his initial surprise, he pressed for more information: "Do you know what Ann wore to church? Whether she'd changed out of her church clothes can give us an idea of when she was murdered."

Jack paused, then: "You could ask some of the people at the church if they saw her or sat near her. Someone may remember what she was wearing."

I was waiting eagerly to hear Hargis' side of the conversation. When Jack hung up the phone, he turned to me.

"There's nothing to clean up," said Jack quietly. "Hargis said the crime scene was completely cleaned."

# Chapter 7

# Who's the Killer

Iva Ray's phone rang periodically with people who were sure they knew who the killer was. Jack's cousin Brenda called to say she overheard a short man talking about the murder at The Pantry, a quick-shop grocery. He was discussing facts about the murder that hadn't been released yet—that Ann was stabbed, that she was wearing her rings. Brenda was Ann's niece by marriage. She and her brothers are related on Carroll's side.

Her mother, Margaret Branson, stopped by to say that Joseph Knight, the crazy renter, had come to their house Sunday afternoon, about 4:00, trying to sell a DVD player. He said he was leaving town fast and would sell it cheap. He was a friend of Ann's great nephew who'd been in and out of trouble.

"Captain Hargis called." Iva Ray came into the TV room where Jack and I were trying to assemble the murder puzzle. "He wants the family to come to the police station tomorrow morning for a briefing."

The next morning, Iva Ray, Jack and I rode to the police station together. We were the last to arrive.

I hadn't seen all the Winstead siblings together in years. Now, here they were, gathered to find their big sister's killer. I glanced around the room, having the same thought I would have for days to come, each time I was in a gathering: One of the people in this room could be the killer.

Grace looked bad. She'd always had a weight problem and, contrary to the way cancer typically emaciates its victims, Grace was even larger than I'd remembered. She looked bloated, sullen and aloof. She was wearing a blond wig and a heavy faux fur coat. She avoided eye contact when we entered the room. I hugged her anyway, and she stiffened.

*Could she be the murderer,* I asked myself. Even in the final stages of cancer, sixty-two year-old Grace seemed strong enough to inflict physical harm and she probably outweighed Ann by more than one hundred pounds. And rage, I knew, gave surprising strength.

Grace seemed to have enough pent-up rage for anything she chose to do. She'd been angry since she learned she had cancer, and the anger only festered and grew. Jack had tried to visit her when she was first diagnosed, but she refused to see him. Terrified and bitter, she'd shut herself off from everyone who tried to help her. She wouldn't let Iva Ray visit either. Iva Ray did research with Alzheimer's patients, and Grace said the old people she was around probably had germs.

Janet was trying her best to make Grace comfortable, but her overtures just seemed to annoy Grace.

Eight months older than Grace, Janet was Grace's high school friend who later married her friend's big brother. Janet liked to be in charge, and that was fine with quiet, easygoing David Winstead. Besides me, she was the only one who wasn't a blood relative, and blood meant a lot in Jack's family.

Janet sat to Grace's left. David sat quietly beside Janet and Earl beside David. I thought I'd covered everyone in the cramped room when I noticed a small, wiry woman sitting alone behind the others. Looking a little out of place, the somewhat tired-looking middle-aged woman with yellow-orange hair sat quiet and detached, pulling her well-worn coat tightly across her chest. No one introduced us, and feeling a little awkward, I simply pretended she wasn't there.

Janet picked up the conversation where it had been before our entrance.

"David called Ann about 8:15 or 8:20 and no one answered. We were trying to find out if she could take Grace for her treatment the next day. But Judy talked to her a little past nine, and Ann gave her instructions for the week. Bob called her at ten o' clock and when she didn't answer, he figured she'd already gone to bed."

"So she must have let the killer into the house right after she talked to Judy," Earl calculated. "As long as everybody's right on their times."

The door opened, and Captain Hargis stepped inside. His eyes rested briefly on Jack, and he registered recognition.

"We'd like to talk to the family now," he said solemnly.

Janet helped Grace up and they struggled through the doorway first—then David and then Earl. Jack and I walked with Iva Ray and allowed her to go through the doorway before us. As Iva Ray passed through the doorway, Hargis closed the door before Jack and I could enter.

Although furious myself, I knew I'd better stifle my anger to avoid fueling Jack's. We were stressed. The police were stressed. So what may have been an unintentional slight sent a message that Jack would not be included in the investigation and wouldn't be considered family when information was doled out.

As I struggled to defuse the volatile reaction I anticipated from Jack, a timid voice reminded us we weren't alone.

"You Iva Ray's boy?" It was the woman who'd been sitting in the back of the room. She approached Jack cautiously.

"Yes, ma'am," Jack answered.

"I'm Judy," said the woman. "Miz Ann's housekeeper."

Jack pummeled Judy with questions.

"Are you sure about the time you talked to Ann?"

"Yeah. The police said I can't be right, that I'm lying. But that's when I talked to her."

"You just tell the truth," Jack assured her. "What about the handyman, Wayne Shelton? What do you know about him?"

Judy's eyes narrowed and she spoke with a passion that caught me slightly off guard.

"That's who *I* think did it," said Judy. "Wayne's mean. He's got a temper. And he was mad at Miz Ann because she wouldn't sign a paper saying he worked for her full-time. He needed it for child support. He didn't work full time, and Miz Ann wasn't about to lie for him. He owed her money, and he cheated her outta money whenever he thought he could get away with it."

By now, Jack was totally focused on Judy, so I took notes for him, knowing he'd want them later.

"Do you know where Wayne was Sunday night?" asked Jack.

"Driving right by Miz Ann's house! He *said*," and she drew out the word, "that he drove by and was going to stop, but decided not to. Wayne stopped by nearly every Sunday night to get his work for the week. Don't know why he'd drive by this week without stopping."

Judy's expression was a mixture of anger and sorrow. "You know what Wayne said when he found out Miz Ann was murdered?" After a reasonably dramatic pause, she added: "He came over about the time they was carrying out the body. He just said, 'Well, what do you know.' After all Miz Ann done for him, that's all he said."

"Is he strong?" I asked Judy. "Strong enough to have killed Ann?"

"Sure," said Judy. "He's just forty-eight, and he's a handyman. He's got a heart condition but it doesn't slow him down. He's real strong."

"Judy," asked Jack. "How tall is Wayne?"

"Kind of small," said Judy. "About five-six."

Jack and I exchanged excited glances, remembering Brenda's description of the man at The Pantry.

"Another thing," said Judy. "He took care of Miz Ann's rent houses. And she kept the patching paint and the house keys in her basement."

"And," Judy cast more doubt on Wayne, "This friend of mine said her neighbor worked at the printer's near Miz Ann's house. He was driving by Miz Ann's about four or four-thirty Monday morning, and he seen a dark-colored truck pulling outta Miz Ann's driveway. Wayne's got a dark-colored truck."

# Chapter 8

# The Nightmare Continues

Driving home from the police station, Iva Ray recounted the meeting with Hargis.

"He didn't say much," observed Iva Ray. "Just that they were doing all they could to find Ann's murderer and that they'd keep us informed."

"They're playing big-city cop," observed Jack, still reacting to being left out of the meeting. "They figured they were supposed to call a meeting."

"They want us all to walk through the house tomorrow morning, looking for anything that's out of place," said Iva Ray. "Then they'll turn the house over to the family."

We spent the afternoon talking to the scores of visitors who stopped by Iva Ray's, people we hadn't seen in nearly twenty years. After a while, we felt as though we were holding an open house, filled with laughter and food, instead of grieving that someone we loved had been murdered.

Earl stopped by later that evening. Though the temperature was barely above zero, he'd been out running. Jack teased him again about staying fit for his younger girlfriend. The two men were laughing and enjoying each other's company so much that I relaxed for a while, too.

With just thirteen years difference in age, Earl and Jack had been close all of Jack's life. Years ago, Earl stayed with Jack's family in Texas while he attended college. Jack's mom was a schoolteacher, so Earl took Jack to school on his first day of first grade. When I'd planned a party for Jack's fiftieth birthday three years earlier, Earl drove down to Georgia to be part of the surprise. They didn't see enough of each other and I knew they wanted, for a few moments tonight, to forget about the nightmare that had brought them together.

They denied the occasion as long as they could. But eventually the conversation turned to the murder.

"The police asked me to find out who'd seen Ann at church Sunday night," Earl offered.

"So what'd you find out?" asked Jack.

"Lots of people remembered seeing her."

"What was she wearing?" asked Jack. Earl shrugged his shoulders.

"Mother," asked Jack. "Do you know what Anna Mae was wearing?"

"No," said Iva Ray, "but I know who sat behind her."

"Do you have their number?" asked Jack as he reached for the phone.

After a short conversation, Jack told us: "She wore a black cape with a leopard skin collar and a black pantsuit under it."

"The cape we gave her for Christmas," I gasped. Then, unexpectedly, I began to cry. I'm still not certain why this news upset me so much.

Iva Ray moved closer to me. "She loved that cape," she told me softly. "I saw her in it a lot the past few weeks."

"Ann sat alone in church," Jack filled us in on more of his phone conversation. "Close to the back. The family sat behind her but didn't notice anything unusual. Church let out about seven and she walked back across the street."

"Do you think she'd just gotten home when she was murdered? Could the killer have been waiting for her inside the house?" I asked.

"Nah," said Earl. "She was wearing some old clothes when she was killed. A pair of stretch pants and a sweater. She wouldn't have worn them to church."

No use arguing with Earl, I thought, but I knew Ann might have worn the old clothes. In fact, she'd have enjoyed throwing the glamorous full-length cape over comfy clothes, putting on one of her many wigs, loading her hands with diamonds, slipping into dress shoes, and walking confidently into the church, with only Ann herself knowing that the cape was a facade.

We'd once sat with Ann at church on a Sunday evening when she was elegantly dressed. She opened her expensive handbag to show me her secret. It was empty. Just a matching prop.

"Was she wearing a wig when she was killed?" I asked Earl.

"Yeah," said Earl. "She had a wig on."

If she'd had time to change clothes, she would have taken her wig off, too. And that late at night, she would have changed into sleep attire instead of pants and a sweater.

It was our opinion Ann hadn't been home long before she was murdered.

# Chapter 9

# The Parade Begins

Midmorning Thursday, we drove Iva Ray to Ann's house. By now, the snowstorm had arrived, blanketing the little town like a fresh coat of white paint and making it appear momentarily storybook exquisite.

"They're releasing the body today," said Iva Ray as we pulled into Ann's driveway. "It looks like we'll have the viewing tomorrow and the funeral Saturday."

"Penny and Dave won't be able to drive up now," Jack told his mom. "Georgia and Tennessee have an ice storm, and it's going to take a while to clear. They can't even make it to the airport. Better not plan on Dave being a pallbearer."

"Janet and David's sons are flying in tomorrow, and we can use them," continued Iva Ray. "Russell can serve, and maybe his sister's boyfriend. Then you and Brenda's brother."

A marked car had stayed in the driveway all night, but the investigating police had not yet arrived. We pulled far back in the driveway to make room for the other cars.

Soon an unmarked police car pulled into the driveway. Out stepped four police detectives, all in black suits, all carrying black briefcases. Three men and one woman.

We followed the officers, the family and Judy into the house. But just after stepping inside, Jack leaned down and whispered to me, "I can't do this. Let's get out of here till the police leave."

I understood Jack's frustration. He knew how an investigation should be handled, and it was torture for him to be left out of this one.

We slipped outside and waited an hour and a half in the sub-freezing car. Then the police left, officially turning the house over to the family.

Entering Ann's house was surreal. Everything was just as she'd left it. A magazine rested on the den sofa, half read. To-do lists and reminders were scattered on the desk where she conducted rent business. A hand towel in the bathroom outside the kitchen was comfortably crinkled where Ann had dried her hands for the last time. It was as though she'd stepped out to buy some milk and we were waiting for her return.

I felt that all these relatives were intruding on Ann's privacy, picking up magazines, leafing through letters, opening drawers. I knew Jack was having the same reaction. We walked gingerly from room to room, respectfully refusing to touch the antiques and furnishings.

The police had taken all of Ann's kitchen knives from the drawers, and they were laid in a row beside the sink. Ann's purse was on the kitchen table.

"The police said her purse was stolen," Judy told Jack. "They said they searched the house twice and couldn't find it. I walked right into the kitchen, and there it was, on the same chair where she left it every night."

Judy continued. "Whenever Miz Ann came back from church or a bridge party or from out shopping, she'd put her purse on the table, and she'd take all her rings off and dump them on the table. Then, when I come in, I'd separate the good jewelry from the cheap stuff. I'd put the cheap stuff in a cup in the kitchen cabinet, and I'd take the good stuff up to her dressing room."

"Was there any jewelry on the table after Ann was murdered?" asked Jack.

"No," replied Judy. "She must have still had her rings on."

"I was upstairs when they was searching Miz Ann's things," Judy continued. "You should have seen them. They couldn't have found anything the way they was searching. It was like they was afraid Miz Ann would come running in the room and tell them to stop messing up her things.

"They'd pull a drawer out just a tiny bit and barely raise up something and peek under it. I watch enough television to know the police are supposed to pull things out of drawers to search."

"A good search can be done without messing up drawers," smiled Jack.

Jack and I walked into the dining room. The black cape with the leopard skin collar was lying across a chair. Directly outside the dining room was a foyer, then the stairs leading to the second level of the house. Ann's hunter green heels were on the bottom step, where she'd slipped them off Sunday night.

We pictured Ann's last moments. She'd come in the front door, which was closest to the church. She'd taken off her shoes, then her cape. She'd walked into the kitchen and put her purse on the chair. Sometime after that, she'd been interrupted.

Jack and I stood motionless at the bottom of the staircase, dreading the climb. The upstairs was Ann's inner sanctum, her personal space. We'd climbed the stairs many times, and we'd slept in Ann's bedroom countless nights. She insisted we use her king bed when we stayed with her, so the room was familiar. But the upstairs was personal, and we dreaded the emotional connection we'd feel when we walked there.

We climbed the stairs one at a time, moving as if wearing those weighted boots astronauts use when gravity is sparse. Gravity and emotional heaviness partnered to make the climb an ordeal, and the effort was nearly unbearable.

At one point in what seemed an eternal climb, we laughed, remembering that Bob was not allowed on the second level of the house. Ann had problems with a faucet recently, and Bob offered to fix it. She'd refused, saying it was improper for him to be in her bedroom.

At the top of the landing was Ann's dressing room, a generous room that consisted primarily of wigs, makeup and jewelry. I glanced in as we turned toward Ann's bedroom. The dressing table was strewn with cosmetics and jewelry, and a light sprinkling of face powder covered the table's surface, giving the impression that Ann was coming right back to remove her makeup and whisk away the dusting of powder with a Kleenex.

Even before entering Ann's bedroom, we saw pictures of me and Jack, Penny and Dave as children and our grandchildren, Taylor and Elliott. The only pictures besides those of our family were a few studio shots of Ann and Carroll.

"We were her family," I told Jack. "You were as close to her as any son could have been."

We moved around the bedroom, lush with peach and gold window and bed dressings. Many times, we had sunk into the thick coverings of that bed after a long drive, falling effortlessly to sleep in its eloquent comfort. But today, we felt like intruders. We stood deliberately in the middle of the room, holding hands, being careful not to touch Ann's personal belongings. We understood the officers' hesitancy to disturb items in the drawers. Everything was so uniquely Ann's, and she had not planned for company.

We paid our respects to the rest of the upstairs rooms. When we had surveyed every perfectly decorated room, we faced the inevitable.

# Chapter 10

# Bloodstains

We headed for the basement. Everything appeared as Ann would have left it. She tended to stack things on the basement stairs, letting Judy eventually put them in their proper places. Right now, pictures she'd planned to frame were stacked on the stairs along with a variety of household clutter. We inched down the narrow stairs, navigating around knick-knacks, newspapers and paraphernalia that had meaning only to Ann.

Like most basements in older homes, Ann's was not designed for company. It was dark, dank and served as her dusty catchall. But today the basement was pristine except for the spot where Ann's body was found. Apparently, blood continued to seep from her body after the killer cleaned the crime scene. Police cut away the carpet and now the bloodstained concrete floor was exposed. The dark spot could have been any type stain, but we were acutely aware that Ann's battered body had lain in the spot now marked by her blood.

We stood motionless on the final step, surveying the basement. Ann kept a small waist-high freezer at the bottom of the stairs, and it was gone. Everything else seemed to be in place: small piles of magazines, boxes of memorabilia and stacks of laundry. Everything was perfectly placed against an eerily clean backdrop.

We moved quietly, almost reverently, around the dark basement. This was the place where Ann's life ended. This was the room where someone hated a 115-pound older woman enough to bludgeon and stab her to death. In the stillness of the basement, I could imagine the thud of Ann falling to her death. I could almost hear the steady monotone of stab wounds to a still body that, even in life, would have been too fragile to fight back.

The killer had walked where we were walking. He'd scrubbed blood off the walls, moved past Ann's mutilated body to the far side of the basement and taken a shower. A washer and dryer stood next to the shower. I imagined the killer washing his clothes while he showered, leaning indifferently on the wall as his clothes dried, and then stepping over Ann's body to climb the stairs.

Jack and I walked over to the old-fashioned shower stall. A slight and continual drip kept the entire stall damp. Jack squatted, shining a light from his key ring into the drain. I knelt beside him and followed the light beam. Hairs and fibers glistened in the light.

Jack used a key to pull the now-useless evidence from the drain. The house had been turned over to the family, and all evidence would now be considered contaminated. We knelt by the shower and stared flat line.

Earl called down the stairs to Jack. "We're going to try to find Ann's gun. Want to help us?"

Earl, Jack and David went back to Ann's bedroom. I walked over to the desk where Ann kept phone messages and notes. Scraps of paper were everywhere, scrawled with names, dates and phone numbers.

I sensed Judy behind me.

"You know what's hard to understand?" she asked me. I looked up and waited for her answer.

"I was the last one to talk to Miz Ann, and they never even searched my house. They didn't ask me to take a lie detector test or anything. It's just weird, that's all."

Jack stormed into the room. He slammed a gold revolver on the table. He doesn't get angry often, but he was furious now. In the past few days I'd seen Jack display as much anger and impatience as he normally displayed in a year.

"I told the cops to call Bob and ask him where Anna Mae kept her gun. That's all they had to do. I called Bob, looked behind the books on the bookshelf—where he said—and found it in three minutes.

"These cops couldn't find their way down a railroad track if they were riding on a caboose." Whether the judgment was fair or unfair, Jack was frustrated and I knew he needed to vent among family.

"Well, you're sure out of control," Grace said in the cutting tone we'd come to expect in recent months.

Jack glared at her. "We should all be out of control. Someone's been murdered. And the victim was your sister and my aunt. This isn't a time to be polite. I want Anna Mae's murderer found. If we sit back while the locals play whodunit, the killer will go free."

"Jack," Janet spoke his name with a slow Kentucky drawl. "We can't make the police angry. They're all we have."

"If we don't do everything—everything—possible to find the killer, then Anna Mae's murder will still be unsolved a year from now," Jack said on his way out the door. "Mother, if you want to stay here a while, maybe Earl can drive you home."

Once in the car, Jack called Captain Randy Hargis. He spoke to Hargis' voicemail as if they'd never met, and I knew he'd passed his edgy stage and was now into full-blown volatility. It was a side of Jack I seldom saw, but I knew the stress of the situation had removed the tiny bits of courtesy he usually slapped on the outside of his abruptness. "Captain Hargis, this is Special Agent Jack Branson. I'm Ann Branson's nephew from Atlanta. Earl Winstead now...has...the...gun...that you and your investigators were unable to find. I found it in a matter of minutes by doing exactly what I suggested you do. I called Bob."

Jack hung up and took an audible breath. This type of fury seemed strange coming from a man who calmly put on body armor and busted down doors as part of a regular day. But this crime was personal, and Jack was hurting as I'd seldom seen him hurt.

We drove in silence for a few moments while Jack regained his composure. "We need to let Hargis know what Judy said about the truck," Jack told me.

"You mean about someone seeing a truck pulling out of Ann's driveway that night?" I asked.

"Yeah." Jack took a breath. "Honey, if I call him again, I'm going to say some things I'll regret—again. Will you call him?"

Jack handed me his phone and I pressed redial. I left a second message for Captain Hargis.

"Thanks, hon," said Jack. We stopped at a red light and Jack turned to me. "You know how I'm feeling. I don't want this to go on for a year or more. I want every resource possible on this case."

"I know."

"And there's a lot I can't do while I'm an agent," Jack continued. "I have access to all kinds of information, but legally I can't use it unless I have an official case open."

"We could hire a private investigator," I offered.

"I was thinking the same thing." Jack reached across the 'Vette's console and squeezed my hand. "It's expensive, and I don't know if anyone else will go in with us."

"I don't see how we can do anything else."

Jack's mom came home about an hour after us. She looked frail and tired. She was barely a size two, and we worried about her on a normal day. Her leukemia caused sores to break out periodically on her arms and legs, and her current stress had caused an outbreak.

"You've got to get some rest, Mother," said Jack.

Iva Ray perched on the arm of a leather recliner and nodded.

"Maybe it'll all be solved soon," she said. "Grace thinks it's Maggie, a friend of Ann's. Grace said Maggie's always been jealous of Ann. Ann loaned her clothes. She didn't have a lot of nice things herself."

"We only met her once," I said. "It was the time you and Jack and I had supper with Ann and another lady at that little restaurant downtown. That was Maggie, right?"

"Yes," said Iva Ray. "I don't know her too well either, but she does seem to have a temper."

"So does Grace," observed Jack.

Iva Ray nodded solemnly. "She certainly showed it today. After you left, she talked so hateful to Judy that she had her crying."

"Mother, until we know who killed Anna Mae, everyone's a suspect. What do you think about getting a private investigator?" Jack asked.

"I guess that's a good idea," Iva Ray said slowly. "I don't know what the others will say. I'll ask them, though."

"That's fine, and I hope they want to go in with us. But Mary and I are doing it anyway," Jack assured her. "With or without the rest of the family."

Later that evening, Jack stopped by The Pantry convenience store to pick up milk. When he returned, he shoved the milk into the refrigerator and slammed the door. Through clenched teeth, Jack relayed his milk-buying experience.

"Two old bags were talking about Anna Mae's murder." When Jack is angry, he resorts to mild name calling. Old bag and old geezer are two of his favorites. "One of them said, 'She had her rings on when she was murdered.' The other one said, 'Oh, no, she didn't.'

"They stood there arguing like two old crows, both of them so sure they were right. Both of them were treating Anna Mae's murder like small-town gossip.

"I finally walked up to them and said, 'She had her rings on. And she was my aunt.'"

# Chapter 11

# Viewing the Body

Friday. Ann's body would be ready for viewing in the afternoon.

There was some concern about whether Ann's injuries could be adequately disguised, but the women of the family seemed determined that there would be an open coffin. Maybe they needed to see Ann's body looking normal so they could imagine she had died peacefully.

A wig would cover the gaping holes in her skull, but it would have to come down far enough to camouflage the parts of her neck that were missing or concave. Iva Ray, Janet and Grace sorted through Ann's many wigs and found one they thought would work.

The ladies communicated throughout the day with the mortician. A "local boy" now in his fifties, he had worked at Barnett-Strother Funeral Home since high school graduation. He now owned the business and conducted it with the dignity and class you'd expect in a larger city. Always quiet and somber, you felt that he shared your grief.

Funeral home staff instructed the ladies to choose a pair of heavy gloves to cover Ann's hand injuries. They found black leather gloves and, from Ann's well-stocked closet, they chose a gray suit with a mink collar to match them. As Iva Ray described the clothing they'd selected, I realized that only the front portion of Ann's face would be visible.

I had never seen Ann wear the drab combination of clothing Iva Ray described. When she'd worn the gray suit, it would have been accented with bright pink earrings and pink floral shoes. Her wardrobe was filled primarily with oranges, purples and tropical prints. She enjoyed color, and she knew she looked good in it. I wished she could have worn a brightly colored outfit when we said our final good-byes.

Earl called Jack and asked if he'd go with him to Ann's house to get the large portrait that hung in her living room. In case the coffin had to be closed, Earl was thinking practically.

The portrait was actually an exquisite twenty-four-by-thirty-inch photo that Barbara Yonts, a local photographer, had taken of Ann. Ann had occasionally allowed Barbara to use her beautifully landscaped yard, with its statues and gazebo, for children's portraits. As a thank you, Barbara had presented Ann with the portrait less than a year ago.

In the portrait Ann is dressed in a pink linen pantsuit and she's holding a pink rose. She's stunning. It's the way I want to remember her.

As Jack was leaving to meet Earl, Judy called.

"Judy's found what looks like blood," Jack said as he hung up the phone. "She took down Anna Mae's portrait and decided to wrap it so it didn't get damaged taking it to the funeral home. There was some bubble wrap in the basement, along with some supplies Anna Mae used for mailing packages.

"When Judy pulled out the bubble wrap, she found a piece spattered with what looked like dried blood."

"I guess it's useless evidence," I observed.

"Yeah," said Jack. "But I still want to let Hargis know about it."

Jack and Earl stopped by Ann's house for the portrait. Jack thought the brownish-orange stain on the bubble wrap looked more like paint than blood, but he and Earl stayed until a police officer picked it up. Jack had taken off his jacket, and the officer noticed his badge and weapon.

"You're the one who's a federal agent," the officer commented.

Jack nodded.

"Maybe you can help me," the officer continued. "Do you know how to get the federal reports that show when people make big purchases?"

"Sure," said Jack. "You can check CTRs and 8300s through the Treasury Department."

Jack had investigated countless financial crimes—high-stakes gambling, money laundering, counterfeiting, prostitution—and using CTRs and Form 8300s was as natural to him as using credit cards was to me. He was glad to help this officer, who so comfortably admitted that he was venturing into unfamiliar territory.

Banks are required to file CTRs (Currency Transaction Reports) with the U.S. Department of the Treasury any time they have a transaction involving $10,000 or more in cash. A conscientious bank often files a CTR for transactions that appear to be avoiding the $10,000 guideline, such as two $5,000 transactions or a $9,800 transaction. These reports are on file with the U.S. Treasury and can be obtained by other law enforcement agencies by subpoena.

If a $10,000 cash transaction occurs with an entity other than a bank, a Form 8300 is filed. Real estate companies, casinos, car dealerships and boat and airplane sales companies usually keep these forms handy for the occasional person who pulls out a wad of one hundred dollar bills to cover a transaction.

During the days of Prohibition and the beginnings of organized crime, the government learned that it was easier to prove excess money than to connect criminals directly to their crimes. While it was impossible to connect Al Capone with his racketeering, proving that he had money he didn't report on his tax returns put him behind bars.

The government finally decided to transfer its work to banks and businesses by requiring cash transaction reports, and in 1984, Uncle Sam set up the CTR/8300 system. At the same time, the government made money laundering a federal crime, and banks and individuals failing to report cash transactions were subject to indictment.

"Can you help me get reports like that?" asked the officer.

"I can do it if I have a case open on someone," said Jack. "Otherwise, those reports are off limits. But you can request them yourself if they're crucial to a case you're working on."

"That's great," said the officer. "I'll do that."

"Wonder what all that's about," Jack told Earl after the officer left. Then noticing Earl's demeanor, he added, "You okay, Earl?"

Earl, with the normally flat-line emotions, was leaning forward in an antique chair, looking as if he were about to jump up and punch someone.

"I was doing alright until now," said Earl. "But anger's set in. When I think what someone did to my sister. ..."

Earl got up suddenly. "Let's get out of here. Come with me to my shop, and I'll give you the gun you found yesterday. Ann would want you to have it."

The family viewing was at 3:00. We gathered in a room next to the viewing room, waiting for everyone to arrive. Then we walked in together.

I pulled Jack aside and squeezed his arm tight. "Honey, we can't let people see her this way. She was too beautiful and feminine. Her features were soft. What's in that coffin looks harsh."

"It doesn't look anything like Anna Mae," Jack agreed. He pulled his mother aside. "People don't need to remember her this way."

Iva Ray nodded, but we knew she wouldn't speak up. She'd go along with whatever the others chose to do.

"Change the lipstick," Janet told a funeral home employee. "Ann wore a lighter shade, more of a pink."

The employee wiped off the red lipstick and put on some pink. The staff had done their best with Ann's battered body, but the wounds were ghastly and they had been unable to artistically cover them. But the family wanted to, had to, believe she looked fine.

"There," said Janet with finality. "That's better."

And so Anna Mae Winstead Branson's loved ones and friends said good-bye to what seemed to me a harsh caricature of the real Ann. Unfortunately, the curiosity seekers had ample reason for assumptions and speculations about the covered parts of her body.

Before long, hundreds of people streamed into the funeral home. We stood near the coffin to greet the endless procession of mourners. Over and over we heard "you don't remember me, do you" as we were reacquainted with people we'd known nineteen years earlier when we moved from Madisonville. And all I could think was that any of these people could be Ann's killer.

Russell brought his three sons from his first marriage. The oldest was twelve. His twin boys were nine. The twins seemed nervous about approaching the body. Russell placed his arms around their shoulders and they walked together to the coffin. I realized again how scary Ann's body appeared.

Pastor Tom Branson and his wife, Connie, nearly filled a row with their children. Tom was not the appointed minister for the next day's service, though he was leading a prayer. However, he and Connie were so used to their ministerial role that they moved among the mourners, greeting and comforting them.

Suddenly a distant family member was beside me.

"Can you imagine!" the family member whispered. "Someone had the nerve to ask me if Ann had been violated."

She leaned even closer and shuddered. "And someone asked if her fingers had been severed."

She waited for my response. When I remained silent, she pressed, "*Were* they?"

# Chapter 12

# Suspects and Other Mourners

By early evening, I found a place alone in a back row of chairs. But soon someone eased into the chair beside me.

"Hi, I'm Russell's wife." I reached out to shake her hand.

"You look as tired as I feel," she smiled. "This is so hard on all of us. I sure wish we'd met under different circumstances. Russell speaks so highly of you and Jack."

Russell's second wife, Terri, was the first person I'd talked to all evening who hadn't sapped my strength. She had a relaxed way of interacting that helped me slow down and take a breath. I liked her immediately.

Slim, attractive Terri was elegantly dressed in a fitted knee-length black dress. In spite of her careful hair and makeup, she struck me as a natural beauty who didn't fret over her looks. I liked her immediately and wished I could hide in the back row and talk with this easy conversationalist all night.

I felt that Terri would have liked to hide as well. Though she and Russell had been married for several years, I could tell she felt like an interloper, a concerned person on the fringe, a non-blood relative. Russell was spending time with his sons, and they'd come to the funeral home with his first wife, Denise. Terri stole occasional glances at Russell and his first family, and I sensed a slight rise in her voice and a subtle shifting of body language when she watched them.

When Judy, Ann's housekeeper, entered the room and stood alone and uncomfortable near the door, I knew I had to make her feel welcome. Reluctantly, I told Terri, "There's someone I need to speak to. But let's talk some more. I'd like to get to know you better."

Judy seemed relieved when I approached her. She was glad to see someone she knew and was eager to talk about the murder. Being one of the people who knew Ann best had elevated her to near-star status. But in spite of her readiness to talk, I sensed that Judy was deeply and truly grieving.

"I know you loved Ann," I told her. "And I know you did a lot to make her comfortable."

Judy's demeanor brightened. "Oh, I did. She loved to go and do and have parties and lunches. And I tried to take some of the work off her. Every week, we'd sit down and talk about her plans. Then I'd put it all together for her.

"I loved Miz Ann. She was so good to me, and to my daughter, too. She's fourteen. Miz Ann would give her big old boxes of makeup. When I told my daughter what happened, she cried and cried."

"Thanks for the information you gave us the other day," I told Judy.

"I'm glad to do it," said Judy. "I want her killer caught. And *I* think it's Wayne. He's not even coming to the funeral home. Don't you think that's strange? When I asked him why, he just said he doesn't do funerals. He doesn't even seem sad about Miz Ann. He just told me, 'Great. Here I am living alone in the country and I don't have any alibi.'

"He tried to make his mom be his alibi, but she wouldn't do it. He stopped by her place and ate some chili and biscuits and left at 8:30. He tried to get her to say it was 9:30 but she wouldn't."

Judy was insistent. "Wayne has a terrible temper. I think he did it. He's got memory lapses. And he's got this heart condition that makes him have blackouts."

"How were Ann and her fiancé doing?"

Judy was solemn. "She wasn't going to marry him, at least not right now. She told me a couple of times. She told me, 'Judy, I just don't feel good about marrying him while Grace is alive, and I told her, 'Then don't you do it.'"

I squeezed Judy's arm. "Judy, after we go back to Georgia, will you contact Jack or me if you think of anything else?"

Judy nodded. "Jack already gave me one of his cards. I'll call if I find out anything."

Judy shook her head in disgust. "I just hope Wayne don't confuse the police. He's trying to shift blame to Russell. He told them Russell stopped by on Saturday and, after he left, Miz Ann told him that the only time Russell stopped by was when he wanted money, and she wasn't going to give him any more.

"That's the craziest thing I ever heard. Miz Ann would have given her family anything she had. All they had to do was ask." I nodded but inwardly wondered if Ann would have given Jack or me anything we'd asked for.

David Branson, Ann's brother-in-law, approached, and he was a welcome relief. Always even-tempered and down-to-earth, he had stories about Ann—and I was hungry to hear them.

"Anybody who's jealous of Ann's money needs to know that she and Carroll earned every bit of it," said David. "Nobody gave them anything. They didn't have two pennies to rub together when they got married, but Ann had class before she had money.

"They lived down near the old home place when they got married, and I used to go over to their house when I was a kid. Ann always fixed things up nice, set the table nice and all. She'd almost always have a warm syrup pie, and she'd cut me a big slice. I can still taste it."

"Syrup pie?" I asked.

"Yeah," said David. "Just what it sounds like. Maple syrup poured over a pie crust and baked."

Hard as I tried to hide my feelings about such a pie, David knew it didn't sound appetizing to someone who hadn't grown up in rural

Kentucky.

"I tell you," David shook his head. "When you're poor and you're craving something sweet, there's nothing like a warm syrup pie."

David was quiet for a moment before summing up his feelings about his sister-in-law. "Ann was a lady, through and through. That's what I'll always remember about her."

As someone else sought David's attention, I searched the room for Jack. He was more comfortable in this crowd than I was. This was his family, and he was catching up with relatives he rarely saw.

"Jack, can I talk to you for a minute?" It was Russell. The two cousins found chairs in the back of the room.

"Jack, do you think they'll catch whoever did this?" asked Russell.

"Yes," Jack was emphatic. But with his mind still on the gun he'd so quickly found in Ann's house, he added, "But I think we're in for a long, involved investigation. This is a small town with limited murder investigation experience and limited resources."

As the crowd began to dissipate, Jack and I were finally able to talk. I'd tried to let him spend time with his friends and family, but now I realized how much I'd missed him. Squeezing his hand was reassuring.

"I'm going to call a private detective," Jack said as we were leaving the funeral home. "I've got to know we're doing all we can.

"The PI I'm thinking of is a former Bureau agent. He was the FBI's polygrapher, and we worked together on a couple of cases. He's tough but fair. He retired a few years ago and started his own PI business.

"He's one of the best. And that's what it's going to take. We're up against more than a tough murder case. I don't want Anna Mae's murder to end up as a case number and a box of evidence on a back shelf in the MPD records room."

# Chapter 13

# Graveside

Friday evening, as Jack and I were getting ready for bed, I was developing those aches, pains and a scratchy throat that can only be described as an "all-over sick feeling."

"I think I'm coming down with something," I told Jack.

"It's probably the stress," Jack assured me. But when the alarm buzzed on Saturday morning, January 18, I was immediately aware that I had a full-blown cold.

I struggled out of bed, overcome with grief, exhaustion, a sore throat and a head cold. Chills ran up and down my fevered body. Then I remembered that I'd be outdoors at the graveside service. My satin-lined leather coat was perfect for the coldest Georgia day, but it would feel like tissue paper in the aftermath of the Kentucky snowstorm.

I swallowed and gagged as my swollen throat rejected even saliva. I staggered the twenty steps to the bathroom and put my head down to rest from the exertion. Gathering courage to face the mirror, I raised my head to see puffy cheeks and nostrils that looked as if someone had smeared red lipstick on them while I slept. I coughed and my chest fought a vice-like grip just to draw another breath. At that moment, I understood how Job felt when physical ailments were added to his already grief-stricken spirit.

In the kitchen, Jack, Iva Ray and I moved as if we were walking underwater. With the same eerie resistance you feel when you move your limbs while at the bottom of a pool, we reached for milk and toast and juice. We heard each other's voices with the echoed distortion of scuba divers communicating under the water's surface. This was a day we wanted behind us, but that closure would come only after hours of small talk and endless lines of mourners.

Pumped full of extra-strength cold medicine, I dressed in my floor-length black velvet skirt and matching top, sprinkled with bright pink roses. Everyone should wear their brightest florals in honor of Ann, I thought.

Ann savored life, and her clothing conveyed her extravagant intensity. Once, when she and Iva Ray took a cruise and their luggage was delayed, Ann pulled an elegant nightgown from her overnight bag—a nightgown that probably cost more than my wedding dress—dressed it up with heels and diamonds, and dined at the captain's table with no one the wiser.

And Earl said she wouldn't have worn the old pants and sweater to church.

As I was fastening my pearls, Jack's hands reached over mine and he connected the clasp.

"Happy birthday," he whispered close to my ear.

"I'd completely forgotten," I answered.

We drove to the funeral home with Iva Ray. Armed with a lace hand-kerchief for show and a wad of tissues for survival, I tried not to talk and spread germs in the car.

"Tom and Connie invited everyone to their house after the funeral," Iva Ray told us. Jack and I glanced at each other, and quickly affirmed that neither of us was up to this gathering at his cousin's house.

"I think we'll skip that," Jack told his mother. "Mary's not feeling well, and it's her birthday."

Iva Ray put her hand on her mouth. "Oh, no. I'm so sorry. We just didn't remember when we scheduled the funeral."

"We delayed it too long, anyway," I reassured her, trying not to project my voice and its accompanying germs. "I forgot it was my birthday, too."

We were barely inside the funeral home when a family member I hardly knew approached me. "If there's anything—anything at all—that I can do to help you all…I worry so much about Iva Ray. She's so frail."

"As a matter of fact, there is something you can do," I responded. "Next time you're making soup or vegetables, take a little dish over to Iva Ray. I'm afraid she eats mostly junk food."

The family member nodded, then asked: "What's going to happen to Ann's personal belongings? I know that will be a real job, cleaning all that out."

"I believe that's taken care of," I replied.

"Well," she said. "I told my kids that when I die, I didn't want anyone going through my underwear drawer! I'll be glad to take that job off the immediate family. You all have so much more to worry about."

I took a breath and answered. "Ann designated who was to receive every personal item. But thanks for offering to help."

The family member looked toward the crowd.

"Oh, I see someone I need to say hi to," she said, moving away without making eye contact.

I breathed a raspy sigh of relief and wiped my now-raw nose just as Judy approached. "I heard you were sick. That little coat you had on last night won't keep you warm at the cemetery. You can wear mine."

I hugged Judy, being careful not to turn my runny nose toward her. I appreciated her gesture, but I told myself. *Keep your guard up. No one's eliminated as a suspect.*

For the service, the immediate family was ushered into a separate room just off the main one—Janet and David, Iva Ray, Grace, Earl and his family, his daughter and granddaughter, Ann's fiancé Bob and me. I sat on the back row, along with Bob.

From the family's room, we could see the ministers and musicians and the first few rows of mourners. We watched as the pallbearers made their way solemnly to the front row. Janet and David's sons had just flown in from California and Ohio, dressed in pricey suits  befitting their professional positions. Equally well-dressed were Russell and Jack. Earl's daughter's boyfriend was dressed in a more modest suit. Brenda's brother wore dark cotton pants, shirt and tie and a navy-colored outdoor jacket.

The pallbearers were stone-faced, as their assignment demanded. Inside the family room, we could weep in private. But the atmosphere was quiet and stoic.

As the minister spoke, I watched Jack's face, knowing that behind the steely stare was a broken, grieving heart. No one but me noticed his slightly set jaw and the rhythmic tapping of his clenched fist against his thigh. Knowing how he was hurting, I told myself that the other family members were hurting, too. And yet, one of them could be the killer.

As the service progressed, Bob began to sob quietly. I wanted to comfort him, but I couldn't bring myself to do so.

After the service, we filed by for a final look at the body—first, the hundreds of mourners in the large room and then the family. Bob walked in front of me, bent over and sobbing. Seemingly from nowhere, Connie appeared at his side. Draping her arm around his frail shoulder, she audibly comforted him.

The snow made for treacherous driving, so Jack drove his mother and me to the cemetery, quickly joining the other pallbearers when we arrived. He walked with his mother and me up the snow-covered knoll to the open grave, then hurried back to the hearse. Snow flurries blurred the pallbearers' vision as they trudged up the small hill to the grave.

At that moment, I was especially thankful not to be a man. Not to have to lift a coffin which contained someone I loved. Jack had done this many times, but today I knew the burden was especially great. Loved ones had died of cancer, heart conditions and other natural causes. Never had we lost someone to a violent crime.

The gray, cloudy sky and scattered snow flurries added to the somber feel of the graveside service. The closer relatives sat in folding chairs under a small canopy beside the open grave. In spite of my cold, I decided not to sit under the shelter—the blood thing and all. There would be one or two who would whisper, even if just inwardly, "What's *she* doing sitting with the family?"

While the others went to Connie and Tom's, Jack and I snuggled up on Iva Ray's couch, eating leftovers from well-wishers and nursing my now fully developed cold.

Iva Ray was animated when she returned from Tom and Connie's.

"The family wants to go in on an investigator," she told Jack excitedly. "You say you have someone?"

"I'm already scheduled to meet with him Monday afternoon," said Jack. "I'll tell him to work through Earl."

# Chapter 14

# In the Valley

I soon learned that I could weep without warning. With minimal emotion, I'd tell five people what we knew so far about the murder. Then, to my own surprise, I'd begin crying as I told the sixth.

I'd walk into the mall with so much rage that I'd hope someone would try to grab my purse so I could attack them with my fists. One day, I told a sales clerk in the photography department of a store—a complete stranger—about the murder.

I became afraid to walk down our basement stairs when I was alone in the house. I couldn't watch murder scenes in suspense movies. I didn't want our grandsons, Taylor and Elliott, to play with their oversized rubber Lego swords any longer.

We brought Ann's portrait home and hung it in our dining room. The first time we had the family over for supper, eight-year-old Elliott pulled a chair in front of the portrait so he could pretend that Aunt Ann was eating with us.

During the meal, Elliott began talking about next Thanksgiving and Christmas. With holiday family stacked up like airplanes over Chicago,

Elliott usually wandered around with his pillow, looking for a bed with space enough for a wiry little boy to crawl in.

"Sometimes I sleep with Granny Ive, and sometimes I sleep with Aunt Ann. It's funny to sleep with Aunt Ann, because her feet are always cold," Elliott giggled. I looked quizzically at Penny.

"He knows," she whispered. "He just thinks if he doesn't acknowledge it, it won't be true."

Older brother Taylor responded openly to Elliott. "She's dead, Elliott. A bad guy broke into her house and killed her. Aunt Ann's not coming at Christmas. You just have to get used to it."

Jack didn't sleep well, and he thought about the murder constantly. Just as he'd start to relax most nights, our phone would ring and the caller ID would indicate a call from Madisonville. And after he talked about the murder, he'd have another sleepless night. His alarm sounded each morning at 3:20 a.m., regardless of how many hours he'd stayed awake trying to focus on anything but Ann lying lifeless at the bottom of her basement stairs.

Neither of us could comprehend how something this horrible could happen in our normal family. But we knew from experience that we can't make sense out of a tragedy while we're in the middle of it. It's only when we reach the other side of the valley that we can look back and see how the path brought us eventually to higher, safer ground. It's only then that we realize that the path set for us is exactly the one we would have chosen – if we could have seen the destination.

I knew we'd be stronger not in spite of what we'd gone through, but because of it. But no one—while walking through the fire—can say, "Let me walk a little longer. The heat will make me strong." But when the fire cools and we see that we're durable and strong, then we understand.

Right now, the other side of the valley wasn't in sight, the fire was still raging and it would be a long time till we could make sense of anything associated with Ann's death.

Part 2

■ ■ ■ ■

# All in the Family

# Chapter 15

# The Tallest Days

Monday, January 20. Jack and I returned to work. We spent the evenings trying to put the pieces of the crime puzzle together. The whodunit overshadowed the grieving process, and I resented not having the energy to mourn. I was a marketing director with a small family of staff. My team was incredibly sensitive and allowed me to talk about the murder when I felt like it and push it to the back of my mind when I could. Mostly, I needed to talk.

As I described the past week to co-workers, I felt a strange detachment. The circumstances were so bizarre that my mind easily denied that they were associated with our previously normal family. It was as if I were talking about a crime film Jack and I had seen the previous weekend.

As I listed the many suspects, I collapsed in a chair.

"It's like a giant game of Clue," I laughed uncontrollably. "Did Colonel Mustard do it in the dining room with a wrench? Or was it Professor Plum in the library with a candlestick?"

I sank deeper into the chair, wiping away tears of hysterical laughter. Fortunately, my friends knew me well enough to realize I wasn't cold and uncaring. My body was just demanding that I release the stress of the past days. We were all surprised when the stress showed itself as laughter instead of tears, but we accepted it as another chapter in the bizarre story that was now the Bransons' lives.

On Monday, Jack had lunch with Sam, the retired FBI agent and private detective he had hired to investigate his aunt's death. Sam had an associate in Kentucky—Burt—and he said Burt would be doing most of the work on Ann's murder investigation.

Jack provided Earl's contact information and told Sam that Earl would be handling everything on behalf of the family.

"I'll overnight a letter of engagement," Sam assured Jack. "We require a $10,000 retainer. As soon as we have that, we'll get started."

The two men shook hands, and Jack returned to his office, feeling as if he'd just transferred at least a small part of his emotional burden to Sam.

Judy called Jack at his office that afternoon.

"I just thought of something you might want to know," she said. "Wayne used to live in Paducah. He had a girlfriend, a married woman. And her husband died under what I hear was suspicious circumstances. I just thought you'd want to know." Jack immediately called Sam and gave him that bit of information.

By Wednesday, we were physically and emotionally drained. We were tired of telling the story of Ann's death. What had at first been therapeutic was now exhausting. We decided to turn in early and try to make up for some of the recent sleepless nights. It was 9:30 when Jack reached for the lamp on the nightstand.

Immediately the phone rang, and caller ID showed that it was Iva Ray. It was only 8:30 in Madisonville, and over the next few months we'd learn to regret the time difference.

"Is everything okay?" Jack asked his mother.

"Yes," answered Iva Ray. "But I got a strange letter today. It was addressed just to 'Branson' and I thought it might be meant for you."

Jack replied quickly: "If you haven't opened it, don't. Let the police. They may be able to lift a print from it."

"I'm sorry." Iva Ray was nervous and apologetic. "It was with a big stack of sympathy cards and other mail, and I ripped it open before I realized what it was."

Hiding his disappointment, Jack answered, "That's fine. It was probably wiped clean anyway. What does it say?"

Iva Ray read the brief letter aloud: "This is true. The maid and the apartment manager are cousins."

Jack: "Is that all?"

"That's it," said Iva Ray. "It's handwritten, but the handwriting is almost childish, like someone wrote it with their left hand. Maybe the person was trying to disguise their handwriting."

"Mother, you need to call the police immediately," said Jack. "If you can't make me a copy before you give the letter to the police, ask them to send you a copy."

Early Saturday, Jack and I bounded out of bed in anticipation of our first normal day in too long. Taylor and Elliott would soon be scurrying in the door, and we knew that somehow their laughter and energy would overflow to us.

Before the boys arrived, however, Earl called. Jack was walking through the living room when his cell phone vibrated, so he sank onto the living room sofa as he answered. When I realized the call was about the murder, I sat down beside him.

After a moment or two of surface conversation, Earl said, "David's here with me. He wants to talk to you."

"We've decided not to help pay for the private investigator," said David in his slow Kentucky drawl. "Janet says the FBI would just run a bunch of reports. And Grace talked to a retired state trooper she ran into at the mall. He said if we got the feds involved, it would make the police mad and they'd slow down their efforts."

"Do you think the police are so uncommitted that they'd slow down their efforts for something that petty?" asked Jack. "I think you're underestimating them."

David was only the messenger and his response was apologetic: "Sorry. That's just the way it is. The family's not going to pay for a private investigator. The police are getting hair and blood samples from the family, so they must have something."

Jack closed his small Motorola phone. We sat on the living room couch, our arms around each other.

"I guess it all boils down to money again," Jack said as he shook his head.

The boys were the innocent and happy elixir we had hoped they'd be. We had several hours of relief from the stress. But we'd had a longtime commitment to attend a retirement party that evening for one of the agents, so Jack drove the boys home instead of tucking them in as usual.

Sam called Jack's cell during the twenty-minute drive to take the boys home.

"Just wanted you to know we have some background information we're putting together on the suspects," said Sam. "And Burt is checking with his sources to see what he can dig up in Kentucky."

"The family's changed their minds," said Jack flatly. "They're saying now that they're not going to pay. Better put the investigation on hold till I figure out what to do."

Jack dropped off Taylor and Elliott and immediately called me at home. As I was changing from a sweater and jeans to a glitzy silver top and black crepe pants, I heard Jack's determined voice: "Let's do it ourselves."

I knew what he meant. I'd just been wondering how long it would take him to realize what I had known earlier that morning. Jack's integrity would drive him to do everything possible to find Ann's killer, with or without his family's support.

Jack had often told me how much he'd admired Davy Crockett when he was a boy. He'd had a coonskin cap and a rifle, just like Davy's. He'd read a biography of Crockett and discovered that his motto was "Be sure you're right, then go ahead." He'd decided to make it his motto, too.

I could easily imagine Jack as a nine-year-old boy, wearing his coon-skin cap, and vowing to stick to his convictions. Because I'd seen him stick to his convictions the entire time I'd known him.

"I don't see any other option," I told Jack. "If there's even a small chance a private investigator can help, we have to try."

"Then I'll call Mother and Earl," Jack answered with relieved determination, "and then Sam."

Jack's messages to his mother and to Earl were the same: "This is strictly a courtesy call. I'm not asking your permission or your blessing. Mary and I are hiring a private investigator on our own."

As I held an array of earrings and necklaces against my top to find the best match, a sad smile crept across my face. Jack had once been inter-viewed by a local newspaper and asked his favorite quote. Half expecting to hear him recite Crockett's motto, I realized that in adulthood, he understood that moving forward with your convictions can be costly.

"The tallest trees catch the most wind," Jack had replied to the reporter. It had never bothered Jack to stand tall, but I sensed now that his tallest days were before him.

76

# Chapter 16

# Suspects and Investigations

The decision to pay for the investigators was easy. Writing a check for the $10,000 retainer was not. If the siblings had gone in with us on the retainer, each of us would have paid only $2,000. We comforted ourselves with the knowledge that we would have had just as much trouble coming up with $2,000 as $10,000.

Jack and I both earned good salaries, but we spent our money as fast as the paychecks could be cashed. We drove two fast sports cars. We lived in a nice house, we ate out nearly every night and we bought our grandkids just about anything they wanted. We liked the good life and we enjoyed our earnings. And now we had till Monday to come up with $10,000.

The next day was tough for us. We talked about the situation intermittently throughout that Sunday afternoon.

"Do you think Anna Mae would have paid for a private investigator if one of us had been murdered?" I had to ask the question.

"I don't know," Jack answered. "I think there's a good chance she wouldn't. She probably would have had the same attitude as the rest of the family. She'd have said just wait and see if the police can handle it before spending all that money."

"But that's not the point," continued Jack solemnly. "We're doing the right thing. That's what we have to focus on."

That evening, the family came for supper. As we passed the meatloaf and mashed potatoes, Jack told our children: "Mom and I are hiring a private investigator to try to find out who killed Aunt Ann."

"The rest of the family was supposed to go in on the cost, but ..." My voice quavered as I struggled to finish. "...they've decided not to put out the money. The PI has to have a $10,000 retainer just to get started."

"I can help with the cost," offered our son Dave. "You can have my tax refund. It's over a thousand."

"I might be able to borrow against my retirement," said Penny.

I began to cry in earnest. But this time, the tears represented gratitude. What we'd tried so hard to teach our kids—that money wasn't as important as integrity—had somehow been "caught."

"Thanks for the offer," smiled Jack. "But Mom and I can handle it."

The next morning, I went to my credit union. The staff had already heard about Ann's murder. I explained why we needed an immediate signature loan and received the check within minutes.

Jack and I decided to meet for lunch so I could give him the check. We met at a busy cafeteria. Halfway through our lunch, Jack got a call on his cell.

I watched Jack's array of expressions, trying to fill in the other side of the conversation. I knew the call was from Sam, and I knew they had someone. I had pictured Jack being ecstatic when the police located a suspect, but the pain on his face told me that he was hearing news he would rather not hear.

Finally, Jack closed his phone. "It was a conference call with Sam and his associate in Kentucky —Burt," said Jack slowly, concentrating on every word, making sure he relayed every shred of evidence accurately.

"The police called in some people for polygraphs. The handyman, Wayne, couldn't be tested. Kentucky law says you can't give a polygraph to someone who's had an angioplasty."

"You're kidding," I exclaimed. "I've never heard of that."

Jack nodded. "It's a state law that applies only to police polygraphs. Burt said he can polygraph the handyman if he's willing."

Jack continued with precision. "Burt's source said that Knight, the crazy renter, failed the polygraph."

"So it was the renter?" I offered cautiously. "Then it will be over soon?"

Jack blinked slowly and continued. "Russell failed the polygraph, too. And he failed it miserably."

I put my hand over my mouth just in time to stifle a gasp. Quietly, almost inaudibly, I said over and over, "Dear God, no. Oh, no. Not Russell."

"Russell was upset after the polygraph—crying, unable to drive himself home. They called Earl, and he drove to the station and picked him up. Earl's claiming the polygraph was given under duress, that the police want to pin the murder on somebody and get the case solved."

"What do you think?" I asked.

"Very possible," Jack nodded. "Especially with the renter failing too, though they both could've been involved.

"I'm not sure who gave the polygraph, or if Russell was questioned before or after. You don't hit a suspect hard with upsetting questions before a polygraph, but if the Madisonville police aren't experienced with the test, they might have done that.

"Only thing …," Jack hesitated. Then: "They've got a motive for Russell. Russell's got a gambling problem, and a big one. Plus, he owed Anna Mae a lot of money."

# Chapter 17

# Escalating
# Stress

Jack filled me in on the rest of the conversation: Sam and Burt had agreed to go to Madisonville the following weekend. They'd do polygraphs on Wayne and Russell if they were willing. And they'd interview Judy and possibly some other witnesses.

We gripped each other's hands as we walked from the restaurant. As we tried to absorb everything we'd just heard, we talked in staccato.

"How much did he owe her?"

"What about Earl?"

"Gambling? Not Russell."

"There's no way."

"The MPD must be mistaken."

Productivity for the remainder of the day was zero. Like human robots, we returned to our offices and went through the motions. When we could finally go home, we nestled in each other's arms, reinforcing each other's disbelief that Russell could be involved.

Jack's mother called later that evening. Though she wouldn't speak out to challenge her siblings, she wanted us to know why the family had decided not to help pay for the PI.

"Grace says she has a will," Iva Ray told Jack, "but no one's seen it. Of course, Grace is due to inherit a fourth of Ann's estate. Some of the family say that if Grace dies intestate, all our money will be tied up for years. Grace doesn't want us to hire a private investigator. If we upset her, she could die before we can find out about her will."

"Money talks," said Jack when he relayed the conversation. "But what it says can be unpleasant."

"But this is Anna Mae's money," I told him. "Money she and Carroll worked hard for."

Jack nodded. "Mother also said that Anna Mae no longer had an insurance policy for Grace. She knew Grace was about to die, so she cashed in the policy a couple of months ago and gave Grace part of the money so she could enjoy it now. But if Ann died first, Grace would still get $90,000 from the estate, to cover what the others received from their policies.

"Grace, at best, has a few months to live. She knows it. She's already bought her grave stone. But she's obsessed with the money. Earl divided a couple of small parts of the estate three ways, and when Grace found out, she threatened to sue him."

"Still," I said, "as long as Grace is alive, a fourth of the estate belongs to her. I don't understand the big rush to divide the estate. If Grace doesn't live to enjoy her share, she should at least be able to leave it to whoever she chooses."

Earl called a few minutes later. He didn't mention Russell and neither did Jack. The two had always been close, and Earl was just running some strange occurrences by him.

"I went to Ann's house this afternoon," said Earl. "And there was a blackbird loose in the house. You know the old wives tale that if a bird gets in the house…"

"Someone's going to die," Jack finished the sentence. "I wouldn't worry about that. I'd worry about how it got in there. Who's got a key to the house? Somebody had to let that bird in."

"Nobody's supposed to have one but me," said Earl. "But Judy or Wayne could have made one sometime in the past."

"And Jack," said Earl. "You remember the diamond ring that was missing?"

"Yeah."

"It's back."

"What do you mean?"

Earl explained that he'd taken some things out of the kitchen cabinet and the ring was behind the cup that held the costume jewelry.

"I don't know how we could have missed it," said Earl. "Janet and Grace looked through that whole cabinet. They would've found it if it'd been there."

"Someone's getting in the house. Lots of people could already have keys," Jack said. "Earl, you've got to change the locks."

"I'll get them changed tomorrow," said Earl.

The phone calls had escalated our stress. We lay in the dark, trying to sleep.

"Honey?" Jack's voice was clear in the sight-and-sound vacuum.

"Yeah?"

"I've been replaying everything in my mind, trying to see if I could make sense of it all," Jack continued.

The room was quiet. Then: "I keep thinking about something that happened at the funeral home. Russell pulled me aside and asked if I thought they'd find the killer. I was so mad at the MPD that I slammed them.

"Right after that, Russell's mood changed. Just a little. At the time, I only noticed it on an unconscious level.

"But thinking back, I realize Russell seemed pleased that the killer might not be caught."

# Chapter 18

# Lies
# and Truth

Iva Ray called on January 28, to say that Grace was getting worse. And she said the family now thought a PI might be a good idea.

"What's changed?" I asked after Jack hung up the phone.

"Well," said Jack. "Grace is dying. An investigator won't hasten her death now. It won't keep the family from getting their money."

"Hmmm," I told Jack. "We've already paid the $10,000 retainer."

The next day, Earl called Jack at work. He wanted to talk.

"Jack, the police are trying to jam up Russell," said Earl. "They called him in and badgered him. Then they gave him a lie detector test and they claim he failed it."

Jack listened quietly as Earl confirmed what our investigators had already told him. "They're determined to pin this on Russell, and he's innocent. They had him so upset, I had to drive him home from the police station.

"They had a search warrant, and they searched Russell's house and took some of his clothes—some jeans and a couple of sweaters. And a claw hammer. They impounded his truck and he needs it to get to work. Is there anything I can do?"

"Does Russell have an alibi?" Jack asked.

"Yeah," said Earl. "He says he can account for every minute of his time. He went to church that night, like he does every week. He and his wife, Terri, took separate cars because he had to drop one of his boys off at his ex-wife Denise's place. After he dropped them off, he went straight home. He and Terri had a late supper and then went to bed."

"Earl," said Jack. "I don't know what to think. The police haven't taken me up on my offer to help. I haven't heard anything since we got home."

"I wouldn't put it past them to plant DNA or blood on the things they took from Russell's house," said Earl. "They just want to finish this case fast and get their publicity."

"Jack," Earl continued. "I'll pay half the PI. We have to prove Russell's innocence."

"Will Russell submit to another polygraph?" asked Jack. "My PI is a retired Bureau polygrapher."

"I'm sure he will," said Earl. "We've got an attorney now, so I'll ask him."

"Tell him to be available this weekend," said Jack. "Our PI will be in Madisonville for some interviews, and he can polygraph Russell while he's there."

Friday morning, Jack said, "Sam's flying to Kentucky to work with Burt this weekend."

"You don't sound excited about it." After thirty-five years of marriage, I read Jack's voice and moods effortlessly.

"It just doesn't seem like we need both of them. They charge a hundred dollars an hour—each. With an airline ticket, travel time, two motel rooms and double expenses, they'll eat up the retainer in a couple of days."

All this PI stuff was new to me, but I tried to think of a reason for the double billing.

"Maybe one has to take notes while the other does the polygraph."

"No, I've seen plenty of people put on the box," said Jack, referring to the polygraph in law enforcement slang. "Sometimes there are two polygraphers, but just as often, there's one."

"Maybe Burt's afraid to be alone during the interviews."

Jack smiled. "Burt's six-foot-four. He was a college football player. He's a retired FBI agent, trained at Quantico. And he was on the FBI SWAT team."

I'd been rushing to get ready for work, talking as I applied makeup and blow-dried my hair. Now I stopped and looked directly at Jack.

"Do you think they're taking advantage?" I asked. "This is a high profile case, and it's been all over the news that Anna Mae was wealthy."

"I guess they're wanting their share, like everybody else," said Jack sadly. "They're doing a good job. But I don't think it's necessary for both of them to go to Madisonville.

"But at this point, I'm willing to pay whatever it takes to find Anna Mae's killer," said Jack. "And, I hope, clear Russell's name."

# Chapter 19

# Truth or Consequences

S am flew to Louisville on Friday morning, then he and Burt drove the 150 miles to Madisonville. That evening, they interviewed Earl for more than two hours.

"The police have a suspect," volunteered Earl. "It's my son, Russell." Earl told our PIs about Russell's grueling six-hour interview and polygraph and how Russell had been so upset that Earl had to pick him up at the police station.

"After the way Russell was treated, I told him not to talk to the police again unless someone was with him," said Earl. "I knew they wouldn't let me be with Russell, so I found him a lawyer. One of the local lawyers recommended a lawyer from Princeton, about thirty-five miles from here."

"Why do you think Russell was so upset when he had the polygraph?" Sam asked.

"Why *wouldn't* he be?" asked Earl. "They were badgering him about killing someone he loved. They were accusing him of all sorts of things. By the time they hooked him to the machines, he was a wreck."

"If Russell was questioned with that severity before the polygraph, there's a good chance it affected his response. Burt here's a retired Bureau polygrapher. He can administer a second polygraph," said Sam.

"Jack mentioned that," said Earl, "and we've been thinking about it. We talked to Russell's attorney about it, and he felt like we ought to be able to do that while you are all in town."

"We could do it this weekend," said Sam. "Do you want to call Russell's attorney now and try to set something up?"

Earl called Russell's attorney, who had graduated from Madisonville High School a couple of years after Jack and me. He and Jack had been members of the same youth club. In a town the size of Madisonville, you could usually find a connection with everyone but the newcomers, and though we didn't know this Princeton attorney well, we knew him.

The attorney confirmed that he had a list of items taken from Russell's house when the search warrant was executed. The list included shoes, jeans, sweaters and a claw hammer. He confirmed, too, that the police were taking hair and blood samples from several individuals, and he assumed they had found usable DNA at the crime scene.

Sam and Burt set Russell's polygraph for Sunday morning.

"What about the housekeeper?" Burt asked Earl. "Can you arrange for us to interview her while we're here?" Earl nodded.

"And the handyman?" Burt continued. Again Earl promised to help.

Earl mentioned the renter that Ann was afraid of. "He's about fifty," commented Earl.

"I finally evicted him because of his crazy behavior. He thought people were after him. And he had delusions. He was always calling the police and calling Ann and me, complaining that people was trying to break into his house. He's staying in a motel now, but I don't know which one."

Then: "Russell's been gambling a lot lately," Earl volunteered to our investigators.

"Where does he normally gamble?" they asked.

"He used to go to the boat—the one in Evansville, right across the state line in Indiana, about fifty miles away. Casino Aztar," said Earl. "But he's been barred from there for winning too much money."

"How much has he won?"

"Something to the tune of $80,000," Earl answered. "After that, he started going to one of the casinos around Louisville."

"That's a long way," observed Sam. "About 150 miles."

# Chapter 20

# An Uneasy Feeling

The following morning, Saturday, February 1, Sam called Casino Aztar, the only casino in Evansville. When he asked the day shift supervisor if the casino banned players for winning too much, she laughed.

"We only ban people for two reasons," she told Sam. "Sometimes they realize they're compulsive gamblers and ask us not to allow them in. And if someone is causing a disturbance, we ask them to leave."

Sam and Burt interviewed Judy at a nearby motel on Saturday afternoon. It wasn't long into the interview before Judy offered up Wayne, the handyman, as her primary suspect.

"*I* think it was Wayne," she stated. "I never knew Wayne to go by Ann's house late in the evening until a month or two ago. But lately he'd been doing that every Sunday night. He told me he'd been trying to borrow money."

Our investigators listened and nodded as Judy continued weaving her story, with Wayne as the lethal thread. "Wayne told me he drove by Miz Ann's house the night she was killed. He said he started to stop—it was about nine o' clock—and then all of a sudden, he thought 'to hell with it' and went on home. Now you tell me why he'd do that." Our investigators indicated that they couldn't.

Judy told us how she remembered the events: "That Sunday night, around 9:00 or 9:30, I got a call from Miz Ann. My adopted granddaughter was talking to a friend. We have that call-waiting thing, and she got off the phone long enough for me to talk to Ann. Then she went right back to talking. The police have been bearing down on me lately, trying to get me to change my story about what time Ann called, but I know what time it was and it was 9:00 or 9:30.

"One of the officers stopped by a couple of days ago, and he told me, 'Judy, if you want to change your story, we'll just tear up your first report and forget we ever wrote it.'"

We had told our investigators about Iva Ray's anonymous note, which prompted them to ask Judy, "How long have you known Wayne?"

"About seven years," Judy responded. "Wayne's daughter and her boyfriend live next door to me. I know from her that Wayne's served time."

Judy told our investigators that Wayne had been at Ann's house the Thursday before Ann was killed, and that he'd told her that Russell had been there, too. "He said that Russell was there when he got there," said Judy, "but he left right afterward. When he left, Wayne claims Miz Ann told him, 'I don't know why he hangs around here. He only comes when he needs money, and I am not giving him any more.'"

"No more?" asked Burt.

"Yeah," said Judy. "He owed her $10,000. He had a CD that was about to mature and soon as it did, he was going to pay her what he owed."

"Why had he borrowed money from her?" asked Sam.

"I think it was for some kind of mining equipment. But Wayne owed her, too. Back around Thanksgiving, Miz Ann told me Wayne had asked her for $2,000, but Ann wouldn't give it to him because he already owed her something like $2,000 or $2,500. Then he asked her to sign a paper saying he worked for her full-time so he could prove he could pay his child support. Well, he didn't work full-time. He was hourly, just like me, and Ann said she wasn't signing anything."

Judy summarized her evidence against Wayne. "Wayne's a cold-hearted person. His daughter's been coming over to see me, and she's said some things about him. His daughter's been in trouble with the law, but I think she just got in with the wrong crowd. She's twenty-five or twenty-six, and she talked Ann into renting to her. She's a good kid and she doesn't have anything to do with this.

"Wayne's a different story." Judy had focused again on her prime suspect. "He's got a temper—a really bad one—and he needs money. And his daughter told me he's been acting weird lately."

From my experience with Judy, I knew she was believable. And I knew within five minutes of meeting with her, that she seemed to believe that Wayne was the murderer. She seemed focused on Wayne to the exclusion of other suspects. Most of her time with our investigators was devoted to elucidating her theory.

"I saw Wayne last Monday or Tuesday," Judy continued. "He came by my house and he seemed nervous. He said he didn't know whether he was coming or going. He came back later that day and said he met with the police. They wanted to give him a lie detector test but since he had that balloon surgery, they couldn't."

Still focusing on Wayne, Judy continued to build her case.

"Wayne talks about a woman that he was seeing. This woman's husband died under suspicious circumstances. I heard his death was ruled a suicide, but Wayne and this woman had been going together, and all of a sudden she shows up pregnant. She had a daughter.

"Well, anyway, the story goes that this woman's husband was working on this barge and just fell off. They said he committed suicide, but most people think he was pushed. And who had a better reason than Wayne?"

Wanting something more than conjecture, Sam asked, "You said Wayne had served time?"

"Yeah, he sure did," Judy snapped back. "When he was about twenty, he robbed a Pantry store and took a girl hostage in his trunk. I think he would have robbed Miz Ann in a minute. She was bad about leaving her purse laying wide open, especially when she was loading the car. She was bad about leaving her keys in the door, too."

Judy's eyes narrowed. "Wayne sometimes talked about how careless Ann was, and how she lived so close to the railroad tracks. He talked about how easy it would be to knock her off."

It was hard to refocus Judy, so our investigators let her talk about Wayne. If he was the killer, she was providing plenty of circumstantial evidence.

"I guess I haven't been too shy about telling people that I think it's Wayne. His daughter overheard me tell somebody, and she told Wayne. He waited till the three of us were together and told her to repeat what I'd said.

"I thought he'd light into me," Judy continued. "But he didn't even deny it. He didn't show any reaction, just like he didn't show any reaction when I told him Ann was murdered."

"What about Knight, the renter?" asked Sam. "Was Ann afraid of him?"

"Yeah," said Judy. "She was afraid of him. But he didn't do it. Neither did Dr. Bob, and some people are saying that."

"You know that for sure?" asked Burt.

"Yeah," Judy pushed back. "Because it was Wayne. Not that she was going to marry Dr. Bob. Miz Ann confided in me, and she told me she wasn't going to marry him. I was the one who suggested the prenuptial agreement."

Judy was obviously pleased to be Ann's confidante, and with no one to dispute how intimate their conversations had been, she made the relationship sound like best friends at a pajama party.

"I wasn't aware she and her fiancé had a prenuptial agreement," observed Sam.

"Oh, yeah," Judy assured the investigators. "I saw it. And the last time I saw it, something was underlined. I couldn't tell what it was, because the paper was upside down. But something was underlined for sure."

Ann told Jack nearly everything about her business and personal affairs. She hadn't mentioned a prenuptial agreement, but it certainly did not sound unreasonable. Ann and Bob were both wealthy. Bob had children who were probably worried about their inheritances. And though Ann had no children, I believe it meant a great deal to her to provide for her siblings, nieces and nephews. In addition to insurance policies for Jack, Iva Ray, David and Earl, Ann had left a sum of $10,000 to each of her nieces and nephews.

Both Ann and Bob would have wanted to protect their estates, but we'd heard nothing about a prenuptial agreement. And as far as Jack and I knew, no one had mentioned finding it in the house after Ann's death.

Judy told our investigators she had known Wayne seven years. The anonymous note Iva Ray received stated they were cousins.

Judy believed that Wayne was guilty and we had questions about his motives as well, but we found discrepancies in her theories about him. The telephone call she said she remembered didn't firm up with the estimated time of death. We knew we had to look further and deeper.

# Chapter 21

# Guilt or Innocence?

Wayne Shelton agreed to be interviewed and polygraphed Saturday evening. He drove to a nearby motel where our investigators were staying. Shelton, a frail, slightly built man of forty-eight, showed up dressed as if he were checking the motel's electrical wiring instead of proving his guilt or innocence in a high-profile murder case. But he was on time, and the three men quickly began an informal interview.

"How long did you work for Ann?" asked Sam.

"About five years," replied Wayne. "When I first started working for her, it was kind of off and on. But for a long time now, I'd been working just for her. She had plenty of work, with her rent houses and all."

"What kind of work did you do for Ann?"

"Anything that needed doing," bragged Wayne. "I did heating and AC. Plumbing and electrical and some carpentry."

"When did you hear about Ann's death?"

Wayne concentrated carefully on his response. "About 2:30 on Monday. Then the next day, a woman detective named Kelley Rager talked to me. Then another detective named Scott Troutman."

"Why do you think they talked to you twice?"

"I can see it," said Wayne earnestly. "I was there nearly every day. People knew I used to drink a lot. I quit three years ago, but most people don't know that. I sure could have been the one, but I wasn't."

Wayne stood and began to pace the small motel room, not with a guilty nervousness but with the restlessness of someone to whom physical labor was so natural that he couldn't sit still for long without feeling a twinge of guilt. But his pacing was slow and his skin was ashen.

He continued talking as he paced the fifteen-foot room. "They told me to come in and take a lie detector test, and I went in like they told me to. But I got a heart problem, and I had that balloon surgery. And I have poor circulation in my legs, because I'm a heavy smoker. The police sent me home. They said they couldn't do a lie detector on me on account of my balloon surgery."

"When was the last time you saw Ann alive?" asked Sam. Wayne realized the importance of this question, and he stopped walking and looked squarely at the investigators.

"I saw her Saturday, January 11, about eleven in the morning," Wayne responded. "She and this friend of hers were on their way to Evansville to see her boyfriend."

"Did you owe Ann any money?"

"Yeah," said Wayne. "Sometimes she'd give me an advance on my paycheck. And I borrowed $1,400 from her two years ago this March."

"When did you repay her?" our investigators hammered back.

"Never did," Wayne confessed.

"When's the last time you saw Russell Winstead?" asked Burt.

"I seen him at Ann's place on Thursday," said Wayne.

"January 9?"

"Yeah. He came over twice that day," said Wayne. "When he left the second time, Miz Ann was really mad. She said he owed her money and he only came around when he needed more. And he wasn't getting none anymore, because he owed her too much already."

As they prepared for the actual polygraph, our investigators asked Wayne to tell them what he did on January 12. Immediately, Wayne began moving around the room like a caged animal sensing a weak spot in his confinement. Finally, he could squeeze through a hole in the fence and escape to freedom. Convinced he had the answers that would open the cage, he began his narrative.

"I dropped my daughter off at her mama's—it's in a town a little over an hour away," said Wayne. "I dropped her off at 6:15, and I got back to town around 7:30. I went to my mother's house. She fixed me some chili and biscuits, and I stayed with her till 8:30 or 9:30. Then I just went home for the rest of the night."

Wayne breathed audibly as he finished his alibi speech. Take it or leave it—that was his full story. Our investigators asked if he was involved in any way with Ann's death. He emphatically denied that he was.

"Look, Wayne," said Burt. "I'm a retired FBI agent, and I was the Bureau polygrapher for years. Kentucky has a law that their police officers can't give a polygraph examination to anyone who's had an angioplasty. But that's a Kentucky law that applies only to their law enforcement officers. I can give you a polygraph if you're willing."

"Fine with me," replied Wayne. "As long as it's not dangerous or nothing. I gave them my hair and blood samples. I'm not afraid, because I'm telling the truth."

"Are you having any chest pains or other heart problems now?" asked Burt.

"Nah," said Wayne. "Not right now. Sometimes, when I've been working hard and it's cold outside, I'll have a little chest pain but nothing right now."

Burt set up his portable computerized equipment as he explained the procedure.

"Polygraphs have been in use since 1924," explained Burt. "'Poly' means 'many' and 'graph' is the report. The polygraph combines a number of different reports to give an overall picture of someone's truthfulness.

Polygraphs work on the theory that when a person lies, their breathing, heart rate and perspiration rate elevate."

"At first," said Sam, "We'll ask you to answer some questions correctly and some incorrectly. This will show us how you respond when you're telling the truth and when you're lying. Then we'll ask you two specific questions, and we'll ask you to tell the truth on those questions. We'll ask you: 'Did you stab Ann on January 12?' and 'Did you hit Ann in the head with anything on January 12?'"

Wayne nodded and sat in the straight chair by the motel desk. Burt fastened small metal plates to some of Wayne's fingers to record sweat gland activity and a blood pressure cuff on his arm to measure heart rate. He fastened rubber tubes around his chest and abdomen to measure breathing. All these measurement devices were connected to a laptop computer.

When the polygraph equipment was operational, Burt asked the preliminary questions, instructing Wayne to answer either truthfully or untruthfully on each. Burt found Wayne to be a capable reactor as he responded to the preliminary questions, so he proceeded to the primary questions.

Burt: Did you stab Ann on January 12?
Wayne: No.
Burt: Did you hit Ann in the head with anything on January 12?
Wayne: No.

Wayne Shelton's reactions quickly created multiple graphs on the computer screen and provided an official report. Burt calculated the responses himself and compared his results to those on the computer. Then he asked Sam to check his work. All calculations agreed. Wayne Shelton showed no signs of deception on his polygraph examination.

# Chapter 22

# Deep Deception

It was late Saturday when our investigators completed Wayne's polygraph. Russell's polygraph was scheduled for the following morning, Sunday, February 2. Sam and Burt agreed to notify us immediately after administering Russell's polygraph.

We woke that Sunday morning without help from the alarm. We were keenly aware that things were happening in Madisonville and that sometime later that day, we'd have a clearer picture of Russell's innocence or guilt.

As usual, Taylor and Elliott spent Saturday night with us. Penny picked them up on the way to their church. Then Jack and I drove quietly to our church.

I taught my Sunday school class the assigned lesson. The topic was heaven. I felt distinctly that Ann was aware of us that morning and that she knew our family's efforts to find her killer.

Some people wanted publicity from Ann's death. Some wanted money. And some just wanted it all to go away. I thought that Ann must be pleased that her favorite nephew wanted justice. That he wanted to honor her in death as he had in life. That he—and his family—wanted answers bad enough to pay for them with money they didn't have.

Right now, I felt that our family was Ann's only voice. And I knew we might continue to be her only voice until justice was done.

I met Jack in the church auditorium. As the music began, we tried our best to concentrate on the service. But our minds were 350 miles away, in a motel room in Madisonville, Kentucky, where the son of Jack's favorite uncle was undergoing a polygraph to see if he had bludgeoned and stabbed Jack's favorite aunt.

Russell had arrived at 9:00 a.m. for his polygraph. His attorney accompanied him. Cramped in the tiny motel room, Sam and Burt began their efforts to get to know Russell and to put him at ease. Then they asked Russell some questions about his habits, behavior and whereabouts.

Our PIs asked Russell when he had last seen Ann alive.

"I saw her on Friday, January 10, about 6:15 p.m.," said Russell. He then offered the information he knew the PIs wanted. "I went to her home to borrow $9,700."

"What did you do with the money?" asked Burt.

Russell was obviously resigned that his gambling habits would soon become public knowledge: "The next day, I went to Caesar's Palace near Louisville, added $300 of my own money, and lost the entire $10,000 that evening."

Ann didn't keep that much cash around the house, so she would have written a check, which Russell would have cashed at a bank or at the casino. Because of Jack's experience with financial crimes, we knew that Russell probably asked her for the unusual amount to avoid a bank filling out a CTR or the casino completing a Form 8300, both reports of cash transactions of $10,000 or more.

Russell said he spent Saturday night in Louisville and returned to Madisonville about 2:00 p.m. on Sunday. Russell went to his ex-wife's and picked up one of his sons. They went to Russell's house until approximately 5:45. Then he and his family drove to church.

He and his son took a separate vehicle so he could drop his son off at his ex-wife's while Terri, his second wife, got her children ready for bed. They were at church until about 7:10. Russell took his son home about 7:20 or 7:25. He returned home no later than 7:40, where he stayed the rest of the night. Russell said he first learned about Ann's death at approximately 3:00 p.m. on Monday, January 13.

Our investigators questioned Russell about his gambling habits. He admitted owing Ann between $65,000 and $75,000. He admitted that he borrowed money from her on a number of occasions, paid back part of the money and then borrowed more. He said that the money he borrowed was always for gambling.

Russell gambled at casinos in Evansville, Indiana, near Louisville, Kentucky, and at Metropolis, Illinois (about ninety miles from Madisonville). He told our investigators that he had never been barred from any casino.

Our investigators asked: "How many times did you frequent casinos in the past year?"

Russell answered, "The police said that between Evansville, Metropolis and Louisville, I'd frequented casinos 236 times in the past twelve months. That sounds about right."

"What about the $10,000 you borrowed from Ann to buy a piece of mining equipment?" asked our PIs.

"There was no mining equipment," admitted Russell. "I used the money to gamble."

"You must be in hock up to your eyeballs," observed Burt.

Russell acknowledged that he was.

"You know you're the prime suspect in Ann's murder," Burt said softly.

"It's because I owed her money," answered Russell. "But I didn't kill her. The Madisonville police said I failed the Kentucky State Police polygraph, but it was because they questioned me so hard before I took it. I'm glad to take another polygraph because I'm innocent."

No one knew better than Burt and Sam that polygraphs could produce false negatives and false positives. Critics claim the polygraph is only 70 percent accurate. Proponents claim a success rate as high as 92 percent. Even the higher estimate allows room for error. Burt eliminated a significant degree of inaccuracy by using the Lafayette computerized polygraph. The computerized scores greatly minimize subjective and often-biased readings by those administering the tests.

Burt acknowledged the possibility that the previous polygraph could have been faulty. "Sometimes, if you're emotionally involved with someone, just hearing their name can alter your responses," Burt explained to Russell. "When I administer your polygraph, I won't use Ann's name. That should put you a little more at ease."

Burt and Sam did everything possible to provide a safe and comfortable environment for Russell. They began the polygraph with preliminary questions and established that Russell was a capable reactor with no physical or psychological problems that would hinder the results of the polygraph.

Then they asked Russell two questions:

Burt: Did you hit her in the head with anything on January 12?
Russell replied, "No."
Burt posed the next question: Did you stab her on January 12?
Once again, Russell said, "No."

The worship service was coming to a close when Jack's cell phone vibrated. He slipped quickly out of the service. The remaining moments stretched unbearably as I waited to join him. At the first chord of the closing music, I pushed past people gathering to chat and reached the outside door. I saw Jack standing beside our car, still talking on his cell. From across the parking lot, Jack's posture shouted the message I'd been praying we wouldn't receive.

When I reached Jack, he put his arm around my shoulder and looked into my eyes. The last time I'd seen that look of loss was when he was carrying Ann's coffin.

We learned that following the examination, Burt conducted a numerical evaluation of the polygraph charts and asked Sam to conduct a separate numerical evaluation. The results of the two evaluations on Russell were consistent.

In addition to Burt's usual Lafayette computerized polygraph instrument, he also generated a computer score referred to as the "Polyscore"—an algorithm-based scoring system developed by scientists at the Johns Hopkins University Applied Physics Laboratory. The combination of scores for these two objective tests provides significant accuracy.

The results of both Sam's and Burt's Lafayette calculations were three times the threshold score needed to fail the polygraph examination. The results of the Polyscore were 100 percent probability of deception on the question about stabbing Ann and 99 percent probability of deception on the question of hitting her in the head. There were no gray areas in Russell's polygraph.

It had cost Jack and me more than $10,000 for the past week's private investigative work, but Russell had been given an independent polygraph, with no harsh grueling before or after. He failed—miserably.

Were the investigators worth the money? We never doubted they were. Without the information Sam and Burt presented, we could not have accepted the MPD's conclusions. But now we knew that they'd come upon the truth.

# Chapter 23

# Evil Steps Forward

Jack participated in a conference call in which Russell's attorney was notified of the polygraph results. His attorney said he was concerned about how Russell would react when he learned he had failed the second polygraph. He was particularly concerned about Russell's emotional well-being, implying that he might be suicidal. He obviously wasn't looking forward to sharing the results with Russell or Earl, but he agreed to do so.

That evening, our children came over for supper. As they left at different times, I walked out to their cars with them and broke the news that, in all probability, a family member had killed Ann. Both Penny and Dave named other family members they thought might have killed Ann. They asked first about one possibility, then another.

I realized then that no one was beyond suspicion. We'd reached the point of comprehending that all of us are capable of evil. We'd lost a trust that we would never fully regain.

Jack grieved for his favorite uncle. On Tuesday, he called Earl to tell him he was thinking of him.

"The polygraph results are wrong," Earl said emphatically. "Russell couldn't do anything so horrible to Ann. He loved her."

Jack has an uncanny way of listening sympathetically while not actually agreeing. He has the ability to communicate *I care, I understand, but I don't agree* in a way that's palatable to the listener. His strong sense of justice wouldn't allow him to agree with Earl, and his sympathy and love for his uncle stopped him from challenging his words.

"Ummm," Jack responded. Earl recognized Jack's noncommittal response as the support and love it was meant to convey. At that moment, the two men strengthened their bond in a way that only two strong, silent and stoic Winsteads could understand.

In what had now become our near-nightly ritual, the phone rang just as we were falling asleep. This time it was Jack's cousin Tom.

"So, what's up?" asked Tom. "Have you heard anything new on the murder case?"

"I don't know as much as I wish I knew," answered Jack. But Tom had news.

"They called me to the police station today," said Tom. "They talked to me for two hours and filled me in on what was happening. Captain Hargis told me that Judy—the housekeeper—didn't have an accurate memory about taking a phone call at 9:00 from Ann. Her daughter had been on the phone for an hour and a half at the time.

"When the police gave Judy the accurate information they'd obtained, she said she had call-waiting and had interrupted her daughter's call long enough to talk to Ann. Captain Hargis said they checked with the telephone company and Judy doesn't have call-waiting."

"Umm," replied Jack. This time his response simply meant *I'm listening*. Tom interpreted it correctly and continued.

"The police also told me that Russell has been leading a double life. He has a big gambling problem."

As Jack talked, I could see his jaw tighten. These once uncommon stress reactions were beginning to seem normal in Jack, and I hoped the cause of the stress would soon be over.

When Tom said that Connie had talked to Iva Ray that day, Jack worried that his mother now knew that Russell was the prime suspect, and he didn't want to add to her stress until or unless Russell's guilt was confirmed.

Jack quickly called his mother to be sure Connie hadn't told her about Russell. She had called while Tom was at the police station, so that's all Iva Ray knew.

The next day, Jack called Sam to tell him about Tom's call. Sam had another bit of information, which was probably the catalyst for the police focusing their investigation on Russell. The police had Ann's most recent financial journal. She'd entered a $12,000 check from Russell on January 12, but the police could not locate the check.

Russell claimed that he had not seen Ann on the day of her death, and he said he had not written her a check. However, he could not account for one of his checks.

Sam said he'd now heard the financial extent of Russell's gambling. During the 236 visits to casinos, Russell had $1.2 million in gambling transactions for a total of $1.6 million in the past three years. The first year on the casinos' records, Russell had $150,000 in transactions. The second year, he had $250,000. In the past year, the cost of feeding his habit had more than quadrupled.

Russell had told people at the casinos that he was a professional gambler, and he'd gambled in a manner that made his lie believable. I could imagine Russell enjoying the perceived glamour of being a professional gambler. Though he was a mining engineer, he still spent time in the underground coal mines that had supported a large percentage of western Kentucky residents for generations.

His cousins were a lawyer, a computer engineer and a federal agent. He was the only one who came home with grime on his face and dirt under his fingernails. But at the casino, he was offered free rooms and expensive food. He was greeted by name. He was somebody.

As Jack relayed our PIs' findings about Russell, I noticed that his voice was matter-of-fact. Polygraphs, investigations, evidence and alibis were part of his everyday world. Now these work words centered on a family member, but at least the setting was one in which he was comfortable.

For me, it was as though I'd stepped into a B movie with too many twists and turns to be believable. Or the elaborate game of Clue I'd envisioned earlier.

Only this was Ann's life and Ann's death. It wasn't a game. We could not put the pieces back into the box and move on to something else when it got tiring. It followed us wherever we went, like a gnawing ache in the stomach, a virus in the digestive system, a feeling of fatigue or depression that wouldn't go away.

We'd faced death before, but this wasn't the natural circle of life. It was Evil, stepping in and stealing Ann's last days, taking away the culmination of a life well-lived, robbing her of the chance to close her life with dignity. Ann had so much living still to do, and I was angry that her last days, which should have been her best, were ripped away.

I was angry, too, that murder had become a way of life for our family. I didn't want our grandsons to grow up thinking that murder was normal. I didn't want to think it myself.

Jack took a business trip, and I was immobilized when I tried to walk down the basement stairs. Our washer and dryer were in the basement, and I would not wash clothes—even during the day—until Jack returned.

And worst of all, an indefinable aspect was no longer part of our lives. Without it, we were never fully relaxed. Without it, we anticipated bad news with every ring of the phone. Whatever was missing, I knew deep down that it wasn't coming back, that it couldn't be replaced or replenished. Whatever was missing, I knew the change was permanent. I believe the quality we now lacked was innocence.

# Chapter 24

# Overkill

Jack decided to tell his mother that Russell was the primary suspect in his mind, as well as with the police. We still didn't fully believe Russell killed Ann, and we understood Earl's reluctance to believe it.

Still, Russell lived only a few miles from Iva Ray. If he were the killer, he could kill again. Jack feared for his mother's safety, so he called her on Friday, February 7, to tell her his feelings and to encourage her to lock her doors. Iva Ray tried to find any solution that didn't involve Russell.

"Could it have been a hit man?" she asked Jack. When he assured her that this was a crime of passion, not the work of a professional, she considered other possibilities.

"As much as it grieves me to say it, I believe Russell killed Anna Mae," Jack said soberly.

The next day, Saturday, February 8, Earl called Jack.

"I wish Sam and Burt had talked to me before they left," he told Jack.

"I'll ask them to give you a call," Jack assured him. At this point, we knew we were paying the entire PI bill and that phone calls were the regular-hundred-dollar-an-hour rate. But if Jack could help Earl come to grips with Russell's guilt, we were willing to spend a little more.

Jack called Sam and asked him to call Earl. Sam invited Jack to be part of a three-way call, but Jack felt Earl would be more open to what Sam had to say if it were just the two of them.

So we were billed for three calls that day, ours to Sam, Sam's to Earl and Sam's call to Jack to report on his call to Earl.

Sam had told Earl that he'd been skeptical about Russell being thrown out of Casino Aztar for winning too much money and had contacted the casino. An employee told him that the casino did not bar people for winning too much.

Earl said that maybe he was mistaken, that maybe Russell gave him another reason for discontinuing his visits to the Evansville casino.

Sam tried to explain how severely Russell had failed the polygraph, that the scores were not in the gray area, that Russell would have had to be involved or have firsthand knowledge of Ann's death to receive such drastic scores.

Earl thanked Sam for his concern, but he said he totally believed in Russell's innocence. He stated that polygraphs weren't 100 percent foolproof, that if they were, they'd be admissible in court. We'd done what we could, but Earl was adamant. And the graphs on Sam's computer weren't changing that.

Jack and I wanted to believe Russell, too. I wondered if he had firsthand knowledge, as Sam said. Maybe a loan shark had demanded money and gone with Russell to Ann's house. When she wouldn't give them money, maybe the loan shark killed her and Russell was too afraid to speak out.

Jack assured me that loan sharks don't work that way. "It's just business for them," said Jack. "This was brutal. Overkill. Personal."

A few days after the call with Sam, Earl—still trusting Jack as his confidant—called to tell him the name of the bank where the remainder of the estate money was deposited. Earl said he was telling Jack "in case I have to leave town suddenly."

In that same phone conversation, he asked Jack if cell phone calls could be traced. Though Jack knew they could, his answer to Earl was vague. If Russell was guilty, Jack wanted him caught, even if it meant misleading his uncle.

March and April passed with no news, no progress and no indictment. We heard from our investigators that the police couldn't locate Russell and assumed he'd left town.

Though our investigators said the renter had failed the polygraph, he'd also left town and no one seemed to know where he'd gone.

Since Ann's murder, Jack had been subscribing online to the *Messenger*, Madisonville's newspaper. On April 17, we read that Ann's handyman, Wayne Shelton, had died of heart disease in the local hospital.

The next day, Jack checked the online *Messenger* court reports:

"The following people pleaded guilty in Hopkins County District Court on April 18: Russell E. Winstead, 38, to violation of a Kentucky emergency protective order, under North Carolina v. Alford. Winstead was sentenced to jail time, discharged for two years on condition he commit no violation of law and pay court costs and fees."

Jack called me to the computer to read the report over his shoulder.

"Sounds like Terri's afraid of Russell," I observed. "Do you think she suspects he did it?"

"I don't know," said Jack. "But an EPO doesn't do a lot of good if someone wants to hurt you. Just makes them mad."

"And if the police think Russell's guilty, why didn't they take advantage of his arrest to hold him for a while?" I asked Jack, not expecting an answer.

We received a call from Iva Ray on May 18. Grace had died. Everyone knew she was in her final days, but the family thought she had a little time left. Hospice had not yet begun its work and, in fact, Earl was signing the hospice paperwork at the time of her death.

According to Iva Ray, in her last days, Grace was saddened that Russell hadn't visited her in several months. Russell had grown up on the same street where Grace lived and they'd been close when he was younger.

Grace had expressed her desire to live long enough to know the identity of Ann's killer.

In the twenty-four hours prior to her death, Grace appeared

suspended between the physical and spiritual worlds, sometimes focusing on aching muscles and dry lips, sometimes seeming to see something wonderful just beyond the view of those around her.

In her last moments, local relatives gathered in her bedroom, rubbing her feet and moistening her lips. They heard a knock on the door. It was Russell.

"Grace, your favorite nephew's here!" exclaimed Janet. "It's Russell."

When Russell reached Grace's side, she was dead. Iva Ray later told me she believed that, in her state between heaven and earth, Grace knew who Ann's killer was and didn't want to see him face-to-face.

On May 20, the day of Grace's funeral, Jack and I drove the six hours to Madisonville. We reached the funeral home only an hour before the service.

It was good to see Earl. He and I stood together, laughing, teasing and reliving happier times. It was, for those few moments, as if nothing had happened.

"I call Bob about once a week," Earl told me, "just to check on how he's doing."

"And how is he doing?" I asked.

"Pretty good, I guess," said Earl. "He's still living in Evansville. Russell lives just a few miles from him, in Henderson."

"No kidding," I said. "So Russell's just thirty miles from here. Does he get home very often?" I wondered if the police knew Russell was thirty miles away.

"Yeah," said Earl. "He was back for a family barbecue about a week ago. And he's going to be a pallbearer today." Now I knew why Earl kept looking past me through the crowd. The funeral would begin in a few moments, and Russell wasn't there.

"Guess I better go check on Russell," said Earl. "See you after the funeral. I think we're all going to Country Cupboard for supper."

I watched as Earl checked the foyer, hoping to find Russell, and I wished this whole nightmare would go away. I genuinely liked Earl and I wanted everything to be like it used to be.

But nothing could ever be the same. Not for Ann. Not for Earl. Not for Russell. Not for any of us, ever again. Our lives were set on a completely different course. We were just far enough down that path to no longer be able to see the starting point. We could no longer remember what normal used to be.

We were nowhere near the end of our emotional journey. We could not yet see our destination. The road before us was foggy, and we were feeling our way through the dark.

I moved through the crowd to Jack. He leaned down so he could talk softly in my ear.

"Earl said Russell's supposed to be a pallbearer," said Jack, "and he didn't show. They had to grab someone at the last minute to fill in."

"He's living in Henderson," I said. "Did you know that?"

"No," said Jack, "and I don't think the police know."

Jack found his seat with the other pallbearers. I sat near the back of the viewing room.

A woman tapped me on the shoulder. She said she was a friend of Ann's and Iva Ray's.

"When those two ladies were bridesmaids at your daughter's wedding, it was the thrill of their lives," she laughed. "The next Sunday, they were as surprised as the rest of us when they both showed up dressed alike in their bridesmaid dresses. Ann was so proud to be a bridesmaid. She told all us ladies about it, right down to the pedicures and purple toenails."

An array of funny, happy, memorable snapshots flashed through my mind: Ann as a bridesmaid. Ann playing Rook to the wee hours. Ann climbing into the cramped backseat of my Trans Am, more limber than someone half her age. Our grandson, Elliott, grabbing his pillow and climbing into bed with Aunt Ann when the house was overflowing with Christmas guests.

Ann telling us about the tonic she drank each morning to stay young and healthy. Ann dipping fondue. Ann at Dave's college graduation. Ann at our wedding thirty-five years ago. Ann visiting us in Denver. In Birmingham. In Indianapolis. In Atlanta.

Ann was a part of who we were and how we defined our family. All those great memories that I'd taken for granted until I realized the reservoir was as full as it would ever get.

"Thanks for sharing that story with me," I said as I squeezed the lady's arm. Another special memory to draw from when I felt the emptiness of times without Ann.

As Jack, Iva Ray and I drove in yet another funeral procession to the entrance of Odd Fellows Cemetery in Madisonville, Jack tapped my arm and pointed as unobtrusively as possible to a silver Crown Victoria parked within viewing distance of Grace's grave. I blinked to let him know I understood, avoiding letting Iva Ray know that the police were surveying her sister's graveside service. They have no idea whether Russell is still in the area, I thought, and they're watching to see if he's a pallbearer.

# Chapter 25

# Fast Getaway

As summer approached, the *Messenger* was again our method of discovering news about Russell. We learned that on June 6, Terri was granted a divorce from Russell.

Iva Ray said that Russell showed up at a Father's Day family picnic. That was the last time we knew of anyone in the family seeing Russell.

Jack and I drove to California in July, a combination business trip and vacation. On Tuesday, July 15, Penny called my cell phone while Jack and I were at Knotts Berry Farm. She'd learned from Iva Ray that Russell had finally been indicted. We celebrated for two days.

We were driving on Interstate 5 North, from Long Beach to San Francisco, when Jack got a call from Captain Randy Hargis. Russell hadn't shown up for his arraignment—his attorney had promised that he would—so the police went to Russell's last known address to arrest him. They learned that he'd left the country.

Jack told Hargis that Russell had attended a family gathering in mid-June, and Hargis seemed surprised. Jack surmised that the police hadn't known where Russell was for a long time. We'll always regret that we allowed the doors closed by the MPD to keep us from calling Hargis two months earlier when we learned Russell was working in Henderson.

Jack closed the cell, shook his head and talked through clenched teeth. He spoke every word slowly and precisely, as he tended to do during his most intense moments. "I...can't...believe...they...didn't...keep... him under surveillance...when...they...knew...he...was...about...to be...indicted."

Six days later, Jack and I were in Oklahoma when we heard from Iva Ray. An article had run in the *Messenger*, stating that the insurance company was holding the siblings' insurance policy benefits until they were all cleared as suspects. We'd received the money from the policy Ann had for Jack several months ago, and we hadn't realized that the other policies had been held.

Iva Ray was crushed that someone might think she was a suspect. Jack assured her that all the policies were held up because of Earl, though realizing her brother was suspected of murder was equally difficult for Iva Ray.

Iva Ray was stressed, too, because a family member had proclaimed that the siblings wouldn't get the entire amounts of the insurance policies because the insurance company would take out legal fees. Jack promised his mother that this wouldn't happen, but she kept repeating that they'd have to pay the fees.

"Mother," said Jack, "I'm telling you that you won't have to pay legal fees. And someday I'm going to say 'I told you so.'" I don't believe I'd ever heard Jack say "I told you so" before, but a month or two later, he did.

When we arrived home, Jack called the Commonwealth attorney David Massamore to ask details of Russell's flight. David said that Russell had applied for a passport in Chicago in May. He was thought to be in Costa Rica.

Jack shook his head as he hung up the phone.

"Costa Rica wasn't a random choice for Russell," said Jack. "It's popular with American tourists. San Jose is crowded with casinos and they have the highest table stakes in Central America.

"And Costa Rica doesn't extradite for capital crimes."

Russell had planned the perfect vacation getaway—financed by Ann's estate.

# Chapter 26

# The Widening
# Circle

Jack retired in September, after twenty years as a federal agent. We sandwiched his retirement between trips to Hawaii and Florida. It was a true time of celebration. An exciting career had come to a satisfying close. A major life work had ended. The curtain was down and Jack was ready to begin the next part of his life.

Vacations, parties, tributes, awards, gifts and cards. Everything pointed to a satisfying closure.

But one part of our lives never closed. We could never file away the ever-growing packet of newspaper articles, polygraph reports and notes from phone calls—the packet that had come to represent justice for Ann.

Weeks and months blurred with only small steps toward bringing Russell back to stand trial. Jack was used to working cases that took years to solve. He and his partner once worked six years on one case before the criminal trial began. But this was so personal that the delays were magnified.

Jack wasn't ready for retirement. His good friend, Buck Jones, was police chief in our suburban town of Cumming, and Jack agreed to work for a while as a detective, with the eventual goal of starting his own private investigation business. He'd worked as a volunteer for the county sheriff before becoming an agent—in the same county where Ann lived and died. He'd been sworn in as a Georgia Bureau of Investigation agent for work he'd done as a federal agent. City law enforcement was the only branch in which he hadn't served.

So he found himself attending police academy with officers younger than our children. Because he drove a Corvette, the other officers nicknamed him the "old rich guy," though he was far from old and even farther from rich.

A week into the academy, Penny called Jack. She'd just received a call from Iva Ray. Earl had been arrested. The police executed a search warrant on his home and found evidence of Western Union transactions to San Jose, Costa Rica. Earl was arrested on the premises.

That evening, we pulled up the front page of the online October 8 *Messenger*. It contained a large photo of Earl being led from his house in handcuffs. To my knowledge, Earl had never even had a parking ticket before that day.

Jack read the article aloud. Kentucky State Police detective Ben Wolcott was quoted in the article. We hadn't heard his name before.

We looked closely at the photo. It included a man in plain clothes, leading Earl out of his house. He was young, tall and sturdily built, clean cut with almost a military appearance.

"Is that a Madisonville detective?" I asked Jack.

"I haven't seen him before. Could be this Ben Wolcott quoted in the article."

Later we learned that the man was indeed Ben Wolcott. That day, as we wondered about the new face, we could not have predicted the change Ben would make in the investigation.

Ben and others had set up a sting operation to catch Earl wiring money to Russell. Earl was arrested on seven counts of first-degree conspiracy to hindering prosecution/apprehension. He was held without bond until his hearing.

Ben stated in the article that the police did not believe that Earl acted alone in helping Russell. He said that the Hopkins County Commonwealth Attorney's office was offering amnesty until the following Friday for anyone involved who would come forward and cooperate with police.

Commonwealth attorney David Massamore was quoted in the article as well. He said local authorities had done everything within their power and they were now depending on national and international agencies. He'd spoken to the State Department and they'd assured him that Russell's passport had been revoked. If he attempted to travel using his passport, he'd be picked up. And Russell was listed with the National Crime Information Center and Interpol, an international police agency.

The week passed with no one coming forward to take advantage of the amnesty offer. But we knew the circle was widening. Russell's flight to Costa Rica had caused Earl to break the law to help him. And, we believed someone was breaking the law by helping Earl.

Captain Hargis was quoted in the article as saying that he hoped Earl's arrest had "cut out a major source of funding for Russell Winstead." We felt that law enforcement at all levels seemed to underestimate Earl's devotion to his son and both Earl's and Russell's resourcefulness.

We took comfort in knowing that Russell was now listed as a fugitive. We felt hopeful that Interpol, as well as Costa Rica, was watching for him. At least now, national and international agencies were involved.

Meanwhile, Jack's new career was progressing. Because of his experience in most areas of law enforcement, he was required to attend only the minimum number of days at police academy, primarily when classes involved Georgia law. On days he wasn't at the academy, he worked as a detective for the city police.

In mid October, on a day he was attending the academy, Jack got a message from the police department, telling him Ben Wolcott had telephoned him. Jack called Ben during a break.

Ben wanted to introduce himself and to be sure Jack knew about Earl's arrest. He said he had unofficially been part of the investigation since the beginning but was now taking a more active role. Jack asked how Hargis was taking the change.

"I think Randy is relieved," observed Ben. "Seems like when the case wasn't solved quickly, the MPD was more open to help."

Jack sensed Ben's determination to solve the case. He kept photos of Ann in his car and on his desk to remind himself that she still needed justice. His wife even made up a song about how determined he was to find the killer. Ben vowed that he was as dedicated to finding Ann's killer as he would be if she were his aunt. While that observation was comforting at the time—and, I'm sure, spoken truthfully by Ben—we would learn repeatedly in the next months that no one cares like the family.

After years of sizing up people's honesty, Jack is the best I've seen at discerning someone's motives and inner self. Jack trusted Ben from the first phone call, and that was good enough for me.

Jack and Ben kept in periodic contact. Over the next months, they both became frustrated by the limited time and money Ben was allowed to spend on Ann's case. They both knew that the other work was necessary, and they both understood budget restrictions. But their experience told them that the trail was getting cold and only time and money would bring Russell to justice.

Ben and Jack even spoke about going to Costa Rica and bringing Russell back. But with three million people in Costa Rica and one million of them in San Jose, they knew that wasn't feasible without a definite lead on Russell's location.

# Chapter 27

# 97 Wounds

Dave called me one day in January, as I was driving home from work. "What about calling *America's Most Wanted?*" he asked.

"I don't know," I said. "*AMW* has a lot of cases to consider and this one may not qualify for some reason. But I guess you could try."

"I'm going to call them right now," said Dave.

"I'm glad," I told him. "Let me know what they say."

Dave called again the next day.

"The request has to come through a police department," said Dave. "So I called the Madisonville police. They connected me with one of the detectives and he said they'd submit it."

We waited. Nothing was submitted.

In February, Jack called *America's Most Wanted* to verify that the show was broadcast in Costa Rica. Dave had already contacted the Madisonville Police Department, so Jack faxed David Massamore and told him that *AMW* broadcast in Costa Rica and he was going to send them a packet.

The next day, Ben called Jack. "Massamore told me to submit a packet to *America's Most Wanted*, and I did that today." The contact had been made, and we were grateful.

I persuaded Jack to follow up with a second packet, because we had inside information and family photos that might make the case more appealing to viewers. On February 26, Jack sent his packet to *AMW* and referred to the packet already sent by Ben.

Ben stayed in sporadic contact with Jack, but his communications were not nearly as frequent as we needed to feel comfortable that progress was being made. Our need for information was insatiable.

I was scheduled to attend a weekend conference in Nashville, Tennessee, March 19-20, and Jack decided to drive me there and spend Saturday in Madisonville—about one hundred miles away—seeing his mother. He mentioned to Ben that he'd be in town, and Ben suggested they meet over coffee and discuss the case.

Jack spent the morning visiting his mother. Then he met Ben at a local restaurant at one o'clock. It was the first time he and Ben had talked face-to-face.

The confidence in Ben that Jack had sensed over the phone was affirmed, as he sat across the table from the young state police detective. Ben was thirty-two, but his actions and demeanor made him appear older.

Ben's openness and honesty were refreshing. He obviously viewed Jack as both a fellow law enforcement officer and a family member of the victim. He understood Jack's need for information and his ability to keep information confidential.

For months, Jack and I had hoped that Russell was innocent. Even as the evidence mounted against him, we continued to hold out a shred of hope that the charges were just an awful mistake, an unlucky series of coincidences, misunderstandings and unfortunate circumstances. However, the hour and a half Jack and Ben spent at the restaurant forced us to put our doubts about Russell's guilt to rest and focus on doing everything possible to bring him to justice.

"We have evidence that's not been released to the public," Ben told Jack. "Russell's second wife, Terri, is willing to talk."

"Does she know for sure he did it?" asked Jack.

"Well," answered Ben. "Just about. According to what she told me,

Russell didn't come home at 7:30 like he said. It was more like 9:00. He was relaxed and quiet. He was clean—no blood—so we can only assume that he showered and washed his clothes in Ann's basement.

"He took a shower and slipped on a T-shirt and flannel sleep pants. Then he called a close friend. His friend came to the house, and he and Russell went to the basement and talked quietly. He left about fifteen minutes later.

"Terri slept in her daughter's room that night. She didn't know if Russell left again.

"After Russell was questioned by the police, he told Terri he and Earl felt that they all needed to be together on their stories. He told Terri that when the police asked, she should tell them that he was home by 7:30. He wanted her to say that he played video games in the basement with her son. Then the kids went to bed, and Terri and Russell had a late supper. They had chili. He had crackers and she didn't. They both had sweet tea."

"Sounds like he pulled together a detailed alibi pretty fast," observed Jack. "Did Terri go through with the plan?"

Ben nodded. "At first she seemed to, but we felt the story was too perfect and too detailed. Who has that kind of recall of an average Sunday night?"

"What made her decide to come forward with the truth?" asked Jack.

"I think, at first, she was confused. Maybe she was scared for her children and afraid of being charged with perjury and going to jail," said Ben. "She came back about a week later with her attorney. She said she wanted to set the record straight, to clarify her earlier statements. The police hammered her with more questions. She finally told the whole story."

"And Russell doesn't know that she's talked?" asked Jack.

"No," replied Ben. "In fact, he tried for a while to keep her on his side. He sweet talked her, gave her gift certificates to jewelry stores and told her how much he loved her. He'd never been violent toward Terri, but he got a little rough when he instructed her about what to tell the police—grabbing her arm and shoving her against the wall. I guess he wanted to smooth all that over, to make sure she wouldn't turn on him. But by the time he got worried, she'd already talked."

"And there's another witness," added Ben. "After the indictment hit the paper, a woman came forward. She said she recognized Russell, that she'd seen him the night of January 12."

"Why did she wait to come forward?" asked Jack.

Ben shook his head. "She didn't. She contacted the MPD right away, but she called on the Crime Stopper line that can't be traced. And she wouldn't give her name. But when she saw Russell's picture in the paper when he was indicted, she contacted the police again. She told them they had the right man, that he was the one she'd seen walking down the street near Ann's house.

"This woman was coming home about midnight. She's diabetic and had to use the bathroom badly. She thought about running the light in front of Ann's house, so she pulled up and checked to be sure a police car wasn't hiding on Noel Avenue. No one was around.

"Just then, the light changed and she turned onto Noel Avenue. Her headlights shined directly on Russell and their eyes met. She thought his car might have broken down, and she considered stopping to ask if he needed help. Since she had to use the bathroom so badly, she didn't.

"She said Russell was wearing camouflage. We asked Terri if Russell owned camouflage clothing. She'd given him a camouflage jacket for Christmas, but a couple of days after the murder, he claimed someone stole it from the back of his truck. He never filed a theft report with the mines, though."

Jack was quiet, reflecting on all the new information and allowing Ben to talk.

"Russell apparently went back to Ann's house and cleaned everything with alcohol. We think he even painted the walls—at that time, we didn't have an alternate light source to check for blood. We poured Luminol [a substance used to detect blood] down the sink and found what appeared to be blood."

"Did you use Luminol on the shower or on the washer and dryer?"

asked Jack, remembering the hairs and fibers he'd found in the shower.

Ben shook his head and spoke with an honesty we had to admire. "No. There was a lot that wasn't done to the crime scene."

Ben continued: "There were no fingerprints and no DNA, at least none that were found. Everything was put back to normal. The housekeeper said she had some hand washable items drying on a line inside the shower, and they were just like she left them.

"The autopsy showed Ann had eaten some beans, maybe bean soup. She must have let Russell in soon after eating. Their encounter had to be brief, because the autopsy showed her food was undigested when she was killed.

"Jack, she was hit with something heavy, possibly a mining pick like Russell would have used to get mineral samples from the mines. And she was unconscious immediately, from the first blow. She was struck multiple times with the blunt object and her throat was slit from ear to ear. Then she was stabbed ninety-seven times. Some wounds were para-mortem -- while dying -- and some were post mortem -- after death. But she never felt a thing."

At this point, Jack, usually stoic like the rest of his family, felt the rare sting of tears. This was the first time he'd heard the graphic details of the murder. The brutality of the crime impacted all his senses.

But the tears were an emotional release, too. He commented to Ben: "The early report was that she struggled, because her hands were cut up."

"It's my understanding that the first blow to the head rendered her unconscious. After a while, he must have just been stabbing randomly," replied Ben.

"We've known that," said Jack. Then he responded to Ben's surprised look by telling him about my experience among the Alabama pines immediately after learning Ann was murdered.

# Chapter 28

# A Solitary Clue

As Jack and Ben ended their meeting, Ben said he suspected some individuals of sending money to Russell, and these people were strong contenders for follow-up or surveillance. But both men acknowledged that there were numerous leads that would never be followed. Like everything surrounding Ann's murder, it all boiled down to money. The Kentucky State Police just didn't have the manpower to cover all the bases, and people cost money.

Jack visited Odd Fellows Cemetery before driving to Nashville to pick me up. He went to Ann's and Carroll's graves. Though the day was cloudy and still, the hazy sky was somehow brilliant with light. It was the sort of day when you expect a sudden electrical storm, but none came.

The scene seemed surreal as Jack walked slowly up the knoll to Ann's and Carroll's above-ground mausoleum. As Jack stood before the marble monument to the aunt and uncle who had been such an integral part of his life, he renewed his promise to be Ann's voice until justice was done.

He now felt that he had an ally in Ben Wolcott, but he also knew that no one cared as much about bringing Ann's killer to justice as he did.

When he picked me up at the conference, I could tell that Jack's day had been emotionally draining. He looked tired and his eyes had a sadness that came from deep inside.

He shared what Ben had told him, and I knew that the information that overshadowed even the excitement of the two witnesses was the detailed description of the murder. Captain Hargis had implied a dozen or so wounds and even that had seemed excessive. But the rage that would cause a six-foot-one man to stab a five-foot-three woman ninety-seven times was incomprehensible.

# Chapter 29

# Extradition Dilemma

On March 26, after several postponements, Earl appeared in court to face charges of conspiracy to hindering prosecution, for wiring money to Russell. He pled guilty to seven misdemeanors and was sentenced to two years' probation. The judge warned him that if he had any contact with Russell, he'd serve two years in jail.

Nevertheless, Jack and I felt that Earl would somehow find ways to get money to Russell.

In late March, the Louisville *Courier-Journal* newspaper requested a quote from Jack for an article they were writing about United States fugitives harbored in other countries. When the article appeared in the *Courier-Journal* on April 8, 2004—and was later picked up by the Associated Press wire service—we learned that Costa Rica was one of twenty countries that refused to extradite for capital offenses. Other families were waiting for justice, too.

We discovered that Costa Rica was one of 117 countries that banned the death penalty and one of at least twenty that refused to extradite to a country that would implement capital punishment. The number of pending extradition cases handled by the Justice Department had increased 100 percent from 1990 to 2000.

United States prosecutors were faced with the dilemma of dealing with extradition from "humanitarian" countries. They had to either promise not to seek the death penalty or allow criminals to escape punishment altogether.

The article stated that, from 1995 to 2000, just fifty-six United States criminals were extradited from Mexico and extradition requests were filed for more than 800. The United States had approximately 2,500 pending extradition requests to foreign countries, some submitted as long as twenty-seven years ago.

The article also stated that the consul general of the Costa Rican Embassy in Washington, D.C., said that Costa Rica had not received a request for Russell. The consul general stated that he knew of no cases in which Costa Rica had refused to extradite, provided the country receiving the criminal promised not to seek the death penalty. In other words, someone, somewhere had dropped the ball and Costa Rica had not received the message that Russell was a fugitive in their country.

The article ended with a quote from Hargis: "Madisonville Police Capt. Randy Hargis ...can barely contain his emotions about the six months it took just to secure a foreign warrant for Russell Winstead. Hargis said police assembled arrest records and other documents and had them translated into Spanish, and may have to go to Costa Rica to help local police get Winstead."

Extradition for capital offenses was a serious problem and, like most Americans, we hadn't realized it until it affected our family.

# Chapter 30

# One Step Forward, One Step Back

By the end of April, Jack and I were talking hour after hour about what we could do to move the investigation forward. Most of Jack's friends were in law enforcement and they talked with him often about the investigation.

A fellow retired agent remembered that Scott Price, a man who had a contract to supply tires for the government, had moved to Costa Rica. And he liked to gamble.

Jack sent him photos of Russell, and Price agreed to pass the photos around. We waited for word that Russell was still in Costa Rica, but we heard nothing back from Scott.

Another friend told Jack that a reporter for the *Atlanta Journal-Constitution* newspaper owned property in Costa Rica. Jack attempted to contact the reporter and learned that he was in Costa Rica at the time Jack was trying to contact him. Again, the photos were sent. Again, no one recognized Russell.

Ben was tenacious in getting *America's Most Wanted* involved in apprehending Russell. He called nearly once a week, reminding them of the request. His contact at the show confirmed in June that *AMW* was interested in covering the case. However, several urgent cases took precedence over Ann's murder and she would let Ben know when the case would be profiled.

Ben said the producer was interested in interviewing Jack, and he asked if Jack could come to Madisonville when the *AMW* crew was there. Jack assured him that he would drop everything and be there on a moment's notice. By this time, Jack had begun Branson & Associates, LLC, a private investigating business and worked once a week as a reserve officer for the Cumming PD. I had taken early retirement in May to fulfill my lifelong dream of writing full-time. For the first time in our adult lives, we were blessed with schedules of our own choosing.

We'd planned a vacation to the West Coast for July and decided to move forward with our plans, knowing that it could be months before *AMW* covered Ann's murder.

While driving through Montana, Jack received a call from Ben.

"Do you know anything about a man taking out an assault warrant on Earl?" asked Ben. He'd heard unofficially that the warrant had been taken out in Hopkinsville, about thirty-five miles from Madisonville.

"Earl's ex-girlfriend lives there," said Jack. "Their relationship's been off and on since Christmas. Maybe he's been bothering a new boyfriend."

Jack called his mother and chatted, hoping she'd mention Earl's recent problems, if she knew about them. After several minutes of conversation, Jack concluded that his mother was unaware of the newest charges against Earl.

We returned from vacation July 31 and before our suitcases were unpacked, Ben called with a bright new rabbit to chase. He said *AMW* was definitely profiling Russell, and would be filming soon.

Ben was in the middle of a murder trial and asked Jack if he could come to Madisonville to help organize the people to be interviewed. Jack was so eager to jump into the middle of all that was happening that he would have driven to Madisonville to flip burgers if Ben had asked him.

"The segment producer wants to come to Georgia to interview you, too," said Ben.

"There's no reason for her to come here," said Jack. "I'd be glad to be interviewed while I'm in Madisonville helping you."

Nevertheless, the producer had requested that Jack call her, which he did on August 10. He got her voicemail and left her a message.

The next afternoon, Wednesday, Jack and I made time to catch a mid-afternoon movie, a glorious benefit of self-employment. Jack's cell vibrated in the middle of the movie and he slipped out to answer.

"They're coming next week, probably Thursday or Friday," Jack whispered, as he slipped back into his seat. But the following day, the producer called back. They were experiencing some scheduling delays in Madisonville and wanted to come to Georgia on Monday.

"No problem," said Jack. When he hung up, however, we looked around the house and laughed. Evidence of both our recent retirements was everywhere—stacks of awards and photos, clusters of gift bags and gag gifts. Somehow, we'd gotten used to the piles, and over several months we'd allowed the memorabilia to become part of the landscape. We'd had family dinners with stacks in the corners of the dining room. We'd learned to climb over or walk around enormous obstacles without noticing.

Then we'd come back from a three-week vacation and allowed more clutter to form. Tomorrow was our thirty-seventh wedding anniversary, and we'd planned a big day and evening out.

The day after that was Saturday. Taylor and Elliott were spending the day and night. Though they both had their own bedrooms at our house, their routine was to "camp out" in the family room, dragging air mattresses, piles of blankets, pillows and half their toys in front of the television and snacking and watching television till they fell asleep.

Sunday was church. And Monday afternoon, our home would be the backdrop for filming a segment for national television.

# Chapter 31

# America's Most Wanted

Too late to give the house a major overhaul, so I hurriedly cleaned the bathrooms and hid the clutter. We assumed the camera wouldn't pick up dust bunnies. About an hour before the producer was scheduled to arrive, we turned on the small light above Ann's portrait. Jack worked on PI jobs and I completed writing assignments as we waited for *America's Most Wanted* to arrive.

The producer, Paula Simpson, and her film crew arrived about 2:00 p.m. They were friendly and professional, and they seemed focused on apprehending Russell. She had told Jack he would recognize her, because she'd be the only pregnant one on the crew, but her thin, athletic build and her assertive demeanor were what we first recognized.

We assumed the crew would set up in the fit-for-company living room, but the light was too bright. Soon they gravitated to the lived-in part of the house, where toys peeked out from under sofas and Sponge Bob stickers decorated the glass on the entertainment center.

"This is much better," said the cameraman. *Better for you*, I thought, as he and the sound man moved a couch to expose a single tiger-head house shoe and a candy wrapper. But everyone was so relaxed and busy that I soon stopped worrying about how the house looked.

The crew clipped coverings to our windows to darken the family room. They stretched cords, moved chairs and tested sound. As they worked, Paula, Jack and I sat at the kitchen table going over details of the crime. She quickly let us know that Russell's case was attractive to *America's Most Wanted*, because he was a white, middle class professional and it was hard to keep a racial and economic balance in their profiles. Jack and I found this a little disconcerting but, at this point, we'd take any "favoritism" we could get.

Jack had talked with Ben a few days before and asked him if any information was off limits to share with Paula. Ben said that he'd shared nearly everything with her already. Jack was still cautious. She good-naturedly coaxed him to drop the cop stance but years of confidentiality training wouldn't allow him to do so.

We learned a few things we hadn't known as we talked with Paula. Jack and I squeezed hands under the table as we dealt with each new bit of information. We realized that Ben hadn't deliberately withheld information from Jack—he'd been open in answering our questions. But we were far away and it was easy to forget to include Jack every time a new piece of information was uncovered.

Paula said Russell's game of choice was blackjack. She commented on small aspects of the crime that we hadn't heard. But the new information that impacted us most was that Russell had gone to the casino the day after he murdered Ann. It was one of those moments when we realized how little Russell was affected by what had changed our lives forever.

She made an astute observation about why Ann never told Jack how much money she'd loaned Russell. I was bragging about what a savvy businesswoman Ann was and how her careful journal-keeping had been the only tangible clue left at the crime scene.

"Maybe that's why she didn't talk to Jack about how much Russell owed her," observed Paula. "She *was* a good businesswoman. And she was probably embarrassed that she'd allowed the situation to get out of hand."

When Paula mentioned that Russell told people at the casinos that he was a professional gambler, I tried to envision the double life he'd led. Did he quickly shower off the dirt from the mines, eat supper with his family and then dress in his most upscale clothes to transform to his "other life"? Did he enjoy being greeted at the casinos by people who knew he was a regular, who catered to him as a high roller, even offering him free rooms and fancy dinners when he gambled late into the night?

On weekends, he kept up his charade of normalcy by teaching youth at church and spending time with his sons, wife and stepchildren.

When did he sleep? Driving back and forth to Evansville would add two hours to his night. Metropolis would add four hours. Louisville, five. And "professional gamblers" don't just run into the casino and gamble for a few moments. Neither do the severely addicted.

Cults often keep their members hungry and sleep-deprived, because it affects their judgment and hinders rational decisions. I imagined Russell driven by an addiction as strong as drugs, his judgment impaired by lack of sleep, frantic about his mounting debt.

I felt sadness for Russell. I could despise what he did while still understanding the downward spiral of his life. Could this have happened to our son or daughter? Our grandsons? Jack or me? Immediately, my mind said no. But now I understood why Earl believed so blindly in his son.

The camera crew nodded that they were ready to film. Jack sat in a wooden kitchen chair. Paula sat in another kitchen chair, behind the camera and facing Jack.

"If I ask you anything you don't want to answer," she told Jack, "Just say, 'Shut up, Paula.'"

Then she laughed. "Actually, you've probably been on the other side of questioning lots of times, so this is payback."

She began asking questions, very calmly, very quietly. Jack's responses were equally calm and quiet. But there was an intensity about his responses that was riveting.

Jack is not a person who looks for opportunities to be in the limelight. The family's biggest complaint about Christmas videos and vacation snapshots is that Jack stays behind the camera. The filming wasn't something Jack was doing to bring attention to himself. He was highlighting a killer in the hope of bringing him to justice, and that mindset was evident.

First, Paula asked a variety of questions, some I'm sure just to create a relaxed atmosphere—what's your name, what's your occupation, what was your relationship to Ann Branson, what is your relationship to Russell Winstead. Jack's replying voice was calm and steady.

Then she asked Jack what he would say to Russell if he could speak to him at that moment. I saw Jack's demeanor change imperceptibly. Most people wouldn't notice that Jack became extremely upset, but I could tell by the tightness in his jaw, the way his eyes narrowed and the slight increase in the volume of his voice.

Jack answered with precise, carefully chosen words. "Russell, you've put your father and sons through enough. It's time to do the right thing and turn yourself in. But I know you won't, because you're a coward."

She asked what Jack would say to Earl. As Jack answered, I pictured Earl surprising Jack at his fiftieth birthday party, Jack and Earl clowning around at family gatherings, Earl's daughter as flower girl at our wedding.

"Earl, as a father, I know you don't want to believe that your son could commit such a horrible crime." Then, with the most intensity yet: "But it's time you remembered what happened to your sister. Russell is guilty, beyond a shadow of a doubt."

Finally, Paula asked, "What would you say to anyone who sees this and knows where Russell is hiding?"

"Russell is dangerous. Don't try to approach him yourself. Contact the authorities. He's killed before and he won't hesitate to do it again. And it will be easier the second time." With his replies, Jack knew he was forever severing some important ties with his Kentucky family. Paula asked the hard questions but she had no idea the price Jack was paying to answer them.

# Chapter 32

# Murder Profile

After well over an hour of taping, Paula wrapped it up. She told the crew to get some shots of Jack interacting with me and just moving around the house.

We flipped through Penny's wedding photos, dwelling on the shots that included Ann. The crew told us to do some things in the kitchen—empty the dishwasher, pull something out of the refrigerator and start cooking. We opened the dishwasher to show the cameraman and soundman that, of course, it was empty. We cleaned just for them.

Then we responded to the suggestion to cook something.

"If you show me in the kitchen," said Jack, "everyone who knows me will realize it's staged."

"Same here," I admitted. "Most of the food in the house is in the basement freezer. TV dinners and ice cream." I opened the refrigerator to show them its contents: milk, a couple of pitchers of tea, a bag of lemons and a cantaloupe.

"How about pouring some tea," the cameraman compromised. "Where are your glasses?"

I hurried out of the kitchen with the producer calling after me. "Where do you keep your glasses?"

"Uh," I hesitated. "In the hutch in the foyer."

"No, no," she said. "We want the everyday ones."

I assumed she could hear the tiny bit of homemaker deep inside me groan. Who wants their plastic glasses—free at the drive-thru if you super-size—on national TV? We compromised with the $3.99/dozen clear glass ones.

The cameraman and soundman shot some footage of Jack on the deck, with me bringing him a glass of tea. We gave them our Christmas videos for the past nine years, each with short scenes of Ann sandwiched in among lengthy shots of Taylor and Elliott ripping open mile-high stacks of packages.

The crew took footage of Ann's portrait and several smaller photos of Ann with family members. Then they were gone, headed for Madisonville to interview people there.

Ben's murder trial had been postponed so he was able to coordinate the filming. Jack and I decided there was no reason for us to go to Kentucky.

Our greatest concern about *America's Most Wanted* showing up in Earl's hometown of 15,000 was that it wouldn't take long for Russell to find out what was happening. We'd mentioned that to Paula, but she didn't seem as concerned as we did.

"We just have to trust the police to notify the State Department, Interpol and the U.S. Embassy in Costa Rica," said Paula.

"I wouldn't be surprised to see *America's Most Wanted* on the front page of the Madisonville paper," she said. "I asked them for a copy of the photo of Russell as a pallbearer so they know we're coming."

She certainly was right about the *Messenger's* front page story. On Thursday, with *AMW*'s approval, the front page featured a color photo of Madisonville's mayor being interviewed on camera for *AMW*. The headline: "TV Show to Profile Branson Murder: *America's Most Wanted* Crew Visits Madisonville."

According to Ben, the filming went well. Ann's pastor let *AMW* film the inside of the church where she'd attended a service immediately before her murder. Casino Aztar allowed them to bring the camera crew inside and stage a blackjack game. Tom Branson was interviewed, along with Bill Frank (the Hopkinsville FBI agent who was also assigned to Madisonville), the mayor, Ben, and totally by accident, Earl.

Earl happened to pull up at the site in his truck where the unmarked *AMW* van was parked. Ben pointed him out to Paula, and the crew rushed over to his truck. When pushed for a statement, Earl said that he had nothing to say.

Paula planned to return to Madisonville August 30 to interview the police officer who had been Russell's long-time friend. Then, the *AMW* profile was scheduled to air October 2, now less than six weeks away.

*AMW* had been responsible for the capture of 805 criminals, about forty a year since it first aired seventeen years ago. That was quite a track record, and it should have made me feel better.

"Honey," I told Jack. "I'm hopeful that Russell will be captured in October. But if this doesn't work, what do we do next?"

Jack winked. "Guess we'll just have to get Hargis to go to Costa Rica and get him."

# Chapter 33

# Ten Most Wanted

B en said Paula had wanted to do a reenactment of the crime but he was hoping she wouldn't. He felt that so much of what happened that night was still conjecture and a reenactment might not be accurate. As a law enforcement officer, Jack understood Ben's hesitancy. As a writer, I thought that the reenactment would help people understand the brutality of the crime.

By Tuesday, August 24, Jack's impatience was escalating.

"I'm going to call the Hopkinsville FBI," Jack said mid-afternoon. "I want an update on what's been done by the Bureau." He got Bill Frank's voice mail and left a message.

Later that afternoon, Ben called with news that quenched our thirst for progress. The FBI had captured one of their Ten Most Wanted, and there was an opening on the list. The Bureau was considering adding Russell to the list, alongside Osama bin Laden and other "dirt bags," as *America's Most Wanted* host John Walsh often called the most despicable criminals. A listing on the Ten Most Wanted guaranteed a minimum $50,000 reward—an enormous incentive for residents of Costa Rica.

That evening, Bill Frank called. He seemed neutral about getting

Russell on the Top Ten list and said it was actually the producer we'd been working with, who was pushing for it. He was simply endorsing her idea.

All I could think was what a difference the reward could make. Ann's murder and the ensuing ugliness were all about money. How fitting if justice also boiled down to the dollar.

Then Bill told us information that put our minds in high gear. There was a chance Russell was in the United States and could be picked up before *AMW* could air.

Ben called later that night with the same information. Understanding that both men were sharing highly confidential information and putting the capture and their careers on the line of his confidence, Jack didn't mention to Ben that the Bureau agent had already called.

Jack and I became preoccupied with the possibility of Russell's capture being imminent. We'd been back from vacation for only four weeks and we reminded ourselves how much had happened in this time span. The case was finally moving again, but each bit of progress was so important to us that we anguished over every moment of delay in receiving it.

The long/short waits reminded me of the impatience I sometimes feel when warming something for forty-five seconds in the microwave, or the way I tap my fingers impatiently as DSL connects my computer. Neither Jack nor I would be classified as patient on a normal day. With the emotional investment we had in bringing Ann's killer to justice, even our minuscule patience was gone.

Jack and I mapped out what we thought would happen in the next weeks. Probable case scenario, *AMW* would profile the crime October 2 and a viewer would call and say that Russell was living next door. Best case scenario, the FBI would pick up Russell in Ocean City, Maryland—where he'd supposedly withdrawn money from an ATM—before *AMW* could air.

As we envisioned how we thought Russell would be captured, I was reminded of a joke I'd once heard: Do you know how to make God laugh? Tell Him your plans.

# Part 3

■ ■ ■ ■

# Redefining Normal

# Chapter 34

## Avoiding Prosecution

By Monday, August 30, 2004, Jack was like one of those springs decorated to look like a snake and pressed inside a can, lid screwed on tight, waiting for some trusting soul to open the can for a handful of peanuts. He called Ben and left a message on his voice mail, inquiring about how things were going and asking Ben to call him back. Monday faded to Friday and no call from Ben. Jack became more and more like that snake-spring waiting to pounce.

We wondered if there was progress on the Ten Most Wanted entry or on anything related to the case. Jack read in the online *Messenger* that Ben was involved in a marijuana bust, so we tried to understand his lack of response. Our impatience, coupled with the distance between Atlanta and Madisonville, made it difficult to understand any perspective but our own.

Jack called Ben again Friday afternoon. We learned that baseball playoffs had bumped the *AMW* air date from Saturday, October 2, to Friday, October 8.

Jack emailed Paula to confirm the change and to ask her to keep us updated if the time changed again. She responded that Fox Network was doing some shuffling to accommodate the baseball playoffs and, though it looked as if they'd still air on October 8, the television business was fluid and things could change. She told Jack to keep his cell phone on when the show aired, and she'd let him know if they got an arrest.

Paula's email made us feel a little better. Just reading words like "I will let you know if we get any arrests" made it seem possible. And we had a great deal of confidence in *AMW's* track record.

Our greatest discouragement was with federal law enforcement. The FBI handles a limited number of murder cases, only UFAP's (unlawful flight to avoid prosecution) and the murders of elected officials and federal agents. They're supposed to make murder cases top priority and we felt this wasn't the case. As Jack well knew, agents have an overload of cases, but a murder file should have risen to the top of the stack.

But some were doing all they could to help. On Sunday of the Labor Day weekend, we saw our friends Sonia and Terry McGowen at church. Now a United States citizen, Sonia was originally from Costa Rica. Earlier, Jack had emailed her photos of Russell, and she'd sent them to her brother in Costa Rica. He circulated them among the casinos.

Now Sonia gave us a printed list of Costa Rican casinos on which she'd handwritten additional phone numbers and email addresses. Jack made plans to contact the casinos the following day.

That evening over supper, Jack and I discussed the investigation. As usual.

"Do you think Russell's in the United States?" I asked.

"It's possible," answered Jack. "When the *Messenger* ran articles saying he was believed to be in Costa Rica and that Earl had wired money to San Jose, Russell may have decided it was safer here. Costa Rica's a small country."

"But how could he get back into the United States?" I wondered. "Surely his passport would have shown he was a fugitive." Jack had told me recently that passports were now scanned and more difficult to fake.

"If he established connections in Costa Rica, he probably could find a way to slip across their border. He'd have to get past the borders in Guatemala, Honduras and Nicaragua just to get to Mexico. But these borders, I'm sure, have places where you can pass, if you have the right connections. And he could have walked right over the border from Mexico into the United States," explained Jack. "They don't check passports when tourists go back and forth across the border to shop. He could easily have just walked across. Earl could have been waiting for him."

"If he's in the United States," I continued, "how do you think he's being supported?"

Jack confirmed what I'd been thinking. "Earl just went to Oklahoma on a motorcycle trip, and Ben told us about others who go out of town periodically. I think he could be wiring money or opening little bank accounts all over the country. Russell could be making withdrawals systematically from each one."

We had no confirmation that Russell was still in Costa Rica and no proof that he was, or had been, in the United States. We would have gone anywhere to find Russell, but we needed a confirmation of his location. Otherwise, we may as well have headed to the middle of the ocean and dived for a lost coin.

# Chapter 35

# A Secret
# Life

Jack spent most of Labor Day emailing Costa Rican casinos and sending the photos of Russell. The Internet sites Sonia provided showed that the actual game of blackjack was banned in Costa Rica. The variation, which they called rummy (or rommy), wasn't a favorite at most casinos. Some casinos had only a couple of blackjack/rummy tables.

According to Sonia, only three cities had casinos: San Jose in central Costa Rica and Quepos and Guanacaste on the west shore. The latter two were small towns. If we got a confirmation that Russell was still in the little Central American country, it would probably be a quick task to find him.

But we still had no confirmation of Russell's location, and Jack knew we needed a definite lead to do anything.

Ben was not responding to our contacts, and we learned he was in Florida, helping some elderly relatives who had experienced hurricane damage during the recent multi-devastation from Frances, Ivan and Jeanne. We visited our mothers in mid-September and were disappointed that we couldn't spend a few moments getting a case update from Ben.

We received an email from Paula while we were in Madisonville. Russell's profile had been moved to November. In spite of the delays, we were encouraged by her information. November was a "sweeps" month and her boss considered Russell's profile important enough to use as a feature during this crucial marketing time.

By the end of September, Jack's short supply of patience was gone. He called Bill Frank, the Hopkinsville FBI agent, to see if he had news on the Ten Most Wanted List or confirmation of Russell's location. Bill returned his call but, unfortunately, had no new information.

"How long can all this take?" I called out in exasperation. "You'd think they'd give a murder case priority!" I was suddenly near a breaking point because of bureaucratic indifference.

Jack and I know instinctively how to balance each other. His patience was strained, too, but when he saw my frustration, he drew the last remaining fragments of patience from his exhausted psyche and shared them with me, like a parent in a concentration camp giving his last bread crumb to his child.

"Everybody's doing the best they can," he said gently. "They're all overscheduled and underpaid."

I took this meager offering in the spirit in which it was intended, wishing I had some crumbs to share with Jack as well. But we were both drained, and I wasn't sure how much longer we could go on with limited communication and discouraging delays.

On Sunday, October 3, 2004, Jack pulled up the *AMW* website, as he did nearly every day. But this day, he found Russell's profile.

Excitement and anger vied for priority as we moved back and forth between "I can't believe they've had this information and haven't told us" to "Thank goodness they've found out more than we thought they had."

We learned from the *AMW* website that Russell had used aliases, that he had quirks that made his gambling style recognizable and that certain personal habits and characteristics made him easy to spot.

Russell had used the aliases of Craig Conway and the name of a woman he was romantically involved with. He usually drank water when he gambled.

He played a specific type of blackjack called Negative Progression, or the Martingale System. In this gambling method, the player doubles his bet each time he loses and drops back to the original bet when he wins. The theory is that eventually, he'll win back his money and make a profit. However, even when he does win, the profit can be miniscule.

Few people recommend this method because it has some serious flaws. You have to have a big bankroll to play. Many players run out of money or reach the table limit before winning. Casinos protect themselves from big wins by setting table limits. For instance, if a minimum bid is ten dollars, the table limit could be $500. If a Martingale player wagers ten dollars and loses, doubles to twenty dollars and loses, then loses four more times with additional wagers of forty dollars, eighty dollars, $160 and $320, he can't double his $320 wager because doing so would take his wager over the table limit. And by this time, he would have invested $630, only to start over.

Some players consider the Martingale System a sure success because you have to win eventually. But if you don't win early and often, your investment in the losing hands will virtually cancel out your winnings.

Jack had provided some of the information on the site during the three hours *AMW* was at our home. Some, we assumed, came from interviews with Ben, Russell's second wife, Terri, or casino personnel. Whatever the sources, it was now all compiled in one location.

Jack—and undoubtedly others—had told Paula that Russell was a thrill-seeker. This translated to "adrenaline junkie" on the website and was a colorful but accurate description. Even as a child, Russell had been reckless and full of energy. When Russell was five, we were surprised when this hefty, oversized preschooler barreled right toward me and hit me in the stomach with his fist. I was eight months pregnant with Dave. His exhausted parents, befitting a family with emotional control, simply pulled Russell away and continued talking.

Jack's grandmother often babysat Russell, and Grace, who lived next door, told stories of the five-year-old urinating in the closet and behind furniture. Russell's unbridled energy also resulted in his running in front of a car when he was six. He was hospitalized with severe head injuries.

But by elementary school, Russell was a subdued, quiet child. After the murder, his first-grade teacher expressed shock to Iva Ray that Russell could be violent because he was always "so quiet and well-behaved."

By his early teens, suppressing emotion may have begun taking a toll. Russell's mom was a hairstylist and cut my hair regularly. Her salon was connected to their home, and on occasion, Russell would be sleeping in the next room while she cut hair. She explained that by age twelve he had such severe headaches that she had to check him out of school and let him sleep all day in a quiet, dark room.

By his early twenties, Russell focused his energy on stockcar racing. He raced in several NASCAR races but was not terribly successful. Ann and other relatives went to his races to cheer him on. When racing didn't prove as rewarding as Russell had hoped, he became the well-behaved businessman who, according to Iva Ray, created disbelief among his co-workers when he was indicted for murder.

"They said Russell was always the one who kept his cool in emergencies," said Iva Ray. Apart from riding four-wheelers with his boys, Russell apparently had no release for his "adrenaline junkie" personality—until he discovered gambling.

Russell's need for excitement, coupled with the Winstead self-control he was expected to have since childhood, may have created a bottled-up rage waiting for release. I imagined now that the overkill of the crime was not just anger toward Ann. It was anger toward every slight and hurt, every disappointment and failure that Russell had experienced in the past thirty years.

I wondered what it was like for a hyperactive, intense boy to grow up in a family where emotion was stifled, where even death was faced without the shedding of tears. Had Russell been encouraged to repress his feelings so long that they finally burst from him in a flood of rage?

We pieced together the new *AMW* information and connected it with what we already knew. In addition to Russell's gambling style and habits, we learned from the *AMW* site that he liked to work out and fancied himself a lady's man. That he might be conning women and that he was manipulative and a compulsive, pathological liar. That he talked openly about his children. With all this new information, we were now able to paint a more detailed picture of Jack's cousin.

The hyperactive little boy had become the quiet-spoken man whose smooth, calm demeanor impressed co-workers and charmed ladies of all ages. Russell Winstead – a quiet man with a secret life that fed his need for excitement.

# Chapter 36

# Rocket Fuel

In October, we made a Kentucky business trip and included visits with our mothers. While at Iva Ray's, we pulled up the *AMW* website on my laptop and showed her the coverage. Over the past few months, Iva Ray had slowly given up hope that Russell could be innocent. Nevertheless, we knew the reality of seeing the *AMW* listing would be painful. But we wanted to keep her gently informed instead of relinquishing the responsibility to town gossips.

Through the online *Messenger*, we'd learned recently that Judy, Ann's housekeeper, had been arrested for theft by deception. We asked Iva Ray if she knew the details.

"I talked to Judy right after she was released on bond," said Iva Ray. "She'd written a bad check and she said the police had treated it like a bigger deal than it was. She feels like they're harassing her, because they assume she's helping Earl."

Between visits with my mom, we squeezed in time to see Bill Frank, the regional FBI agent. We made an appointment for early afternoon on October 6, so we grabbed lunch at the Madisonville Dairy Queen before heading for Hopkinsville.

Ann and Carroll had built the new Dairy Queen a few years before they retired. The current owners had remodeled and created a mural from an enlarged black-and-white photo of Carroll standing in front of the original Dairy Queen. For so many Madisonville residents, that photo was a reminder of the 1950-1985 Branson-DQ connection. For Jack and me, the photo now created a painful backdrop for our whodunit conversation. To avoid dwelling on the murder, Jack forced himself to recall pleasant memories of times with Carroll.

"One of the saddest things about this murder," said Jack, interrupting himself, "is that our most vivid memory of Anna Mae will always be the way her life ended. I have so many wonderful childhood memories, but the murder always comes to mind first. Even after Russell is brought to justice, the murder may still be the first thing I remember about Anna Mae."

We arrived in Hopkinsville a few minutes early, but Bill was in his office and ready to talk. A relaxed man of forty-two, he was dressed casually in wool pants and an open shirt, his badge and gun fastened to his belt. Crayon drawings and family photos intersected with Bureau logos and plaques on his office wall.

Bill and Jack talked backgrounds and assignments for a while. Then we focused on Ann's murder. This was the first UFAP Bill had dealt with in his thirteen years as an agent. Like small-town law enforcement officers, federal agents assigned to small towns can have limited experience. But unlike local law enforcement, a federal agent has the training to handle his or her part of the case and a federal agency to fall back on for assistance.

Bill's part of the case was a small but crucial link in bringing Russell to justice. His assignment was to help bring Russell back to face prosecution and he concentrated on that. As we talked with him, we realized that he knew very little about the local investigation. He wasn't involved, or even greatly interested, in the details of the crime or investigation.

We thanked him for the part he was playing. "Ben's the one who has the main role," said Bill. "He's doing a great job." We nodded.

"Any news on getting Russell on the Top Ten?" asked Jack. "I check the site periodically and there's still an opening."

"Haven't heard anything about the Top Ten, but he's supposed to be listed as an October fugitive," offered Bill. "Don't know if the October listing's up yet."

"He's not listed on Interpol," said Jack.

"Hmmm," said Bill. "I didn't know that. He's definitely registered, and he has an Interpol number."

"Yeah, I know," said Jack. "But he's not on the site."

Bill seemed concerned and said he'd check into it.

Bill was surprised when we told him that Russell was now listed on the *AMW* site.

"Some things we saw on the *AMW* website were news to us. And knowing them would have helped," I told Bill.

I realized Bill hadn't seen the site yet, so I explained. "They listed some aliases."

"Those were just names Earl wired money to," said Bill. "One of them is a woman's name."

"The site also told about Russell's gambling habits," I snipped. "We've been contacting casinos in Costa Rica, and it would have been helpful to have that information." I realized that wasn't Bill's part of the investigation, but I was tired of our struggle to get information and I vented unfairly.

Jack attempted to change the uncomfortable direction of the conversation by bringing it back to shop talk. As the two men talked generally about federal law enforcement, I mentally recounted the value of the visit. We now knew to check the FBI website for Russell's profile. Bill knew to give Interpol a nudge. Not much for a seventy-mile roundtrip and two and a half hours of time, but we were desperate for information. It was time well-spent.

We drove back to Iva Ray's and pulled up the FBI site. Though Russell was not listed in the Top Ten, there was still an opening. And he was listed with the October fugitives. The Bureau was offering an unspecified reward and Russell was now characterized as "armed and dangerous."

Russell had become an FBI fugitive in February. Finally, in October, he was listed on their site. We felt like we were crawling through mud. But here he was, finally listed. And we were grateful.

Later that day, we stopped by Brenda's ministry center to donate some books. Brenda's mother, Margaret, shared some of the rumors blanketing the small town.

"Terri told some people at her church that Russell came in that night soaking wet, like he'd taken a shower in his clothes." Ben had sworn Jack to secrecy that Terri was a witness, so we remained expressionless.

"And somebody else said Russell went home and called a friend to go back to Ann's and get the knife. The friend got the knife from between the mattresses of the bed."

"That's a rumor you can squelch," said Jack, assuming Margaret was talking about Ann's bed. Jack had helped search Ann's bedroom for her gun, looking between the two clean mattresses.

As we were leaving for home the next day, Jack called me to the laptop. He'd received an email from the producer at *AMW*. Paula was letting us know that Russell had been moved to the Dirty Dozen, host John Walsh's pick of the twelve fugitives he most wanted to bring to justice.

Our exhilaration skyrocketed. Thanks to *America's Most Wanted*, we felt that Russell's freedom days were numbered. Since they'd taken an interest in the case, everyone else had focused, too. Without the anticipation of national coverage, Russell hadn't shown up on the FBI fugitive list. Now he was an October fugitive. And Paula was encouraging Bill to suggest Russell for the FBI's Ten Most Wanted List.

I was beginning to feel that *AMW* was the fuel for the rocket aimed straight at Russell.

We had hoped to see Ben while we were in town, but he was tied up with a double homicide. We had a list of thirty questions we felt only he could answer. Things we didn't understand about the investigation. Leads we wanted to be sure had been followed. Information gaps we needed to close. We rescheduled for the Friday before Thanksgiving and psyched ourselves for another wait.

# Chapter 37

# Fading Hopes

In late October, we learned from a reliable source that Ann's former neighbors had created an elaborate Halloween scene in their front yard. Their house, like Ann's, faced Main Street, the most traveled thoroughfare in the town. It didn't take long for most Madisonville residents to learn of the murdered "woman" in their front yard.

These neighbors had formed a "body" by stuffing women's clothing and using a pumpkin for a head. The side of the pumpkin had been bashed in and a knife was protruding from the dummy's chest. The house had concrete steps leading to the sidewalk, and the "dead body" was sprawled halfway down the stairs.

For several days, the dummy remained on the stairs. Then late one night, a friend of Ann's family parked his vehicle behind First Baptist Church, crossed the street to the neighbor's, and spirited away the dummy.

"I guess I would have been arrested if someone had seen me running down the street with the dummy over my shoulders," smiled the friend. "But I'd have gladly paid the price."

We'd hoped Russell would be home by Christmas. But by the end of October, our hopes were fading. Jack called Ben to check in.

"Paula was scheduled to come back to Madisonville to do a reenactment of the crime," said Ben. "But things are up in the air right now. It might be as late as February before Russell's profile airs. John Walsh is thinking of filming from Costa Rica."

Jack and I spent most of the evening dealing with yet another change in the air date. We ate supper at one of our regular restaurants, and the poor waiter heard bizarre snippets of conversation, as he replenished water glasses and delivered entrees.

"I don't think I can stand it if *AMW* doesn't do the profile till February," I said.

"If it's not on till February, that will be six months from the time *AMW* filmed at our house," said Jack.

I was exhausted by the "if's" and "maybe's."

"What if we took out a half-page full-color advertisement in the San Jose newspaper and ran Russell's wanted poster?" asked Jack.

"It might work," I answered. "It's worth a try."

"I'll contact the paper tomorrow and get prices and guidelines."

"We'll need the advertisement in Spanish and English," I told Jack. "I read recently that many areas of Costa Rica don't speak English."

And so we added the possibility of an ad in the San Jose newspaper to our repertoire of solutions to the case, with *AMW* always surfacing as our brightest hope.

As we left the restaurant, Jack commented as casually as he could. "Let's apply for passports Friday. My government one's no good anymore. You never know when we might need them."

Jack had PI cases to work on Thursday, but he squeezed in time to investigate placing the ad. San Jose had two newspapers—one was English, the other, Spanish. It would cost us more than $1,000 to run a third-page ad in each.

"We need to have the advertisement written, designed and translated," I said. "I'm sure Sonia would translate it."

"I'll let Ben and Bill know what we're thinking," said Jack.

I was driving back from buying Taylor a Halloween costume when I got an email from Jack on my BlackBerry. He hadn't been able to get hold of Ben about the ad, so he sent him an email.

But he'd talked to Bill. Not only was Bill in favor of running the ad, but he also thought the Bureau would pay for it. As appealing as that sounded at first, we soon realized that if the FBI took responsibility for the ad, we could expect a long wait as they moved the request up through stack after stack on desk after desk. We had someone willing to translate the ad, and we knew friends who would design it. But bureaucratic hoop jumping would turn this idea out too slowly for a family desperate for justice.

The following Monday, November 1, Paula confirmed that the profile was delayed until February, commenting, "Right now, the bosses are mulling over possibilities, because they like the story so much. Unfortunately, it's looking like February. Fortunately, we may go down to Costa Rica to look for him. I will keep you posted."

On Thursday, Jack and Ben confirmed their meeting for the Friday before Thanksgiving, and Ben told Jack about an anonymous tip that Russell was in the United States. Someone checking the *AMW* website called the informant hotline to say they'd seen someone who looked like Russell leaving a tanning salon in Virginia.

"With a reward being offered, why would someone give an anonymous tip?" I asked.

"Maybe they don't know about the reward. It's mentioned on the FBI site, but not on *AMW*'s," said Jack. "Or it could be some nut who made it all up, someone who gets sick pleasure out of hiding in the bushes and watching an FBI SWAT team rush into a tanning salon."

# Chapter 38

# A Rage-Filled Episode

The week before Thanksgiving, Jack and I drove to Kentucky to visit my mom and to bring Iva Ray back for the holiday. We blocked off a full day to talk to Ben.

Ben arrived early at Iva Ray's house, and by 9:00 a.m., we were drinking coffee and discussing the case. It was the first time I'd met Ben, and I was immediately comfortable talking with him. Hoping we'd gain new insights, we asked if he'd start from the beginning and tell us about his involvement in the investigation.

"When a body is discovered in a small community, news travels fast," Ben began. "I heard on the police radio that a body had been discovered on North Main. I went to Ms. Branson's house to see if I could be of assistance. The police said they had things under control."

Ben carefully articulated the details of the investigation, sitting at near-attention in the plush chair meant for relaxing. Only countless appearances before a grand jury and endless hours of cross examination could develop such professionalism in a thirty-three year old. Yet, mixed with his formal demeanor was a sensitivity and warmth that allowed him to share details that were probably meant only for the police. He'd dealt with enough victims and their families to understand their need for the "why's" and "how's" of the crime. And he was fully aware of Jack's background and training in confidentiality.

Ben revealed that evening, that "Randy Hargis called me at home. He said they were in over their heads. None of the three MPD detectives had ever worked a homicide, and Randy hadn't worked one in years."

I had to interrupt. "I'm amazed that you were welcomed so quickly into the investigation. That's so contrary to how he responded to Jack's offer to help. Guess he considered you a local."

"Madisonville's my hometown. I've lived here all my life," observed Ben. "My responsibilities with the Kentucky State Police include seven counties, but I live in Madisonville."

In spite of our frustrations at never knowing as much about the investigation as we hungered to know, Jack and I were encouraged to learn that the investigating officers were immediately dedicated to solving the crime. The night the body was found, five officers and the Commonwealth attorney made a pact that they'd find Ann's killer. None had seen a crime scene as brutal as the one in the home where Jack and I had spent the night, drank spiced cider and watched the Christmas parade from the upstairs landing.

In the days following the crime, Ben spent time alone in Ann's house, using all his senses to try to relive the crime.

"The thing that struck me most was that the crime scene was spotless," said Ben. "The amount of blood that should have been 'cast off' blood from the movement of the knife wasn't there. I knew we weren't dealing with a vagrant."

At first, Ben was involved in the case in an advisory capacity. Though he'd never investigated a complicated homicide ("Mostly drug deals gone bad"), he nevertheless had more experience than anyone else in the county, with fifteen homicide investigations to his credit. He was never officially assigned to lead Ann's murder investigation. However, as time passed, he became the primary law enforcement officer who kept the case alive.

But initially, it was the MPD who determined Ann's actions the night of her murder, spoke with witnesses, identified people with whom she'd had financial disputes and questioned people she'd evicted.

As I listened to Ben's account, I realized how differently we would have proceeded if the police had talked openly with us early in the investigation. If we'd realized the extent of damage to Ann's body, we would have quickly eliminated most suspects. Most could never have wielded a knife for so long and with such force during the rage-filled episode.

Ben described how during the first week of the investigation, Hargis got a phone call from a confidential source. The confidential informant and Russell were regulars at the Casino Aztar in Evansville, and they'd recently ridden in a limo to the casino in Metropolis, Illinois. The informant said Russell lost a lot of money and, on the way home, his demeanor became desperate. He brought a handgun in the limo, taking it from his pocket and laying it on his lap. The informant was concerned that Russell would kill himself. The MPD had learned that Russell had a gambling problem and that he was emotionally unstable.

Ben was unaware that Jack had offered help, but he assisted as best he could from his end. He obtained help from Cyndy Noble of the Kentucky State Police intelligence unit. Noble investigated Russell's gambling habits and within a week had reports from all three casinos he frequented.

"Russell had a growing addiction," said Ben. "The casinos showed he'd been gambling for three years and in the last year, his gambling transactions more than quadrupled, to $1.2 million."

The KSP focused on Russell's movements the week before the murder. Indiana has state police officers assigned to the casinos, and they assisted with the investigation. The KSP learned that Russell went to Caesar's in Harrison County, Indiana (near Louisville, Kentucky), the night before the murder.

"The police talked to Ms. Branson's hairdresser, her fiancé and others," said Ben. "They all knew she was giving money to Russell."

Ann had reached the end of her patience, I thought. Telling family business wasn't her style. But if she was that exasperated, why did she loan Russell $9,700 the day before her murder? The answer, I believe, lay in her emotional makeup, formed early in childhood.

# Chapter 39

# Craving Affection

Jack's grandfather —Ann's father— was a good man who cared deeply for his family, but he was the unemotional patriarch who had shaped the stoic family. With a father who was unwilling or unable to show emotion, I believe Ann grew up without confidence in her father's love. She married an introverted, self-absorbed man. In his own way, Carroll loved her passionately, but his love for Ann was rarely his priority.

After Ann's death, we found this handwritten note in her personal belongings, written on her birthday years before:

"Sunday, November 30, 1975

"I am waiting out a broken knee, so I had a very exciting day of lying on the couch. Evelyn called and wished me a happy birthday. She was the only one that even mentioned my birthday today.

"Carroll's getting ready to leave on his trip and he's pleasant and nice to me, but he really don't know or care what's on my mind, for as usual he's more interested in what he's thinking than I'm thinking, and as long as I don't try to tell him what I want or think or to demand much from him, everything is okay.

"So all I'm expected to do is not expect nothing, not want anything and don't open my mouth about any of his shortcomings.

"So my fifty-eighth birthday came and went. My question is what have I gained all these fifty-eight years. For all these years, my main thoughts have been what's best for us, and now I'm realizing there is no us. Just you and me living together."

We also found a short correspondence between Ann and Carroll that painted a picture of a loving couple who struggled to meet each other's emotional needs.

"Have a safe trip," Ann wrote on a small slip of paper. "I love you, but I don't like to see you act so miserable. Makes me wonder sometimes if maybe you would be happier if I wasn't around. Guess I'll always wonder for I'll be around until my toes turn up."

"I wish I could help it." Carroll wrote his answer on the other side of the paper. "I feel so bad. I realize I'm not much pleasure to be around. Sorry.

"I love you and always will. Without you, I wouldn't have any reason to live another day. I'll assure you I don't have any other reason for living.

"Please try to understand that and get on with your life. You can be sure that I'm on your side all the way.—CGB"

I could understand the unconscious plan Ann devised to get the affection she craved. When Ann cared little about a person or was confident in his or her love, she could be strong, even ruthless, in her financial dealings. When she felt she had to win their love, she was apparently willing to purchase it. She'd mentioned to several people that Russell visited her only when he wanted money, so money was the way to make sure the visits continued. Without the emotional fulfillment from the men she loved most, I believe Ann was too easily flattered by Russell's sporadic attention.

Ben's voice brought me back to the present. "We began to hear from other people, saying Russell had been borrowing money from them."

"Like who?" asked Jack.

"Friends, co-workers," replied Ben. "One day Earl's girlfriend, Betty, got a call from Russell saying he was in town and asking if he could stop by and see her. He was only in her living room a few minutes before he asked if he could borrow $30,000. She told him if he needed money to ask his father."

**Top:** Madisonville, Kentucky's original "Best Town On Earth" sign, erected in 1927.
**Bottom:** New town sign erected in celebration of Madisonville's 200th anniversary.

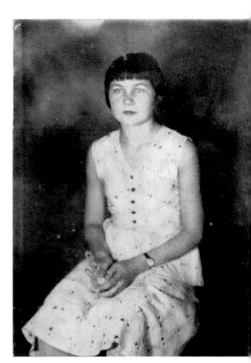

**CLOCKWISE FROM TOP LEFT:** The Winstead family L-R -Ann, father I.E. Winstead, sister Iva Ray and mother Nora; Ann at twelve; Photo of Russell at Jack and Mary's engagement party in 1967 playing with Mary's niece.

**CLOCKWISE FROM TOP LEFT:** Ann and Carroll Branson, circa 1944; Carroll at their first Dairy Queen in 1963; Ann Branson in her DQ uniform circa 1983; Ann standing in front of her photo portrait, 2002; Ann and Carroll at 50th wedding anniversary, 1985

**CLOCKWISE FROM TOP LEFT:** Special Agent Jack Branson; Mary and Jack at the grave of Ann Branson; Mary and Jack pictured separately with Ann in August 2002, five months before her death; Ann with Jack and Mary before Mary's senior prom in 1967.

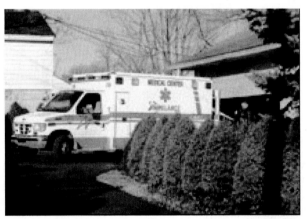

**CLOCKWISE FROM TOP LEFT:** The home where Ann Branson was murdered; ambulance waiting to transport Ann's body from the crime scene; casino surveillance photo of Russell gambling the day after Ann's murder; excerpt from Ann's journal detailing her loans to Russell

# WANTED
## BY THE FBI

**UNLAWFUL FLIGHT TO AVOID PROSECUTION - FIRST DEGREE ROBBERY AND MURDER**

### RUSSELL EARL WINSTEAD

Photograph taken circa late
2002 to early 2003

**Aliases:** Russell Winstead, Russell E. Winstead, Craig Conway, Milena Perez

### DESCRIPTION

| | | | |
|---|---|---|---|
| **Date of Birth Used:** | February 4, 1965 | **Hair:** | Black |
| **Place of Birth:** | Hopkins County, Kentucky | **Eyes:** | Brown |
| **Height:** | 6'1" | **Sex:** | Male |
| **Weight:** | 170 to 185 pounds | **Race:** | White |
| **NCIC:** | W465589909 | **Nationality:** | American |
| **Occupation:** | Coal Mining Engineer | | |
| **Scars and Marks:** | None known | | |
| **Remarks:** | Winstead reportedly is a seasoned gambler and is likely to frequent casinos and gambling institutions. Winstead may have travelled to Chicago, Illinois; Dallas/Fort Worth, Texas; and San Jose, Costa Rica. | | |

### CAUTION

Russell Earl Winstead is wanted for his alleged involvement in the murder of his 86-year-old aunt in Kentucky. On January 12, 2003, Winstead allegedly went to his aunt's home in Madisonville to retrieve a check that he had written to her to repay money he previously borrowed. Winstead also allegedly asked his aunt to loan him additional money, but she refused. Later that day, the victim's body was found in her home, having been stabbed over 80 times. Also, the check was missing from her home.

Winstead was charged with first degree robbery and murder in a state arrest warrant which was issued on July 15, 2003, by the Hopkins Circuit Court, Madisonville, Kentucky. On February 26, 2004, a federal arrest warrant was issued by the United States District Court, Western District of Kentucky, charging Winstead with unlawful flight to avoid prosecution.

### REWARD

The FBI is offering a reward of up to $10,000 for information leading to the arrest of Russell Earl Windstead.

### SHOULD BE CONSIDERED ARMED AND DANGEROUS

**IF YOU HAVE ANY INFORMATION CONCERNING THIS PERSON, PLEASE CONTACT YOUR** LOCAL FBI OFFICE **OR THE NEAREST** AMERICAN EMBASSY OR CONSULATE.

The FBI Most Wanted poster that displayed the identifying photo and description of Russell Earl Winstead while he was on the lam in Costa Rica.

Photograph courtesy of InsideCostaRica.com

Earl's arrest.

Russell's arrest in Costa Rica on May 3, 2005.

Center Photographs courtesy of Jack Branson

Coal company where Russell worked as an engineer.

The home of Earl Winstead.

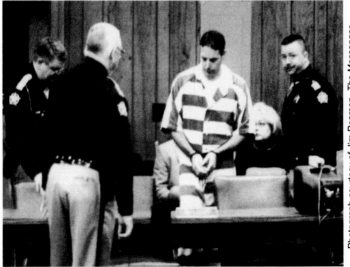

Photograph courtesy of Jim Pearson, *The Messenger*

Russell at his arraignment in March of 2006.

Mr. Winstead,                               12-29-06

    I'm writing you today to ask you
for forgiveness. I'm the reason you have
lost a sister, and 3 years of your sons
life. I have no way to replace what I
have took from you, and your family but
I can help make things right by owning
up to what I have done. I know by
doing this it's not going to bring her
back but maybe it will give some peace
back to your family. I have been living
a complet nightmare and now it's time
I confront this nightmore. by letting
everyone know that I'm guilty of killing
Ann Branson. I hope you believe me when
I say that I'm deeply sorry for the pain
you have all endured. if you have anything
to say please write.
                          Sincerly
                          Fred Roulette

**CLOCKWISE FROM TOP LEFT:** The letter that Russell bribed his cellmate Fred Roulette to write "confessing" to the murder of Ann Branson; Earl Winstead on the witness stand at his son's trial; Russell Winstead looking distraught at trial.

Ben said that when evidence started mounting against Russell, they avoided arousing suspicion by interviewing the whole family and asking everyone for hair and blood samples. When Russell came in to give samples, Ben and Scott Troutman interviewed him.

"We caught him in several lies," said Ben. "He brought detailed notes of his activities that weekend, which seemed strange. We questioned him about financial transactions he'd had with Ms. Branson. He said he'd received money from her on birthdays and at Christmas, but that was it.

"We knew from the financial ledgers that she'd given him a lot more money," said Ben. "From what we can piece together, we think Russell wrote Ms. Branson a check for $12,000 and said, 'This is a deposit on what I owe. Don't cash it till Monday. But I need another $9,700 or they'll put Terri, the kids and me out of our house.' He may have asked for a little under $10,000 so there'd be no federal record of the money.

"Russell cashed Ms. Branson's check for $9,700, then immediately called Caesar's and said, 'Book my table. I'll be there tonight.'

"He put $300 of his own money with the $9,700 and lost it all that night. The casino comped him a room. The next morning, Sunday, he wrote a personal check for $500 and lost it immediately. After he lost the money, he knew he was in trouble. His bank records showed that he barely had enough in the bank to cover the $500. He sure couldn't have paid Ms. Branson back.

"Terri works at a bank. If the check to Ms. Branson had cleared, Terri would have been alerted that Russell was spending so much money."

Ben continued his story, the details such a part of him that he could rattle off dates, facts and figures without referring to notes. Now I knew that Ben lived Ann's murder, too, though not with the same intensity that Jack and I lived it.

"On the way home, Russell made a string of cell phone calls, mostly to a friend," continued Ben. "That night, Russell and Terri drove separate vehicles to church so he could drive one of his sons home.

"Russell's church and Ms. Branson's church both let out at seven. Russell dropped his son at his first wife's, then went immediately to Ms. Branson's. He had to get the check back, any way he could.

"We used the detailed notes Russell brought to the police station to check his story. We asked about his cell phone calls the night of the murder, including one to Terri. He said he called her from their basement to bring him a glass of water, just horsing around."

"But Terri believed his story?" asked Jack.

"Yeah, at first," said Ben. "The same day we interviewed Russell, we scheduled an interview with Terri. While Russell was having a polygraph— I was with him— other officers questioned Terri. Her answers were similar to Russell's. I felt Russell recalled far too many details for an average night, but the officers played along.

"We did an extensive polygraph. All in all, it lasted an hour. The level of deception was extremely high. In other words, Russell failed miserably.

"We videotaped the polygraph and the interview that followed. The KSP polygrapher interviewed Russell."

The evidence seemed solid against Russell, yet Earl had sacrificed his reputation and his finances to protect his son. Our PI had tried unsuccessfully to convince Earl that Russell was guilty. Jack asked Ben if Earl knew enough of the additional information to realize that Russell was guilty.

Ben nodded. "He knows everything we know, except about Terri and the other lady agreeing to testify. I sat down with him one night at the police station and told him just about everything. I tried to persuade him to get Russell to turn himself in, but he didn't respond."

Jack nodded and Ben continued his description of Russell's interrogation. "The interview lasted about an hour. Then Randy Hargis and I interrogated Russell for the next six hours. Russell and Randy have known each other a long time. They played softball together and rode all-terrain vehicles. It was hard for Randy to be put in that role, but he did it.

"Since Randy had a better rapport with Russell than I had, I decided to leave, hoping Randy could get Russell to confess. Six hours of interrogation, and he never did."

"Russell's a gambler," observed Jack. "If there's even a small chance of getting away with the murder, he'll take it."

"You're right about that," said Ben.

# Chapter 40

# Fleeing Prosecution

Over the next six months, the police continued to gather evidence on Russell. Russell knew that Terri had given them the initial statement, but he didn't know that she'd talked to the police a second time. He became worried that she would reveal all that she might have heard, seen and surmised. He became physically abusive—pushing her against the wall, grabbing her wrist— and emotionally abusive and threatening.

"Russell stalked her," said Ben. "Everywhere she went, she saw Russell. One day, he climbed a telephone pole and looked in her parents' window."

"We encouraged Terri to take out an Emergency Protective Order (EPO)," Ben continued. "We knew that as soon as Russell was served with an EPO, he'd violate it. The police watched his residence and, within an hour, they saw someone who fit his description going into the house. He carried out some items, including a small safe. The police stopped him and discovered it was a friend of Russell's. The friend was similar in build, and Russell had talked this man into going to his house. We didn't catch Russell, but we found out a lot.

"They took the friend to the police department and talked to him. He said Russell had asked him to go back to his house to pick up some items for him, including a knife from between his mattresses and a safe.

"The safe contained insurance policies on the children and a suicide letter from Russell to Terri, apologizing for cheating on her and telling her what to do with his possessions.

"The knife matched the stab wounds in Ann's body. The lab took it apart, but found no DNA. It had been thoroughly cleaned, probably with bleach."

By this time Ben, Jack and I had been talking for more than three hours. No one looked at their watches and no one fidgeted. There was an overdose of information, but we were hungry to hear it, and Ben was generous in telling it. We continued the conversation that would last another hour and a half.

"We obtained an arrest warrant that night for violation of the EPO," said Ben. "Kentucky EPO prohibits the adverse party from disposing of or damaging any of the property of the parties involved. When Russell sent his friend to the house he'd shared with Terri and told him to retrieve the knife, safe and other items, Russell violated his EPO. The sheriff's department had served the EPO, so the same deputy got the violation order, arrested Russell and lodged him. Earl bonded him out immediately.

"Russell was trying to keep his wife on his side. He sent her love letters and gave her gift cards to buy jewelry. He had no idea she'd already talked."

According to Ben, Earl began calling the police multiple times, wanting to know when Ann's rings would be returned so the estate could be settled. Ben felt it was just an excuse to keep in contact with the police and that Earl was more interested in when the DNA studies were completed than in getting back the jewelry. When the studies were completed, Ben reasoned, Earl would know he had to get Russell out of town.

Earl and Russell were making plans for the return of the DNA results. In early May, Russell applied for a passport in Chicago. Then in June—a month before he was indicted—Russell flew American Airlines from Nashville, had a layover in Dallas/Fort Worth and then traveled on to Costa Rica.

On July 16, 2003, Russell was indicted. In the first days after the indictment, police had no idea where he was. His attorney promised that Russell would be present for the arraignment. So the investigation continued.

"The only item missing from Ms. Branson's home was the $12,000 check," said Ben, which answered our question about the original report that a fur was missing. "Ms. Branson went to the bank a couple of times a month. In between bank visits, she put her money and checks in a container under the sink. The check was logged into her journal, but it was missing. Because of the missing check, we were able to charge Russell with first degree robbery along with murder."

We asked if Earl had a valid passport, and Ben said no one had checked. "Has anyone followed Earl?" asked Jack.

"I was able to do one two-week surveillance," said Ben. "But that's all I had permission for. I also followed Russell's first wife, Denise, for a while. Nothing came of either surveillance."

After a time of reflecting on the influx of information, Jack said: "I'm surprised Russell kept the knife. What do you think he did with the camouflage jacket?"

"At the time of the murder, the mines were filling in a mine shaft with pure concrete," said Ben. "Someone saw Russell and his gambling friend, Mike, at the mines in the middle of the night. Russell may have asked him to hold the evidence for a while and then they tossed it down the mine shaft. It would be sealed forever in solid concrete."

Our minds were on overload with all the new information, and we felt as though Russell was as close to being captured as a goldfish in a jelly jar.

"In a recent *Messenger* article, you mentioned that you'd actually gone with an informant to wire money?" I asked.

"Yeah," said Ben. "An attorney called Hargis. He said he had a client who owned a liquor store in a nearby town. Earl had asked this client if he wanted to earn a little money on the side by wiring money to Russell. The client agreed but called the attorney to report Earl's offer.

"We wired the CI when he met with Earl to discuss what Earl wanted him to do. They met, and Earl got into the CI's truck. Earl gave him two blank Western Union forms and $2,600. The CI followed our instructions to the letter. We told him to play dumb about filling out the forms and to get Earl to fill them out.

"Earl told the CI to drive to Missouri to wire the money, because he'd already burned Indiana, Illinois, Kentucky and Tennessee—meaning, I guess, that he'd already wired a lot of money from those states and was afraid of arousing suspicion."

"Couldn't you have had someone waiting to grab Russell when he picked up the money?" I asked.

Both Jack and Ben looked as though I'd asked an elementary question. Patiently, Ben explained: "Unfortunately, Western Union doesn't require identification to pick up money. The system is supposedly in place to protect people who lose their billfolds while away from home. The sender can create a password, which the receiver uses to pick up money at any location worldwide.

"When we wired the informant and went with him to send money on forms handwritten by Earl, we got the evidence necessary to convict Earl of first-degree conspiracy to hindering prosecution. That's the best we could hope for."

"So you know of $2,600 that Earl wired to Russell?" I asked.

"Actually, more like $5,600 that we can document," answered Ben. "But I'm sure that's a small percentage of what was wired."

# Chapter 41

# Disappointments and Slowdowns

Interspersed with our time with Ben, we found some disappointments and frustrating slowdowns in the investigation. But overall, we were encouraged, primarily by the dedication and determination we sensed in Ben. Regardless of his overwhelming schedule, it was obvious that he thought about Ann's murder case every day. In spite of budget restrictions, he found ways to move the investigation forward. And without his openness, Jack and I would have had very little information about the investigation.

We were relieved to hear that the death penalty had not been lifted if Russell were caught in the United States. More and more, we felt that he could be closer to home than anyone imagined, and we could only estimate how many women were ready to welcome him back.

Earl, apparently, wasn't as lucky with the ladies. Betty, his girlfriend, continued to date him immediately after Russell's indictment. But she told him she didn't want to know anything about the murder case. In the first year, they broke up, got back together and eventually broke up permanently. When she found a new boyfriend, Earl reacted with a physical altercation.

The new boyfriend filed misdemeanor charges—the charges Ben had called about during our vacation. Earl pled guilty to a lesser charge and was placed on probation for two years, with an order of no contact with his ex-girlfriend or her boyfriend. Earl now had two probations and no one seemed to notice that the episode with Betty's boyfriend compounded Earl's original probation. To me, the second run-in with the law seemed like the perfect time to put Earl behind bars and cut Russell's financial umbilical cord.

I wondered why Terri wasn't suspicious when Russell was away from home 236 nights in one year.

"Did she know Russell gambled?" I asked.

"Just socially," said Ben. "When they went shopping in Evansville, he'd sometimes run over to the boat while she shopped. But that's all."

"But the people on the boat knew him?" I knew the answer before I asked the question. Russell must have spent more time on the boat than he spent at home.

"Yeah," Ben said. "When the pit bosses in Evansville went on duty, they could look at the table limits and tell whether Russell was on the boat. They lowered their limits to run him off." That, I thought, probably was what Earl had interpreted to our PIs as Russell being banned from the boat.

Jack and I had a few questions still unasked, so we fired them in quick succession:

Why had Russell chosen Costa Rica? A local attorney told him they don't extradite if the death penalty is an option.

Had anyone found the prenuptial agreement that Judy, the housekeeper, told our PIs about? Ben wasn't aware that one existed.

Why was the freezer removed from Ann's basement? Ben said the freezer had some areas sticky with blood and they hoped to lift fingerprints or DNA. No fingerprints had been found, and the only blood was Ann's.

Was it blood on the bubble wrap Judy found in the basement? Ben hadn't heard about the bubble wrap.

Had the anonymous note sent to Iva Ray been checked against Russell's handwriting? Ben knew nothing about the note.

"Ben, I don't see how this investigation has dragged on so long. How

Russell was able to flee the country," I said. "What went wrong?"

Ben paused as truth and diplomacy wrestled. Carefully, he responded: "Too many chiefs, conflicting personalities, the investigators' lack of experience and people leaving or changing jobs—the whole continuity thing."

"If you could do it all over," Jack asked. "What would you do differently?"

"Better processing of the crime scene," answered Ben without hesitation. "I'm sure there's still evidence in that basement."

# Chapter 42

## The Fugitive

Jack, Ben and I took a break, but we continued talking while we ate fast food burgers in Iva Ray's dining room. Ben told us of his plans to bring all the major players before the grand jury to stir things up again.

Jack nodded. "Maybe some of the ones who've been loyal will break if they think there's new evidence."

"What kind of gossip do you hear, Ben?" I asked. "What's the attitude of most of the people in town?"

Ben set his jaw almost imperceptibly, and he fixed his gaze on a vase of flowers a few feet away. "I don't hear much. A lot of people think Russell and Earl are on the right track."

Incredulous, I asked, "You mean they think Russell's innocent?"

Ben nodded. Nice clean-cut professional, falsely accused of a heinous crime. A determined detective will stop at nothing to prove his point and bring the nice young man back to face murder charges. It all sounded like *The Fugitive*, the old television series in which kind Dr. Richard Kimble was pursued by ruthless Lt. Philip Gerard. We all rooted for the fugitive because, of course, he was innocent.

There's something in all of us that wants the Robin Hoods of the world to win. Add the image of a dedicated and loving dad and who could help but root for the bad guy?

We closed our time together with Jack agreeing to do a background check on Russell's gambling friend, Mike, and Ben amusing us with a story about Russell's concern that his charm wouldn't last forever.

"At the time of the murder, Russell was just beginning to go bald, right here," said Ben, as he touched the upper back portion of his head.

"The traditional Winstead pattern," nodded Jack, who instead had inherited the Branson hairline.

"The people in Russell's office said he had a second computer monitor set up behind him so he could see the reflection of the back of his head in his monitor. He was constantly checking his bald spot," said Ben.

The Tuesday after Thanksgiving, Jack woke to a voicemail message from eleven o' clock the night before. It looked like they had Russell's location!

"Someone contacted *AMW* and said they saw Russell coming out of a grocery in Louisville. The Louisville police contacted the Hopkins County Sheriff's Department and asked them to fax a copy of the arrest warrant," said Ben in the message. "It may be nothing. We'll just have to see. I'll keep you updated, my friend."

When we received the message, it was 5:30 a.m. in Madisonville. In case Ben left his phone on while he slept, Jack agonized three hours before calling him back.

Ben returned his call at 10:00 a.m. The call requesting a copy of the arrest warrant had come from the Lexington police, not the Louisville police. The deputy who took the call got the cities mixed up, not only when he reported the call to Ben but also when he faxed the warrant. The deputy eventually faxed the warrant to Lexington as well, but the lead proved false.

Jack and I grabbed lunch at a local cafeteria and talked about the case. As we were finishing eating, Earl called.

"I'm helping a doctor's widow here in town sell a couple of old pistols, and I knew you could tell me how old they are and what they're worth," Earl told Jack.

When Jack heard the serial numbers, he knew the guns were valuable. "Nine or ten thousand is what I'd guess, off the top of my head," said Jack. "And they were probably made around the time of Custer's Last Stand. I can do some checking tonight and get back to you."

Earl agreed to call Jack that evening to verify the value.

"I hadn't talked to Earl since his indictment a year ago," said Jack, "and now twice in a couple of weeks." Earl had seen Jack's car outside Iva Ray's the last time we were in Kentucky and he'd stopped by to say hi. I'd already gone to bed, but Jack said they spent a superficial hi/how-about-the-weather ten minutes before shaking hands awkwardly and promising to keep in touch.

"Maybe he's trying to rebuild the relationship," I suggested. "Maybe all his friends have said 'enough is enough' and he's looking for someone to help him send money to Russell."

"I hope so," said Jack. "I'd be glad to be wired and 'help' him all I can."

During his daily checks of the *AMW* and FBI websites, Jack discovered that Russell had been profiled on the AMW radio program. It had aired the day before, on November 30, which would have been Ann's birthday.

Jack immediately emailed Ben to be sure he was aware of the airing. Ben wrote back that he'd called Paula, *AMW*'s producer, on November 30 to ask her to add another alias—Hugh Simmons—to Russell's web profile, and she'd told him about the radio profile.

Jack received an email from Bill Frank, saying there had been a few more Russell sightings—in Virginia, Florida and Indiana—but they'd all turned out to be look-alikes.

Jack emailed Ben, Bill and Paula before Christmas, asking if they knew an *AMW* air date for Russell. Ben answered before leaving for Florida with his family. He had no new information but promised to share anything he found out with Jack.

Bill emailed to say he had a Quantico assignment for January but that he'd work on the case while he was there. We received a Christmas card from *AMW*, signed by Paula, with this note: "Hope we get Russell in 2005!"

We received a Christmas card from Earl, too. He'd handwritten: "Merry Christmas and Happy New Year. Hope to see you soon."

# Chapter 43

# Time
# Flees

Christmas 2004 came and went, and Russell was still free. We drove Iva Ray home on the twenty-seventh and saw Earl's tractor in Iva Ray's driveway. Jack trudged through the snow to Iva Ray's garage just as Earl came out. I saw the two men shake hands with just a trace of awkwardness. After they talked a few minutes, Earl walked down the driveway and motioned for me to let down the window of Iva Ray's Cadillac.

Earl's voice was weaker and raspier than I'd ever known it to be. Straining to understand him, I learned that he'd broken a cotter pin on his tractor and was on his way to get a new one. The driveway would be impassable until he could grade it.

As Earl was talking, Judy—Ann's housekeeper—drove up in a late model car. "Judy's driving me to the hardware store," said Earl. He nodded good-bye and trudged through the snow to Judy's car.

While I visited my mom the next day, Jack drove from the road where Russell and Terri had lived to Ann's house. The three-and-a-half-mile trip took only five minutes driving normal speed in mid-afternoon. He drove from Olive Branch Baptist Church to Russell's first wife Denise's home and from Denise's house to Ann's. The cozy small-town cluster of buildings made it easy to see how Russell could leave church at seven o'clock, drop his son off at Denise's, arrive at Ann's just moments after her own arrival, commit the gruesome murder, take a shower in Ann's basement and return home by nine o'clock.

Jack completed his drive with a trip to Odd Fellows Cemetery, as he did each time we were in Madisonville, visiting Ann's grave and renewing his promise to find her killer.

That evening, as we were climbing into bed, Iva Ray's security system malfunctioned. The house was filled with ear-shattering siren-like sounds. Jack and I rushed from the bedroom to find Iva Ray scrambling to turn off the security system.

"Will the security company call you?" I asked.

"No," said Iva Ray. "They're not set up to call the house with the security system. They call a friend or relative—and the police. I have Earl listed for them to call."

Within moments, we saw headlights in Iva Ray's driveway. Earl arrived, even before the police. Still the protector who graded snow from driveways and checked when security systems malfunctioned, Earl was faithful to care for his one remaining sister.

The next day, Earl stopped by to see Jack and show him the gun he'd called about recently. It was the first time I'd seen him in good lighting and without snow blurring my vision. He looked twenty years older than when I'd seen him at Grace's funeral.

We still had no definitive date for *America's Most Wanted*. In January, Jack emailed Ben to ask if he'd heard and to see if he'd made progress on getting some of the key players before the grand jury. Ben replied that he had plans to bring several witnesses before the grand jury, including Russell's gambling friend, Mike. He said *AMW* was planning to tape a reenactment, but still no definite air date.

He ended his email:

"The anniversary is fast approaching. I think about Ann every day...Her picture stays close to me. As does Russell's." –Ben

# Chapter 44

# Anniversary of a Murder

Wednesday, January 12, 2005, marked the second anniversary of the murder. Jack woke up with Ann's murder foremost on his mind. Our daughter, Penny, sent an e-card to her dad, letting him know she was thinking about Ann, too. Our son, Dave, called.

To our knowledge, no one else remembered. It was just another day for everyone but our immediate family. Ben emailed that morning to tell us that *AMW* was scheduled to come to Madisonville the next week to film the reenactment. A February profile still seemed possible, but after five months of waiting, we'd stopped marking dates on the calendar.

By the first of February, *AMW* had been back to Madisonville to do the final filming, taking its investment in the segment to well over $100,000, according to Ben. In response to an email from Jack, Ben gave us an update on the *AMW* profile:

"The script continues to grow and increase in over-all length. Tomorrow I am sending them videos of interviews I did with Russell (polygraph and PD). Our plan is to flood the viewership with Russell's actual face and features, while using the actor to recreate special scenes.

"I know for a fact that the producers/directors are on a timeline to finish this story and get it aired. They will positively finish with taping in DC this month and I would anticipate an air date of mid to late February.

"I'm ready for this chapter to be over. Working with the show has been like another full-time job at times. I have enjoyed the experience, but I am ready to reap the benefits of fourteen million people seeing Russell's mug on national television and multiple foreign countries.

"Keep your respective fingers crossed down there. Tonight I plan to watch the videos of Russell's interviews here at home. It may sound sadistic to watch such material, but to me, it is an avenue to recharge my batteries for the final drive to catch our man. The end is near, Jack.

"Just a few more days until all of America, and then all of Hopkins County, will find out things that only a few have known."

Jack checked the *AMW* and FBI websites daily. On Friday, February 11, he called me to his computer. "They're getting ready to profile Russell."

Both websites had moved Russell front and center. Four videos were added to the *AMW* site: one of Jack's interview, one of Russell's former best friend and police officer Jeff Jewell's interview, and two of Russell's interrogation by the MPD. Jack described the encounter with Russell at the funeral home, when Russell asked Jack if he thought the killer would be caught. Jack expressed his concern about how quickly the killer would be caught, and how with Jack's words Russell's mood had lightened.

Jewell's interview described the way he felt he could always tell when Russell was lying: A bone on the side of his face, near his right eye, twitched. This was more new information for us.

The two interrogation videos were a good choice for the website. Though the police would have had a mug shot of Russell when he was arrested for violating the EPO, the photo used on the FBI wanted poster and for all other reports of the crime was Russell's driver's license photo. Russell had lost weight since that photo was taken, and the interrogation videos showed a more accurate build.

The videos also provided Russell's voice. Though he could alter his appearance, his Kentucky drawl would be hard to disguise. His voice could be the clue that solidified a viewer's suspicion that they knew the killer.

Jack consistently made sure to tell Ben and Bill everything he knew, and he called Ben as soon as he saw the websites. Ben returned his call, acknowledging that he already knew that the case would be profiled February 19. His email to Bill resulted in the same information. *AMW*'s standard procedure is to invite the investigating officer to the studio the evening the profile is aired, so they can help follow up on leads. Ben was making plans to drive to Washington. As the FBI agent closest to the case, Bill was planning to go to Washington, as well.

Jack followed up his phone conversation to Ben with an email, emphasizing that he wouldn't tell his family about the broadcast date because he didn't want Earl to be aware of it and tip off Russell.

Ben responded by saying they planned to conceal the air date "until as late as possible. Maybe an article in the Friday *Messenger*. We obviously want the public to know about the program, however, we want to maintain confidentiality as long as possible." Jack paled as the words impacted him. Then, in his signature make-every-word-count manner: "They're... going...to...notify...the...*Messenger*...about...the profile. Earl will call Russell as soon as he reads the story."

"I imagine Russell will take off," I said soberly. "You've got to ask Ben to reconsider telling the paper."

"I can try," said Jack. "I'll send him another email."

I watched as Jack typed: "Thanks, Ben, for the reply. Do you think Earl (or someone else) might tip Russell off if there's advance notice of the broadcast in the paper?"

We waited nervously for two hours before Ben replied: "Jack, I'm sure that if or when Earl finds out, he will alert Russell. However, my guess is that based on my surveillance of Earl last year, he normally makes a trip to Daytona for the race festivities. If he is in town, he'll find out about the episode approximately twenty-four hours prior to its broadcast. Even for the best of criminals, that is not much heads-up to go into hiding. If that is all the time he gets for a head start, I will be satisfied.

"I don't anticipate anyone else finding out about the date unless we tell them. I have not even told Russell's second ex-wife, Terri. I feel like we are in good shape right now."

"How quickly could you run if your life depended on it?" I asked Jack.

"Thirty seconds," he replied.

I wondered if Russell was prepared to leave on a moment's notice. I imagined him leaving home each morning with a duffel bag. If he returned to find police surrounding his living quarters, he'd simply drive away. If he left clues, they would be decoys. Ever since the *Messenger* ran the story that *AMW* was profiling him, my guess is that he's been living out of a suitcase.

I felt that Jack and I knew something crucial about his cousin that Ben and *AMW* didn't. Russell was smart, cunning and driven by a strong survival instinct. If Ben was focused on Ann's murder case, thinking about it first thing every morning and last thing every night, wouldn't Russell be even more focused? Wouldn't he have an escape plan ready to execute?

# Chapter 45

# Loving Boy to Killer

Jack and I constantly talked about our fears that a story in the *Messenger* would give Russell enough warning to go into hiding. "Would it do any good to ask the *Messenger's* editor not to run the article?" I asked.

"It might," said Jack. "I don't mind calling Tom. I'll wait until Wednesday, a little closer to the air date, and ask. But if he runs the article anyway, I certainly won't fault him. He's a news reporter and this is news, probably from an official *AMW* news release."

Paula, the *AMW* producer, called on Monday to make sure we knew that Russell would be profiled and to ask us to warn family members that they might not want to watch the reenactment.

"It's pretty graphic," she said.

By Wednesday, we were thinking and talking about the show constantly. As we got ready that morning, I asked Jack, "Are you going to call the *Messenger* editor today?"

"I guess," said Jack. "I'm not sure what good it will do, but we have to try everything. I'll call him after I have my coffee and check my email."

A few moments later, as I was blow-drying my hair, my BlackBerry vibrated. It was a forwarded message from Jack. I turned off the dryer and read what he just wrote. No use calling the editor. The online *Messenger* for Wednesday, February 16, featured a front-page article announcing that Russell would be profiled on Saturday's *AMW*. The article stated that *AMW* had indeed spent more than $100,000 on the segment. And the article quoted Ben as saying, "Announcement of the segment's airing was withheld until so late because authorities did not want Winstead alerted and given an opportunity to withdraw from any social situations he may be involved in."

Unfortunately, the early story gave Russell three days, not one. To our dismay, many online newspapers also printed early information about the *AMW* profile. The Kentucky State Police issued a press release and MSNBC ran a feature about the upcoming profile.

Jack and I had supper Wednesday night at Dawsonville Pool Room, a local landmark about ten miles from our home. Though the dining room has two pool tables as "props," the establishment is now a down-home restaurant with a NASCAR theme. NASCAR driver Bill Elliott is from Dawsonville, as the "Awesome Bill from Dawsonville" signs remind you. The restaurant is filled with news clippings, racing T-shirts and four-foot trophies.

As Jack and I chose between their signature burgers and meat-and-vegetable plates, I nodded toward the Elliott memorabilia and commented, "This could have been Russell. He tried to make it in NASCAR, but he just wasn't that good."

"Anna Mae used to go to his races and cheer him on," recalled Jack.

"Bill Elliott and Russell probably have the same high adrenaline level," I said. "They both crave over-the-top excitement, but they found different ways to achieve their highs. I wonder where Russell would be now, if he'd been a successful NASCAR driver."

"He'd probably never have started visiting casinos," observed Jack.

That evening, Jack got out one of Ann's photo albums that she'd given us a few months before her murder. As we flipped through the pages that told her life story, we paused in unison. Jack removed a photo of Russell as a preschooler. An older cousin was crying, and Russell was reaching up to comfort him, his face communicating compassion.

As we stared at the picture, I was struck by the contrast between the little boy—loving, empathetic, filled with potential—and the man now on the run. Between these two Russells was a life path of nearly forty years. And somewhere along the way, the loving little boy became a killer.

# Chapter 46

## Location
## Found

We awoke on Saturday, February 19, 2005, full of anticipation. "Twelve hours and forty-five minutes till it airs," said Jack as we brushed our teeth.

"Ten and a half hours till it airs," said Penny when we picked up the boys for their weekly overnight visit.

We made sure the boys were settled on their air mattresses, prayers spoken and snacks on hand earlier than usual. We didn't want them to watch the reenactment, and we didn't want to be interrupted by requests for popcorn while we were watching. By 8:30—thirty minutes before the show—I could hear the stereo and steady breathing from the bundles of blankets on the air mattresses. I climbed the stairs and settled into bed next to Jack, nearly nauseated with anticipation.

As the opening music began, Jack and I fervently hoped someone who knew Russell would call the show and end our twenty-five month torment. Finally, viewers across the world, including wherever Russell was hiding, would see a reenactment of his horrible crime. They would see that the charming young man with the easy smile had a dark and dangerous side. We hoped the *AMW* profile would convince those closest to him to expose his whereabouts.

Though we'd resigned ourselves to the need to show the horror of the crime, we were relieved that apparently, in the last-minute cutting of the feature, the graphic scenes had been deleted.

Ben did a great job. His short intermittent interviews were clear and articulate. His description of Russell as feeling "ten feet tall and bullet-proof" was powerful and accurate.

The profile included Russell's polygraph and the information that the results had shown 100 percent probability of deception. And in the end, after the reenactment, there was Russell. His face was broadcast worldwide, and *AMW* pleaded with viewers to contact them if they knew Russell's location.

Now all we could do was wait.

Both Penny and Dave told us to call anytime Saturday night or Sunday morning if Russell was arrested. Jack and I stayed up till a little past midnight after the profile aired. As we turned out the lights, we discussed whether to leave Jack's cell phone on. Since we hadn't heard by midnight, we decided not to. Jack turned off his cell and we slept for seven hours.

But we awoke to a voice mail message at 2:46 a.m. from Ben. They'd had a good night, according to Ben, and "we know where Russell is."

We wanted to be optimistic, but we doubted the FBI was as close to catching Russell as Ben thought. We called Penny and Dave but cautioned them that there was no reason to celebrate yet.

Ben returned Jack's call just as our church service began, and Jack slipped out to take the call. Two years and one week earlier, I'd sat in the same church, on the same pew, when Jack slipped out to take a call from our investigators. We'd found out that day that Russell was most likely Ann's killer. As the service progressed, I prayed Jack was finding out that Russell was captured.

I anguished through the service, then hurried outside to meet Jack.

"He's still in Costa Rica," said Jack. "Ben said he's living with a woman and has his own blackjack table at one of the casinos. U.S. Marshals are on their way to Costa Rica now."

We drove the five miles home in relative silence. No tears of joy. No celebrating. All we could think of was that Russell had, thus far, escaped the death penalty by staying in Costa Rica and the three days' notice Earl surely gave him was more than enough for a desperate man to relocate.

We updated Penny and Dave and cautioned them to keep Russell's location quiet until we told them otherwise. Days passed with no capture. On Tuesday, we headed to California for a writing seminar I'd registered for months earlier.

We hungered for more information, so we exchanged voice mails with Bill Frank on Thursday. He told us that about a dozen phone calls had come in about Russell. Bill said two people who gambled with Russell at the Horseshoe Casino in San Jose had called *AMW* to say they recognized him. He had not altered his appearance. He was going by the name David, but they didn't know where he lived.

Bill Frank called on April 21 and said the Marshals would not, should not, make contact with Russell without having the provisional warrant. He said the FBI agent stationed in Panama was now in Costa Rica, and border personnel had been notified of Russell's alias. Bill was optimistic that an arrest was imminent.

But I was more skeptical. I was sure Russell was getting ready to leave Costa Rica if he hadn't left already.

"He probably has a passport under the same name he used at the casino. He's smart enough to have more than one alias," I said. "He's probably the one who arranged all the false sightings, and he probably made sure the tips got back that he'd altered his appearance. They're dealing with a smart and desperate man, not a bumbling crook.

"He had three days' notice. Three days! He probably was making arrangements to hide in some obscure cabin, with a new girlfriend bringing him supplies. And if he left any clues for the feds, they're probably pointing them in the opposite direction. They keep underestimating him!"

"You're underestimating Russell, too," Jack said when I finally took a breath. "You're underestimating his gambling addiction. Honey, it's as strong an addiction as crystal meth. Russell has to get to a casino. And that's how they can catch him."

There still was no word on Russell as we checked into a motel when we arrived in Anthony, Texas, just west of El Paso, on Saturday evening, February 26, on our way to California on business.

As we drove down Interstate 10 toward California the next morning, Jack and I talked once more about our options for pursuing Russell. "I don't want to do anything right now. I want to give the Marshals a chance to handle this. When we get home, if Russell's still not caught, we may need to rethink our plans."

Jack called Ben and asked him for an update on the case. Though Ben was always willing to provide information when we asked, he seldom called to offer information.

Ben said the paperwork had just gone through giving the U.S. Marshals authority (as opposed to the FBI) to bring Russell in. So now, after ten days, the surveillance would finally begin.

"I can't understand their waiting so long," I said.

"The delay is probably okay," said Jack. "Right after the broadcast, Russell may have decided to lay low for a while. He'll need to resurface soon because he has to feed his habit. It's where he'll resurface that's in question, but I think there's a good chance it will be the Horseshoe."

"He'd have to be stupid to do that," I emphasized again. And then softly: "And if the Marshals give up and go home and everyone turns their focus elsewhere, what happens then?"

Jack was driving at full speed across the Arizona desert and he kept his gaze on the highway. He spoke his next words with the same level of emotion he would have used to ask if I wanted to stop at the next exit and get a couple of Cokes. "How would you like to take a trip to Costa Rica in late May? That would give the Marshals time to find Russell if they can. If not, we can try.

"I'd have to go unarmed, but we know Russell as more than a mug shot. We'd recognize his build and his mannerisms. San Jose has a million people, but if we spend all our time searching the casinos, we just might find him."

# Chapter 47

## Seeking
## Closure

On February 23, the online *Messenger* included an editorial, written by executive editor Tom Clinton, which summed up the frustration of an entire community.

"...In the case of one of our most beloved citizens, Madisonville and Hopkins County are looking for closure in connection with the January 2003 death of businesswoman Ann Branson.

"Her brutal murder in her North Main Street home, not long after she returned from Sunday evening services across the street at First Baptist Church, left us stunned, deeply saddened, angry, questioning and determined that the person or persons responsible be brought to justice.

"...Eventually, police announced their chief suspect was one of Branson's nephews, Russell Winstead, who had been a pallbearer at her funeral. But before police could arrest him, he apparently fled the country after obtaining a passport. It has never been clear how authorities, if they saw him as a suspect for some time, did not see his passport application as a tip he might be attempting to flee and avoid prosecution.

"...Once he 'got away,' getting him back to face trial would not be an easy process.

"...Despite what we are told has been limited intervention by federal and international authorities, Winstead remains free and Branson's family and community remain concerned. We are seeking closure. We want Winstead to face trial for this horrible crime. A jury of his peers will decide his guilt or innocence. He deserves to face trial, whether guilty or innocent, just as those who are feeling his aunt's loss so deeply deserve to know that justice has prevailed.

"...The longer a murder goes unsolved, the more difficult it is to prosecute. In this case, it was seven months before a Hopkins County grand jury handed down indictments charging Winstead with first-degree robbery and murder in connection with his aunt's death. The advantage police have here is their feeling that Winstead is the man responsible. His flight and continued avoidance of police builds a stronger case for prosecution, though it obviously does not convict him.

"...This family and this community want an arrest and trial sooner, not later. We are seeking closure."

# Chapter 48

# A Treacherous Slip

When Penny and Dave were small, our family bought some fertilized duck eggs. Jack and I thought it would be educational for the kids to watch the ducks hatch, but we were the ones who became emotionally involved in the project. We set up a box with a warming lamp and eagerly waited for the fuzzy additions to the family.

One morning, Jack called excitedly: "The eggs are moving!"

We huddled over the box and watched the wiggles and rolls of the eggs. Finally, we heard muted pecking noises, and eventually, tiny beaks made even tinier holes in the shells that separated the ducks from freedom.

As evening approached, the ducks were halfway out of their shells. They were weak from exhaustion. We agonized with them as they struggled to complete the hatching process. We had planned to eat supper out, and right before we left the house, Jack said, "Let's help them. They're about ready to die. They can't keep this up." He leaned gently into the box and carefully pulled a few large pieces of shell from the ducks' exhausted, damp bodies. It seemed to help.

We re-attached the warming lamp, loaded our two- and four-year-olds in our car and grabbed a fast-food supper. When we returned less than an hour later, we hurried to check on our baby ducks. They were dead.

Some struggles take time. And even the painful parts are necessary for a healthy ending.

We didn't wait patiently for Russell's capture; we agonized. We didn't hope for a close to this chapter of our lives; we begged God to end our ordeal. But deep in our subconscious, we somehow knew that each faltering step needed a treacherous slip backward. And in some indefinable way, we realized we were growing stronger. We determined not to give up.

We arrived home from California after nearly three weeks. We had heard very little from Bill and Ben during our trip. On March 17, Jack called Bill and asked for an update. Bill returned his call the next afternoon and said Russell would receive a fifteen-second *AMW* profile the next evening, March 19, as one of the four fugitives in their "Fifteen Seconds of Shame" feature.

We watched the fifteen-second highlight with minimal emotion. If forty times the exposure a month ago didn't result in a capture, we weren't putting our hopes in a quick flash of Russell's face. We called Bill the next week and confirmed that the mini-feature had brought no response.

We drove to Kentucky for a few days to visit our mothers. While in Madisonville, Jack and I drove Russell's route again. We drove to Olive Branch Baptist Church, where Russell and Terri attended church. Driving just under the speed limit in midday traffic, we drove from Olive Branch to Denise's house in eleven minutes and from Denise's to Ann's in five. We ended our drive by visiting Ann's grave.

"Earl was wondering if you'd be here tomorrow night," Iva Ray said on Tuesday. "He said he'd like to stop by and visit for a while."

That evening, we showed Iva Ray a DVD of Russell's *AMW* profile. When the producer had told us it was going to be graphic, we warned Iva Ray not to watch.

When 9:00 p.m. came and went, we began to think Earl wasn't stopping by after all. But finally, we heard a car pull into the circular driveway and saw its headlights beam through the drapes. Jack greeted Earl at the door, and the two men came into the family room where I was working at my laptop.

After the acceptable amount of small talk, Earl pointed to Jack's badge and asked, "How can I get a badge?"

"A federal badge or just a badge?" asked Jack. When Earl shrugged, Jack explained: "It's illegal to possess a federal badge unless you're a federal officer, but you can pick up city and county badges just about anywhere. A lot of people collect them."

"I need to get one," Earl said quietly, letting his voice trail off. I listened casually as the two men talked, only joining in for an occasional laugh or nod. My overall impression of Earl's end of the conversation was that he had changed. The Earl we'd known seemed now buried deep inside the cynical, jaded barrier we felt he'd erected to protect himself and his son.

We left Kentucky Thursday morning. As I packed last-minute items, Jack did a quick email check. A moment later he called me to the laptop. I sensed anticipation in his voice.

"Look at this email I got last night," said Jack. "I can tell from the address that it's from someone at the Department of Justice, but otherwise it's vague. I have no idea who this is." I leaned over his shoulder and read:

"Sir: Please call me when you can. XXX-XXX-XXXX cell XXX-XXX-XXXX thanks and be safe"

"Do you think it's about Russell?" I asked.

"Possibly," said Jack. "But it could just as easily be about a case I worked on before I retired."

Jack answered the email and then called both numbers.

"This guy's with the U.S. Marshals Service," said Jack after he'd heard his voicemail message. "He's a supervisor of the investigative services unit for South Florida. I think we can assume his email is about Russell."

We waited all day in quiet desperation, but the U.S. Marshal supervisor did not return Jack's messages. When we arrived in Georgia about six, Jack could no longer contain his eagerness. He called the numbers again. When he finished the conversation and stepped into the bedroom, where

I was unpacking suitcases, his expression could only be described as bewildered.

"He…doesn't…remember…why he called me," said Jack. "He said he'd had a busy day and couldn't recall. He did, for some reason, remember that we're from Atlanta."

"Did you ask if it was about Russell?"

"I should have. I was taken by surprise," answered Jack. "The last thing I was expecting was 'I don't remember why I called.' I just hung up, flabbergasted."

Jack tried to call him back and got his voicemail. He left a message and followed up with an email, asking if he'd contacted him about the UFAP on Russell. He did not return Jack's communication.

On Monday, Jack called again. The supervisor said he'd been trying to email Ben and emailed Jack by accident. Jack gave him Ben's number. Jack said that if the case didn't progress, he and I were planning a trip to Costa Rica. The supervisor was elusive about what, if anything, the Marshals were planning. He only said he'd hate us to do anything to "spook" Russell.

Jack called Ben and told him to expect a call from the U.S. Marshal's office, and Ben said he'd already had some dealings with him. They'd been in contact immediately after *AMW* aired, and at that time, the supervisor said he didn't think the Marshals would be able to "do anything."

On Easter, we rustled the air mattresses in the family room and whispered good mornings to the boys. We customarily had to drag ten-year-old Elliott off his air mattress in a sleepy stupor, but Taylor was usually up before the alarm. This morning, waking twelve-year-old Taylor was difficult. He told us he'd slept only a few hours the night before.

"I had a dream last night," said Taylor, still groggy and a little disoriented. I sensed the dream had been upsetting, so I sat on the couch and gave him my full attention.

"I dreamed I was at Aunt Ann's house when she was killed," said Taylor quietly. "I saw the man who killed her, and I killed him. But nobody believed me. They thought I killed them both."

I hugged Taylor for a moment and said nothing. There was no

answer, no comfort, no solution for the nightmarish dreams we'd all had for more than two years. But as I stroked Taylor's hair, I was angry once again that this tragedy was part of the boys' lives. As much as we tried to talk in whispers and codes, they'd lived with the murder for too long.

Jack had an agent friend, Ed Williamson, who was planning a trip to Costa Rica. When we heard of no progress in catching Russell, Jack asked Ed if he would take Russell's wanted poster to Costa Rica. He agreed, so we sent him a copy.

Ed was a friend of Scott Price, the man who had once had the contract for tires for government vehicles and now lived in Costa Rica. We'd sent wanted posters to him earlier, but now Scott and Ed were planning to spend time hunting for Russell.

Every day involved some sort of task but few days involved progress. Often Jack followed leads that went nowhere.

He evaluated bank records that federal law enforcement had left unexamined for weeks, while they proceeded on the assumption that the records indicated that Russell could be in the United States. The subpoenaed records eventually ended up on Ben's desk, and Ben acknowledged to Jack that deciphering them was beyond his expertise. Jack eagerly volunteered to study them, and Ben sent the records overnight to Georgia. With his experience with money crimes, Jack needed only a few moments to say definitively that the records were a false lead. Tragically, by then, time and money had been wasted.

When we heard that Russell was rumored to have dyed his hair, we asked an artist friend to create photos of Russell with various styles and colors of hair. Jack provided them to Ben and to the *AMW* website.

While our daughter Penny was visiting Iva Ray, Earl called and said he wanted to stop by to visit with her. Penny called her dad immediately. Jack coached her in what to do if Earl asked her to wire money to Russell. Earl ended up not stopping by, so when Dave visited Iva Ray a few weeks later, Jack coached him on the same possibility. Both Penny and Dave were not only willing to be wired; they were eager for the opportunity.

Friends gave us names of bounty hunters, and though the thought of bringing Russell in by this method seemed bizarre, Jack contacted them.

Jack attempted to place advertisements in Costa Rican newspapers and contact woman who might be associated with Russell. He checked his PI data bases daily for information on everyone associated with the murder. He wrote our congressmen. He wrote the Costa Rican consulate and got hundreds of others to write.

None of these efforts brought results, but they sapped our strength and clouded our focus.

We were constantly weary of the turn our lives had taken. But living in the middle of a manhunt was now standard and we endured it.

One day, I mentioned to Jack that I remembered reading an article in the *National Post* about Winnie Roach Leuszler, the first Canadian woman to swim the English Channel. In the summer of 1951, Winnie nearly drowned in frigid water. Her body was raw from jellyfish stings. Her vision was blurred from sweat. And her waterlogged ears could barely hear the encouragements of her father/trainer, who called to her from the accompanying guide boat.

When Winnie was just one hundred yards from shore, she was overcome by exhaustion. Her father reminded Winnie that her daughter was at home and wanted her ice cream. In other words, "Finish this task and you can get on with your life."

Winnie pressed forward. Then the tide turned and swept her several miles back toward France. She watched as the shore got farther and farther away, despite her struggle to reach it. But she eventually finished, to the cheers of her father and her country.

Winnie later said, "I can't say I ever once thought I wouldn't finish. I just thought, 'How long is it going to take me?'"

We felt as if we'd seen the destination several times in the past two years and, like Winnie, had been swept back before we could reach it. We never thought of giving up, but over and over we asked, "How long is it going to take us?"

Part 4

■ ■ ■ ■

# Justice
# for Ann

# Chapter 49

# He's Out There

Jack had just received an email from Ben Wolcott. "I hope this mail reaches you and Mary in good times. I just spoke with [the U.S. Marshal representative] and wanted to pass along some events that are taking place. According to [this representative], his 'people' are in the country and actively looking for Russell. I don't know if these are Marshals or informants, he didn't say and I didn't ask; but he said that a plan is in place to have a detail set up on the Horseshoe Casino this weekend (Friday, Saturday, Sunday). He has my numbers in case we catch a break.

"I don't know what changed over the course of the last few weeks that they are now on board, but I'm not complaining. Keep your fingers crossed for a productive weekend!!!

"I'll, of course, be in touch with any activity. Give my best to Mary and have a good weekend, my friend. –Ben"

The message produced a mixed reaction from Jack and me.

"Do they really think he's still at the Horseshoe Casino?" I asked.

"He may very well be there," said Jack calmly. "He's got to gamble."

"Maybe, but will he go back to the same casino? When his life depends on it? San Jose has plenty of other casinos."

"The Horseshoe has the highest stakes," replied Jack. "He needs the big rush."

"I know I'm not an investigator," I pressed, "but Russell's instinct for survival has got to be strong. I think there's a forty percent chance he's left Costa Rica. Nicaragua and Panama have gambling, too. And there's got to be plenty of places along the Costa Rican borders where he could slip across unnoticed, or pay someone to let him cross over.

"And I think there's a thirty percent chance Russell's moved to another casino in San Jose, a twenty percent chance he's moved to one of the coastal cities that has gambling, and less than a ten percent chance he's still gambling at the Horseshoe. He just has too much to lose."

Jack was tolerant of my carefully assigned percentages. But we played the "where's Russell" game many times each day, and I knew he didn't agree.

On Monday, April 4, Jack and I worked in our office—Jack on two skip traces for an attorney in a neighboring state and I on a writing assignment.

Midday, Jack's cell phone vibrated. "It's Ben," he told me as he flipped open the phone cover.

"Hey, Ben, what's up?" said Jack as he quietly slipped out of the office so I could continue concentrating on my work. Suddenly, I saw Jack twirl around and rush back into the room, sinking into his desk chair.

"What?! That's great! Ben, that's terrific!" Jack smiled and nodded affirmatively at me as he talked.

Ben was so excited that I could hear his voice, too. I couldn't make out every word, but I could tell it was good news about Russell. Jack thanked him profusely for keeping him informed and for letting him know as soon as he heard the news. Then he closed his phone, turned to me, and said quietly, "They've got him."

"Well, not exactly," qualified Jack. "The first words Ben said to me were, 'We've got him.' But he's not picked up yet."

After so many false leads and unsuccessful attempts, my unconscious refused to let me celebrate. I felt only a strange numbness.

"They know where he lives, and they know what he drives," Jack continued. "The Marshals played blackjack with him Saturday night at the Horseshoe."

"Then why didn't they arrest him?" I asked.

"Ben said the Marshals don't have the paperwork ready."

I shook my head in disbelief. "He was profiled on *AMW* more than six weeks ago. Why weren't they ready?" I felt Jack's comforting hand on my shoulder as I continued to vent. "So now, do they just wait for Russell to resurface?"

Jack nodded. "Ben said they'd probably go for an arrest later this week. I'd better call Bill to be sure he has the latest update."

After Jack left a voicemail message for Bill, he called Ed. "I think Ed's back home now, but I'd better get him to call Scott Price. If they're getting ready to make an arrest, Scott doesn't need to be showing the wanted poster."

Jack called Ed's cell and his home phone, asking him to call as soon as possible. Ed returned his call around eight that evening.

Ed was still in Costa Rica. He and Scott had, by Ed's description, "hit the ground running," spending a great deal of Ed's vacation scouting out the casinos and calling the U.S. Embassy. Scott was a regular at the Horseshoe, and they'd shown Russell's photo to people Scott knew. Everyone seemed to know him. "Sure, that's Eddie. He gambles during the day and at night. And he gambles for hours at a time."

Just as the FBI wanted poster instructed, Ed notified the U.S. Embassy that they'd spotted Russell. He talked to the head of security at the Embassy and asked if he was familiar with Russell's case. The security head pulled out Russell's file, which included the wanted poster. Ed asked why they didn't pick up Russell.

"Do you know how many fugitives we have down here?" asked the security head.

Ed was persistent. "This one stabbed a lady almost a hundred times. The victim was my friend's aunt. And my friend is a federal agent."

"We'll get him," promised the head of security. When Jack relayed this conversation, all I could think was: *With all our struggles, how much worse was it if an agent's family wasn't involved?*

Scott played cards at the table next to Russell on Friday night. Russell was drinking water and playing blackjack, just as the *AMW* website described. He was losing, but he was relaxed and calm. Eventually, he and three other men went upstairs, where there was additional gambling.

Ed said the Embassy head of security told him the paperwork was complete and Russell could be picked up at any time.

Jack immediately called Ben and Bill. Ben said he had connected with a judge in San Jose, and the judge was passing around the wanted posters, too. He was unaware that the paperwork had been completed and said he would call the U.S. Marshals to be sure they knew. Jack got Bill's voicemail, but he left him a message.

Jack and I sat quietly after the series of phone calls. Jack was more confident in an arrest than I was. And he graciously didn't say "I told you so" that Russell was still gambling at the Horseshoe.

Tuesday was uneventful until late afternoon. Bill did not return either of Jack's calls, but around four-thirty, Jack got an email from Ben.

"Jack,

I look for something to go down tomorrow evening. According to people I've talked to a plan is in place to snatch him as he enters the casino. An *AMW* film crew is in place to capture the takedown. Keep your fingers crossed. This might actually be it!!!! Leave your phone on tomorrow night and I'll call, hopefully with the news we've been waiting so long for. –Ben"

# Chapter 50

# Spooked

Within twenty minutes, Ben emailed again.

"Jack,

Disregard the last e-mail about Wednesday night. There are too many people asking too many questions about Russell. He's spooked. So we'll see what happens in the next few weeks.—Ben"

"If they know where he lives, why don't they just pick him up?" I asked.

"I just hope the Marshals aren't delaying the capture until *AMW* can get there," said Jack.

"I thought Ben's email said *AMW* was in place."

"It did. But Ben said on the phone that they weren't there yet, and that the Marshals told them to put their filming on hold." Jack tapped his fingers as he contemplated the situation. That's definitely a good thing. If Russell saw the *America's Most Wanted* cameras, he'd bolt for sure."

"For sure?" I asked. "I thought Ben said he'd already been 'spooked.'"

"It's a good thing I called and talked to Ben directly," smiled Jack. "Emails can be a little sketchy. Actually, the Marshals are just assuming Russell suspects something's up. They don't have proof.

"And they're not standing down. They're at the casino and ready to make an arrest if he shows."

"Anything else?" I asked.

"Ben doesn't think they actually know where Russell lives."

I watched Jack's face to see if he'd gotten the same impression I had. "When Ed went down and was willing to take the posters, we'd have been crazy to say no."

Jack nodded. "I don't regret anything we did. We had to do something. Ben had someone passing out posters, too. We were operating with limited information, even though I talked to the Marshals a few days ago. I think better communication might have prevented all this."

The next day, Jack got a call from Ed. Ed was back in the states. His special agent in charge had received a copy of a memo from the Embassy questioning his actions. The Horseshoe was a family-owned business and Scott knew the owner and felt comfortable asking him about Russell.

The necessary paperwork to pick up Russell was a provisional arrest warrant, and Ed said the Embassy security head told him that the warrant was complete and Russell could be arrested on sight.

Within minutes of Ed's call, Ben and Bill both called. Ben said the information Jack gave him the day before was enough to ease the Marshal's concerns. Bill knew the Marshals were finally in place, but he did not have the newest information until he listened to Jack's voicemail.

On Thursday, April 7, the number of *AMW* captured fugitives was up to 835—thirty more than when the film crew first came to Madisonville. It had been nearly a year since we'd first contacted *AMW*, eight months since the first filming, and nearly two months since the on-air profile.

On the morning of April 13, the capture number moved to 837 on the *AMW* site. The photos showed the latest capture being led away in handcuffs. *AMW* just happened to be there when the arrest went down. I'd seen these types of photos before on the show and never thought about the choreography of taking them—crews had to be in place and sometimes it was rumored arrests were delayed until the crews got there. I remembered that the front page article in the *Messenger* showed Earl being led out in handcuffs when he was arrested more than a year ago.

"How can they do that?" I asked Jack.

"Most newspapers have a source on the local police force that gets them to the arrests in time," Jack explained. "But I think when arrests cross international lines and involve armed and dangerous fugitives, stakes are too high to be slowed by media."

As a family member, I was frustrated by the delays the media had created in capturing Russell. But as a viewer, I understood the need for closure. If *AMW* and police departments wanted to encourage and keep citizen participation, they had to include those citizens in their successes.

Jack called Ben to see if he had an update. Ben's latest word was that Russell had not been back to the casino.

"I hope Ed and Scott didn't scare him off," Jack lamented when he hung up.

After two long years of frustration, I didn't want Jack to feel guilty for taking action in the midst of what we interpreted as a vacuum. As soon as he'd heard that the Marshals were finally in place, he'd called Ed and told him to stand down. Some good friends called Jack "Action Jackson" and I was proud that was true. He was never a lukewarm life observer, and I was glad he'd done what he could to bring Russell in.

"If Russell backed off because Ed and Scott were checking around, what you did was unintentional," I reminded Jack. "And why wouldn't we do anything we could when we'd heard of no progress in the six weeks since *AMW* aired the profile?"

Bill Frank called on April 21, and agreed that the Marshals would not, should not make contact with Russell without having the provisional warrant. He said the FBI agent stationed in Panama City, Panama, was now in Costa Rica and working with Interpol and the Costa Rican equivalent to our state police. But he'd been told that Russell was not surfacing, because a federal agent had been showing his badge around the casino and scared him off.

"Interpol has photos of agents playing cards with Russell," Bill told Jack. "They're watching the borders and don't think he's left the country. They think he'll resurface soon."

Bill told Jack they had reason to believe Russell was still receiving money.

"Earl's on probation," Jack told Bill. "If he's the one wiring money, he'll go to jail." Bill hadn't known that Earl was on probation.

A few days later, Jack called Scott in Costa Rica. He asked Scott to either call him collect or to call the U.S. Embassy in Panama if he spotted Russell. Scott agreed.

On Friday, April 29, Scott called Jack about 4:00 p.m. He was planning to spend as much time as possible that weekend at the Horseshoe Casino. If he spotted Russell, he would call Jack. Jack said he'd leave his cell phone on day and night.

We slept with Jack's cell phone on the nightstand throughout the weekend. It didn't ring.

# Chapter 51

# Gotcha

May 3, 2005, marked the day that the running stopped. Jack and I drove to Madisonville on Monday, May 2, to visit our mothers. On Tuesday morning, Jack drove me to visit my mom in Owensboro, Kentucky, forty miles northeast of Madisonville. He planned to meet us for supper that evening.

"What are you going to do while I'm at Mom's?" I asked as we drove into Owensboro.

"After I stop by the cemetery, I think I'll go by to see Earl," said Jack. "I'd like to hear what's on his mind. All this has got to be hard on him."

Mom opened her Mother's Day gifts, and I went with her to a doctor's appointment.

"Let's stop at that little shop where all the cards are fifty-nine cents," I said as we pulled out of the clinic midmorning. "Then we can grab an early lunch."

As I thumbed through the stacks of cards, I felt my BlackBerry vibrate. When I saw Jack's name appear on the monitor, I thought, *He probably wants to change our meeting time for supper.*

"Hi, Babe."

"Honey," Jack said. "They got him. Russell's captured."

I froze in the aisle as I tried to comprehend Jack's words.

"No way." After more than two years of waiting, I wish I would have had a more profound response.

"They picked him up in Costa Rica and they've already matched fingerprints and confirmed his identity. Ben didn't have any other details, but he said he'd call back as soon as he did."

As I talked with Jack, I moved quickly through the aisles, looking for my mom, wanting to tell her the good news.

"Honey, do you know where I was when Ben called?" Jack asked. After a pause, he continued: "At Anna Mae's grave. Each time I go, I talk with her. I know she's not there, but I feel close to her when I'm at her gravesite. I always tell her, 'We're gonna get him.' I'd just whispered those words and started to walk away. After I talked to Ben, I went back and I told her, 'We got him.'"

"I asked Ben if he wanted me to tell Earl, but he said he wanted to," said Jack. "He said to go ahead and tell the rest of the family, so I'm going to try to catch Mother before she goes out. She said this morning that she'd be out most of the day."

"Do you want me to call the kids?" I asked. Jack said he did. We exchanged "I-love-you's" and confirmed our meeting place for supper.

Just as I hung up, I rounded an end cap and saw Mom. I rushed over to her.

"Russell's captured," I said with so little emotion that I surprised myself. We hugged as Mom whispered, "Honey, I'm so glad, I'm so glad."

"I need to call the kids. I'll slip closer to the door so I'll have better coverage," I told Mom.

Penny and Dave were both working, so I left voice mails and then hurried back to Mom. Her eyes were filled with tears.

"Mom, what is it?"

"I was just thinking about Mrs. Branson," said Mom, referring to Iva Ray in the manner of her generation. "This will be so hard on her."

The rest of the day blurred. I didn't hear from Jack again. I was eager to know if he'd learned more details of the capture, how his mother took the news and if the arrest had hit the Madisonville media. But I realized he was informing his family of the capture and I didn't want to catch him at an awkward moment.

We met for an early supper at Owensboro's Ponderosa Steak House. I saw Jack's blue Corvette as Mom and I pulled into the parking lot. I hurried out of Mom's red Toyota Tercel and met Jack halfway between our vehicles. I hugged him and whispered, "It's over."

What had been our lives for two years, three months and three weeks—bringing Ann's killer to justice—was now officially over. A momentary wave of relief passed through me. And then I thought of what came next – the trial.

# Chapter 52

# Captured

W hen Jack and I bumped elbows at the salad bar a few minutes later, he told me, "*AMW* called. They asked if Paula could call us on Friday to set up an interview about the capture."

I shrugged.

"I told them yes," said Jack. "It was tips from their viewers that confirmed Russell's location. The FBI thought he was back in the States."

I nodded agreement at Jack's observation, but said, "I don't want to be on camera. All this has taken its toll. I just want it to be over." I changed the subject.

"How's your mother?" I asked anxiously.

"Okay," said Jack. "She didn't say a lot. She has a senior adult volunteer appreciation banquet tonight. ..."

I nodded. "I wonder if she'll still go. It'll be hard to deal with all the whispers and stares."

"She'll have to sooner or later."

"Any more news from Ben?" I asked.

Jack shook his head. "Guess he hasn't heard anything more."

But we received a great deal more information on the 6:00 news, along with the rest of the small town. Russell was captured by Interpol and Costa Rican police in the early morning hours. Initial reports said Russell was coming out of the Horseshoe Casino.

Iva Ray had said she'd be home from the banquet by seven, so when she came in well past nine, Jack met her with, "We were worried about you."

"Earl called a meeting with Janet and David and me," explained Iva Ray. "He handed over some responsibilities from the estate and divided the money from the sale of another house."

"How did Earl react to Russell's capture?" Jack asked his mother.

"No one mentioned it." Sometimes it's easier to ignore an elephant in the living room than to clean up after one.

Iva Ray seemed tired as she asked, "Was it on the news tonight?" We nodded.

"I assumed it was," Iva Ray continued. "Everywhere I turned at the banquet, someone was giving me a forced smile."

The next day's *Messenger* provided more information. The article quoted Ben as saying that Russell had been arrested around midnight outside the Horseshoe Casino. Russell had entered the casino that afternoon and then left. He returned that evening and was arrested as he left the casino for the second time that day.

The article also stated that Russell had been using a false name of an American living on Costa Rica's Caribbean coast. Russell was living in Cariari, a gated community that was considered an expensive area by Costa Rican standards. He was not known to have a job.

Ben Wolcott said "I know for a fact that he continued gambling almost on a daily basis." Fred Astaire and Ginger Rogers could not have choreographed the arrest better than the media, and urgency and justice certainly weren't the dance steps.

A Costa Rican Security Ministry news release was quoted in the article as stating that Russell had lost one million dollars in gambling in one year alone. Not bad for a man living in luxury housing with no visible means of support.

Jack folded the newspaper and said, "I think I'll call Earl. I just want him to know I'm thinking about him."

Jack advised Earl not to fight extradition. "The government will eventually win, and you'll pour a lot of money into the fight, money you could spend on the trial." Earl agreed.

Jack had an agent friend who had interviewed a Costa Rican prisoner for a case he was working on. "The prisons in Costa Rica are bad," Jack told Earl. "Russell will be better off in the United States."

Midmorning, Jack and I packed our suitcases and headed for home, with plans to swing through Mississippi for a night. When Jack and I arrived at the motel and logged onto email, a friend had sent multiple Associated Press and television news stories about Russell's capture. One story from a Costa Rican publication included a photo of Russell being arrested, surrounded by a Costa Rican television camera crew. We'd already read that Russell entered the Horseshoe, left and was arrested when he returned.

I stared at the photo, trying to recognize the tired, sad man as the cousin we watched grow up. A trace of the old Russell was evident—his build, his facial structure—but he looked at least ten years older than when I'd last seen him two years earlier.

We pored through the articles, finding multiple contradictions. Russell was alone when he was picked up. Russell was with a "North American man" who was questioned and released. Russell was arrested without incident. No information was available about whether Russell had resisted arrest. Costa Rica will not extradite if the United States seeks the death penalty. Costa Rica will keep Russell in the San Jose jail until the United States not only agrees not to seek the death penalty but also agrees not to seek life without parole. And everyone was quoted as having major responsibility for the arrest—from the Madisonville Police Department to the Kentucky State Police, from the FBI to U.S. Marshals to Interpol, from *AMW* to the U.S. Department of State to the Costa Rican police. We felt the real heroes went unsung.

We were introduced to one of those heroes through a phone call from Paula that evening. She told Jack that three *AMW* tipsters had identified

Russell's location. Two were interested in the reward. The third not only wanted to remain anonymous but wanted the FBI reward, if he qualified for it, to be donated to charity. Real heroes were still out there, and it was good to know of one who was associated with *AMW* Capture 842.

# Chapter 53

# Justice
# Delayed

On Wednesday, May 4, we read the *Messenger* account of reactions to the capture. Bob showed his elation in knowing Ann's killer would be brought to justice, but added: "'I had my doubts sometimes if authorities were doing enough,' Fenneman said. 'We'd go for long periods of time without hearing anything.'"

Though Jack had already told David Branson and, in fact, was with him when the *Messenger* called, David was dutifully "surprised" when a reporter told him Russell was captured.

And the article included a truth I needed to remember as I dealt with my frustrations. Kentucky State Senator Jerry Rhoads, a friend of the family, stated: "Justice delayed is better than no justice at all." The actual quote is "Justice delayed is justice denied," but I wanted to believe Jerry's version created a healthier outlook.

Ben called about three on Thursday. It was the first time we'd heard from him since the capture. The *AMW* crew was still in Madisonville and wanted to take footage of Ann's grave. Ben was calling to ask Jack for directions. Ben had told Paula that Jack was at the gravesite when Ben called with the news of Russell's capture, and she liked the filming possibilities.

*AMW* filmed at our house on Friday. I made an appointment for a haircut that morning. Jack called after they left.

"It was very low-key," said Jack. "The producer didn't ask me to credit *AMW* with the capture. Instead, she asked what I'd say to the tipsters, and of course, I was happy to thank them for bringing closure for our family. It's scheduled to air a week from tomorrow."

Iva Ray said Earl was out of town for two weeks, and we assumed he'd gone to Costa Rica to see Russell. If leaving the country violated his parole, we were sure the DA would ignore the infraction. The quickest way to lose public sympathy was to stop a father from visiting his son.

Jack, our kids, our grandkids and I marked the capture by eating out at a steakhouse. Strangely, the mood wasn't celebratory. We were glad this portion of the ordeal was over, but we weren't happy.

Jack and I headed to Texas on Wednesday and watched *AMW* from a hotel room in Fort Worth.

Russell's segment began with portions of the dramatization from the previous airing. Then they showed video of Russell walking confidently through the Horseshoe Casino, changing money, playing blackjack with a spread of money on the table in front of him and even fondling two cocktail waitresses. Some footage appeared to be taken by a surveillance camera, but other footage—such as a close-up of the money in front of Russell—looked as though it had been taken with a telephoto lens.

*America's Most Wanted* acknowledged that police allowed Russell to leave the casino. He was arrested when he returned. A local television crew was in place.

At one point, *AMW* showed Ben walking up to Earl's door and Earl answering. When the camera zoomed in on Earl, Jack and I felt as if we were voyeurs to a father's grief. Ben was wearing the same shirt he had on in other scenes, and I wondered if Earl had been called to the door some time after he was officially notified of the capture. Ben stated in the *Messenger* that he'd originally told Earl about the capture over the phone.

*AMW* had not been in Costa Rica for the capture and, in fact, Jack had shown Paula the photo from a Costa Rican newspaper, showing the camera crew filming Russell. She asked Jack to email the photo to her. Jack and I assumed *AMW* contacted the Costa Rican television station and asked to use its footage.

As I watched the man who, moments earlier, had sauntered around the Horseshoe and flirted with cocktail waitresses, now handcuffed with his head down, I realized the powerful impact of filming the capture. And I understood how, for so long, I'd chosen to ignore the logistics behind such filmed captures in exchange for the emotional payoff I received as a viewer. The payoff could be huge, and it kept viewers searching the crowd for America's most wanted. If a savage killer could be apprehended, I knew it was worth the price.

The segment ended with Jack's account of hearing the news while he was visiting Ann's grave. After Jack repeated his words to Ann—"We got him"—the camera cut to Russell, head down, one wrist shackled to a metal bench. And host John Walsh, with his signature phrasing, said he was glad "that scum" was captured. My mind drifted back to the photo we'd found recently in Ann's album: Russell, the compassionate preschooler, comforting his older cousin. I felt sure that somewhere inside the gambling, womanizing "scumbag" was a confused little boy with an addiction so strong it terrified him.

David Branson is a chaplain at Kentucky's maximum security prison in Eddyville. He reminded Jack that he'd be in contact with Russell if he was sent to Eddyville.

"How's that gonna work?" Jack asked after the arrest.

"I'll put him on my regular list to visit," said Ann's brother-in-law. And we knew David would be as concerned for Russell as he was for every prisoner under his care.

# Chapter 54

# Ongoing Impact

Iva Ray had been diagnosed with leukemia in 1999, and the disease overtook her quickly in June 2005. Russell intruded even on this portion of our lives.

We took a short trip to Kentucky to take Iva Ray to a Louisville hematologist on Thursday, June 23. The doctor was encouraging, noticing only a common heart problem—arterial fibrillation with rapid ventricular response—and suggesting she see a cardiologist the following week. Iva Ray was encouraged, and she even asked to stop by a shopping mall in Evansville, Indiana, on the way home to look for burgundy apple-shaped candles for a holder she'd gotten from her friend for Christmas.

She slept on the family room couch that evening, and by morning she was too weak to leave the couch. Earl stopped by on his way out of town for a motorcycle trip to Colorado and Utah. Iva Ray didn't open her eyes the entire time Earl was there. We'd been taking turns checking on Iva Ray—Penny and the boys left the day before we arrived and Dave was scheduled to arrive on Saturday, the same day we planned to leave. Earl saw that we were giving her round-the-clock care, but he also saw that she was critically ill.

Two weeks earlier when we'd visited Madisonville, Earl stated that he didn't think Iva Ray had long to live, that she couldn't survive too many days in her weakened state. And this time, he admonished us not to leave Iva Ray alone, that she looked bad. He decided, however, to continue his plans for the cross country motorcycle trip.

"How's Russell?" Jack asked Earl as they stood near the couch where Iva Ray slept. "Are the Costa Rican prisons as bad as I'd heard?"

Earl was matter-of-fact as he replied: "Actually, he's treated pretty good. They treated me good when I was there visiting, too." We had our answer to whether Earl had a valid passport.

"There's an exercise room and a library at the prison," Earl continued. "Russell's allowed four hours with visitors once a week. His girlfriend quit her job to deliver him home-cooked meals each day. And still no news of extradition."

Iva Ray slept most of Friday. When we awoke Saturday, we knew we couldn't wait for Monday's cardiology appointment. I helped Iva Ray dress, canceled her hair appointment, and Jack and I drove her to the emergency room.

In the emergency room, her temperature shot from 97.7 to 102.5 and her pulse rate skyrocketed—often going above 200. X-rays showed that cancer had spread through her chest cavity and a large tumor had collapsed her left lung. That evening, doctors inserted a breathing tube as they attempted to shrink the tumor with massive doses of chemo.

One of the medical personnel who was involved in both Grace's and Iva Ray's treatments observed privately to me that, in their professional opinion, both women's deaths had been hastened by the stress of Ann's murder. As we watched Iva Ray's life slip from her, we thought often of Russell.

Dave drove to Kentucky and visited his beloved Ive. When we saw how much he agonized over her condition, we insisted he return to Georgia. Penny and the boys had seen Iva Ray earlier that week, so we encouraged them to hold that positive memory and allow Jack and me to use the two visitor passes allotted to patients in the critical care unit. With our children in Georgia, the only visitors we approved were David, Janet and Earl.

Janet and David visited Iva Ray on Sunday afternoon and again on Monday. Janet asked if she could call Earl. "He'll never forgive me if I don't tell him." We said that, of course, she could call him.

Early Sunday evening, Iva Ray's oncologist acknowledged that, while the chemo seemed to be working, Iva Ray's kidneys were shutting down and the prognosis was not good. Most patients, he explained, do not live much longer than twenty-four hours after kidney failure.

"If there's anyone who needs to say their good-byes," said the doctor, "they need to get here quickly."

Jack called Earl's cell phone and left a message: "If you want to see your sister alive, you need to come home now."

That Sunday evening, Earl returned Jack's call. Again, Jack emphasized the seriousness of his mother's condition.

"Iva Ray's a fighter. She can beat this," was Earl's response. "I'm going to go ahead and finish my 1400-mile loop."

Saturday through Tuesday, Jack and I were at Iva Ray's side at each visitation time, holding her hand and rubbing her feet. After Monday, she seemed unaware of our presence, and it was painful for Jack to see her struggle for life. But he stayed by her side, in the slight chance that she knew he was there.

Iva Ray had a living will, and she'd stated that she wanted no form of life support. Three doctors concurred that the primary death process had begun and that her situation was irreversible. We gave permission to remove the breathing tube, asking that she be heavily sedated so she felt no pain. The breathing tube was removed Wednesday, June 29, at 8:30 a.m., and the doctor predicted that death would be quick. Jack did not want the memory of watching his mother breathe her last breath so, since she was heavily sedated and no longer aware of his presence, Jack decided not to go to the hospital after the breathing tube was removed.

We spent the morning pacing, talking to Penny and Dave on the phone and calling the critical care unit to check on Iva Ray. Until about 1:30 when Judy, Ann's former housekeeper, rang the doorbell of Iva Ray's house.

"Earl called," Judy announced as soon as the door was cracked open. "He asked me to go to the hospital to check on Iva Ray."

Jack's frame of mind, as he waited for news of his mother's death, made him uncharacteristically passive. He simply listened as Judy described how horrible Iva Ray looked, how she struggled for each breath. I walked into the next room and called the CCU nurse assigned to Iva Ray. I was not kind.

"The instructions on my mother-in-law's chart state that only my husband and I, her two brothers, and her sister-in-law are allowed to see her," I spoke through clenched teeth. "There's a woman in our house right now telling my husband that his mother is struggling to breathe."

The nurse assured me that Iva Ray was resting quietly, that Judy had slipped in before he could stop her, and that she'd been quickly escorted out. But the damage was done. Jack now had graphic mind-pictures of his mother's last hours. We hurried to the hospital to confirm that Iva Ray was heavily sedated. She was.

Less than a half an hour after we checked on Iva Ray, she passed away quietly. Earl didn't make it back in time to say good-bye. He didn't make it back in time for visitation, but he arrived late the night before the funeral. After the funeral, he flew back to Colorado to ride his motorcycle back home.

Visitors to the funeral home had many words of condolences, but some variation of this thought was repeated most often: "My first thought when I heard that Iva Ray had died was 'Thank God she won't have to go through the trial.'" Jack and I had the same thought in the days after his mother's death.

After the funeral, Dave, Penny and the boys met Jack and me back at Iva Ray's house. As we sifted through the awards, clippings and photos that represented my mother-in-law's active life, the emotions of the last few days caught up with me.

"I regret that I didn't ask Ive more about what *she* was doing," I told Dave. "She was always asking about us, shining the spotlight on us. I didn't take enough time to find out about all her interests."

"Are you kidding?" said Dave. "We did plenty for Ive. We turned that stiff little board into a hugging machine."

Dave's response, insightful and compassionate, helped alleviate the inevitable guilt we feel when replaying what we did and didn't do for someone we loved. And it also reminded me what our demonstrative family had done to alter Iva Ray's emotional DNA.

# Chapter 55

# Building
the Case

In early October 2005, Jack received a letter from Commonwealth attorney David Massamore. David said the Department of Justice was projecting that Russell would be extradited within the next three or four weeks. He asked if Jack could meet with him and the senior investigators to discuss the case.

Jack and I had a business trip scheduled in Washington, D.C., and planned to swing back through Kentucky to see my mom. Jack arranged to meet David on November 4, while I was visiting Mom.

The meeting was scheduled for 11:00 a.m., and Jack arrived fifteen minutes early. Jack and David had an opportunity to talk before the others arrived.

David was a six-footer with salt-and-pepper hair, a Vietnam veteran and an officer in the Army National Guard.

"Would you like to see the crime scene photos?" David asked casually as the men walked to his office. Jack quickly answered that he did not. He could talk about the brutal crime, dissect it moment by moment, discuss the weapons and the stab wounds. But seeing actual photos of Ann's body was something he chose not to do.

"Ben's been promoted to the governor's protection detail," said David when they were seated, "and it's a well-deserved promotion." Jack quickly agreed. Ben wouldn't be at today's meeting, but David assured Jack that he planned to participate fully in the trial.

When the others arrived, the meeting moved to a conference room. The others were Marc Boggs, Scott Troutman, first assistant district attorney Kathy Senter, and the Commonwealth's victim's advocate.

Marc now was a captain with the Madisonville Police Department. He took over as head of the detective division when Hargis retired. He was one of the first officers on the scene when Ann's body was discovered. Jack had known him for years, and he was the one Jack called from Georgia when we learned of the murder.

Scott was formerly an MPD detective and was also one of the first officers on the murder scene. He was now a detective with the Hopkins County Sheriff's Department.

The meeting lasted an hour and a half, with Massamore laying out the case and his strategies. A dry marker board behind the table was covered with facts about the case and boxes of evidence were piled in the corner. It was obvious that this was the "war room" where the trial was being methodically planned.

David said he was ready to go to trial immediately when Russell returned to the States. All discovery items had been copied and were ready to turn over to the defense attorney. Witnesses were ready.

As they went over each day associated with the crime, Jack commented that Ann was buried on my birthday. Scott said she was murdered on his.

David said he knew Janet and David and had lived close to them at one time. He asked what Jack's relationship was with them.

"Good," said Jack. "The only relationship that's strained is the one with Earl. He knows I've been talking to Ben and that I've been involved in the investigation.

"In my opinion, at the very least, Earl should have stepped down as executor of the estate when he was arrested," Jack continued. "Ideally, he should have stepped down as soon as he realized Russell was a suspect." David agreed.

Jack asked about the bubble wrap found in Ann's basement, which Judy said appeared to have bloodstains. Scott Troutman said he thought the spatters ended up not being blood after all, but he promised to check.

Though David was deep into the investigation and Jack felt confident in his abilities, the puzzle was complicated. Jack realized that David was still collecting information and, finally, he was grateful for the extra time.

As the team went over our investigators' report, David seemed surprised that Earl acknowledged Russell's gambling problem just weeks after the murder and that Russell admitted he'd visited casinos 236 times in the past year.

As Jack went over his understanding of the events of January 12, 2003, he mentioned that he thought Ann had worn the black cape to church and left it on during the service. David asked where he'd gotten that information. Jack explained that he'd simply called the man who sat behind Ann during her final worship service, and asked what Ann had been wearing. Jack sensed this was new information for David, who wrote on a legal tablet while Jack spoke.

David had copies of the polygraphs our investigators had done, and he asked Jack to send copies of the entire report, including pre-polygraph interviews. He asked Jack to recommend an expert witness on Luminol. It appeared that Russell had used bleach to clean up, and bleach made Luminol tests difficult to read. Jack said he knew an expert and would send the contact information when he sent the investigators' report. He followed up as soon as we returned home.

"We think Russell used bleach to clean the knife," said David. "We believe the knife Russell used was a presentation knife that was part of a set given to some employees at the mine where Russell worked. It's perfectly clean, but soaking a knife in bleach would eradicate every trace of blood."

Jack had learned that Earl was now saying that Ann had kept $20,000 under a rug, and it was missing. The problem with that theory was that a robber would have no way of knowing money was under the rug, which would point right back to family members. And with Jack being Ann's favorite nephew, it's hard to imagine he wouldn't know about such a large stash of money. We wondered why Earl wouldn't have told police about the money immediately.

Jack also learned that Russell had some printed materials in his house on how to beat the polygraph and that he'd researched several possible places to flee, including Iraq.

Russell had been caught lying several times during the six hours of videotapes, which were admissible as evidence.

However, some of what Jack recalled hearing that day was contrary to what he'd been told in the past. The investigators said Ann had already taken off her wig and placed it on a wig stand in the kitchen—Earl had told us Ann was wearing a wig when she was murdered. David said Hargis and Ben had cleaned the basement, and there was blood.

But Jack felt sure he remembered Hargis telling him when I'd offered to clean, that the killer had cleaned the basement. Nevertheless, Jack left the meeting feeling confident that the prosecution's strategy was solid, and they were anticipating all approaches the defense could take. It was the first time Jack had met David Massamore, though they'd corresponded by fax, letter and phone. Jack was impressed by his professionalism and felt a renewed confidence in the outcome of the case.

And finally, Jack understood how Russell had managed to leave the country while under investigation. David wanted to wait for DNA results before indicting so they'd have as much solid evidence as possible.

# Chapter 56

# Extradition

In late August 2005, Jack called me to his computer to show me a *Messenger* article. An elderly woman in Dawson Springs had been stabbed multiple times. She died while attempting to reach the police station, just a few yards from her home. The killer had not been apprehended.

Jack shook his head. "Russell's defense attorneys will try to make a connection between the two crimes. Two elderly women, both stabbed. And the second one killed while Russell is behind bars."

The November 12, 2005, *Messenger* ran the news that Russell might have married again in an attempt to avoid extradition. A spokesman for the U.S. Department of Justice stated that getting married would not impede extradition.

The article explained the options for Russell's sentencing if he were found guilty. The Commonwealth had to agree to Costa Rica's terms, which included no death penalty and no imprisonment of more than fifty years. Kentucky law said he'd have to serve at least twenty-five years if convicted of aggravated murder.

A December 15, 2005, *Messenger* article said that Russell's motion to remain in Costa Rica had been denied. He had up to two appeals, which could take two months, but the major hurdle was passed. We readjusted our hopes of extradition and focused on late February 2006.

January 12, 2006, the third anniversary of Ann's murder, nearly passed without us marking it. It was late that evening when Jack mentioned it. I had forgotten. A part of us was trying to put the three-year ordeal behind us, but each time the wound scabbed over, some shard of news reopened it.

On February 2, Jack received an email from Ben stating that Russell's appeals had run out, and Ben was completing the paperwork to travel to Miami to pick him up. The next day, a *Messenger* article confirmed Ben's email. *The Messenger* stated he'd be back in the states "within two weeks" and that "the specific date will be kept a secret until Winstead is actually back." Ben had estimated three to four weeks, and we assumed his conservative estimate was closer to reality.

On Tuesday, February 21, Ben called to say that he'd be picking up Russell on Thursday. U.S. Marshals were bringing him from Costa Rica to Miami and then to Louisville. They were keeping the pickup quiet and taking extra security measures. Ben said he'd call when they had Russell lodged in the Hopkins County Jail.

Jack and I hugged each other, but our voices were silent and our body language showed very little satisfaction. We were just tired.

On Thursday, we heard nothing from Ben. At 1:00 a.m. Madisonville time, Jack checked Friday's edition of the online *Messenger*. Russell was in Kentucky, at an undisclosed location. Kentucky State Police were taking extra precautions and considering having Russell appear for his arraignment via video. He was currently in solitary confinement, and two guards were with him anytime he had human interaction, including when he had visitors.

Each night we stayed up until *The Messenger* downloaded news for the following day. We learned that Russell had been moved from Louisville to Hopkins County on Friday.

I emailed the article to Penny and Dave. Though they rejoiced Ann's killer was finally behind bars, they also released a little anger. Though our daughter was usually gentle and forgiving, she was also a criminal justice major. She emailed back, "He looks like the sociopath he probably is. I hope the Hopkins County Jail is a stink hole." Dave called and said he was going to visit Russell in jail when he was in Kentucky. When I asked why, he said, "Just to spit on him." We'd all had it, and we wanted justice.

Jack handled the wait with reasonable dignity, until my mom relayed an interview she'd seen on an Evansville, Indiana, television station. She tuned in after the interview had begun, but she soon realized that the unidentified elderly woman being interviewed was claiming to have known Ann and Russell all their lives. The woman said she did not believe Russell could have hurt Ann, and she hoped "they" would not be harsh with Russell—that Ann would not have wanted that.

Jack and I were driving as I talked to Mom. I repeated each thing Mom said so Jack could follow our conversation. Jack's fury increased with each new bit of information. Suddenly he slammed his fist in the air.

"What does that old bag know?" he shouted. "Anna Mae and I discussed the death penalty more than once. She supported it."

We watched Russell's arraignment on an Evansville, Indiana, television station's website. He was dressed in a black-and-white striped jail uniform and only vaguely resembled the confident young man who'd carried Ann's coffin across the snowy cemetery thirty-eight months ago. His face and voice were expressionless.

As the video faded to black, I felt that the case was doing the same— at least temporarily. Russell's trial was set for September 6, 2006, so we had a six-month wait.

"By the time we have a verdict, we'll be approaching the fourth anniversary of Ann's murder," I told Jack. At that time, I couldn't have imagined that the end would be much farther away.

Part 5

# The Prosecution Rests

# Chapter 57

# Jail Time

Russell made use of his time in the Hopkins County Jail. He gambled with fellow prisoners and, according to some of them, bragged about his notoriety. His lawyers requested—and received—two delays, taking the time from murder to trial to four years, seven months and two days.

Motions flew, trial dates changed and the jury pool was called into question. Could a dozen jurors and alternates be found in Hopkins County who had not been tainted by press coverage of the case?

Our suitcases were already packed when we learned that the judge had granted a delay for the September 6 trial, agreeing with the defense's claim that they had not had adequate time to prepare. Since Russell had enlisted his attorney's services just weeks after the murder, we found the request for a delay discouraging. Where was the victim's right to a speedy trial?

The trial was rescheduled for January 3, 2007. On December 20, 2006, we learned of the second delay. A new judge was elected in November, and he felt he didn't have adequate knowledge of the case to move forward in January. On January 26, the new judge—James Brantley— granted a change of venue, and the trial was set for August 14, 2007, in

Greenville, Kentucky, the Muhlenberg County seat. According to *Messenger* reports, the primary "evidence" that Madisonville residents could not deliver an impartial verdict was a drawing left by an anonymous artist on a portable chalkboard in the anteroom adjacent to the Hopkins County Circuit Courtroom—a room with minimal traffic and limited access.

The defense attorneys entered a photo of the chalkboard drawing into evidence, stating that pretrial publicity had tainted the jury pool.

The photo showed a stick drawing of a man hanging from the gallows, with these words: "Clue: Guilty as the devil." Below the words were eight underlines, like the spaces used in the children's game Hangman. All but the first space was filled in: I-N-S-T-E-A-D. Below the partial name was written: "If you win, you get to hang him."

According to *The Messenger*, Judge Brantley "studied the picture at length and termed the evidence as 'persuasive.'" The defense also pointed out that the *Messenger* had published approximately fifty stories on the murder and that *America's Most Wanted* had covered the case.

In February, we learned that there were allegations that a technician had taken undisclosed evidence from the evidence room. According to the *Messenger*, this technician was the sole guardian of the valuable and crucial evidence for all local cases and the only person with a key to the evidence room. Many cases were now in jeopardy because of missing and compromised evidence. In locking the proverbial barn door after the horse was stolen, MPD Chief James Pendergraff told the *Messenger*, "It's our full intention to correct this so it doesn't happen again."

In the midst of the delays, Russell's attorneys requested a bond hearing, which was scheduled for April 18. Their premise was that, though by Kentucky law no bond could be granted if capital punishment was a possible sentence, their client could not possibly receive the death penalty or even life in prison without parole. Therefore, they reasoned, he was eligible for bond. Jack and I were amazed to see the defense attorneys try to capitalize on Russell's flight to Costa Rica and his escaping the death penalty.

It was up to the Commonwealth of Kentucky to prove a

preponderance of evidence, and David Massamore did just that. Bond was denied on April 25.

However, delays weren't the only activity generated from the county jail. We heard that Russell had allegedly charmed a female guard. According to the rumor, another guard noticed the developing relationship and reported it to her supervisor. We also heard rumors that the female guard had been dismissed.

Undaunted, Russell asked a pastor to smuggle a hacksaw and a file to him inside a Bible. We felt we were stuck between the pages of a dime novel.

But his biggest scheme was delivered right into his lap when Fred Roulette became his cellmate. Roulette had been indicted for killing a seventy-two-year-old woman in Dawson Springs, twenty-five miles from Madisonville, in August 2005. The victim had multiple stab wounds to the head, upper body and hands—just like Ann's wounds. Nothing was stolen from her home. At one point, the woman managed to break free from her attacker and stagger toward the police station, just one hundred yards from her home. She collapsed and died on the street. Roulette called 911 to report that he'd heard a woman screaming for help. Then he asked his girlfriend to wash his bloody clothes. He fled to Indiana, where he was arrested in October after his girlfriend turned him in. It was the case Jack had predicted would surface as part of Russell's defense.

Now here Russell and Roulette were, together in a jail cell. One man already confessing to the stabbing death of an elderly lady and facing life in prison, and the other awaiting trial for a similar, savage crime. They had endless hours to talk and plan and negotiate. The result was Russell allegedly  offering Roulette a deal: Confess to Ann's murder and benefit financially. According to Roulette, Russell promised to provide two $20,000 trust funds for Roulette's children, $5,000 for his girlfriend, and to make regular deposits into Roulette's commissary account when he was moved to Eddyville State Penitentiary.

Roulette claimed that Russell pushed him to rehearse the crime over and over. According to Roulette, Russell drew a diagram of Ann's house and described the crime, stating that he'd chased Ann down the stairs and killed her.

Roulette signed a confession but later recanted. He was able to prove he was in Indiana at the time of Ann's murder.

For his protection, Roulette was moved to a nearby jail. Russell received a new cellmate, who was also accused of murder. After this, except for regular card games with other prisoners, Russell languished in the Hopkins County Jail until his trial date, set for August 14, 2007.

# Chapter 58

# The Trial Begins

We traveled from Georgia to Kentucky on Friday, August 10, 2007, leaving behind our nine-day-old granddaughter, Kayla, Dave's first child. We celebrated my mom's eighty-fifth birthday on Saturday, our fortieth wedding anniversary on Monday, and the beginning of the trial on Tuesday.

On Tuesday morning, with temperatures approaching triple digits, we drove from Madisonville to Greenville, arriving a half hour before the *voir dire* (jury selection). Greenville is a mining town of 12,000, about thirty miles southeast of Madisonville. The residents are friendly, hard-working country people. When we arrived, the elegant new courtroom was filled with prospective jurors, many in blue jeans, T-shirts and shorts.

We found a seat on the row behind the prosecutors. Russell, now forty-two, was already seated at the defense table when we entered the room. He looked older and paler than I'd anticipated, with deep circles under his eyes. He sat between his defense attorneys, both dressed in dark suits. Russell was wearing a long-sleeved light blue oxford shirt, open at the neck. This type of shirt, in various colors, would be his attire for the entire trial.

Russell sat solemnly, with hands folded in a vice-like grip, his six-foot one-inch frame seeming a little too big for the fabric-covered molded plastic and metal chair. It was the first time we'd seen Russell since Ann's funeral, and Jack and I were surprised that disdain was the only emotion we felt when we saw him. Over the past four and a half years, most of our raw feelings had scabbed over.

At the prosecutor's table sat Commonwealth Attorney (Kentucky's title for district attorney) David Massamore, assistant district attorneys Kathy Senter and Bryan Hart and Kentucky State Police detective Ben Wolcott. Kathy and Bryan looked New York professional. Ben appeared military tough with his rigid posture and ultra-short haircut. David blanketed the team with experience and calm. The entire prosecution team was quietly intense. We sensed a confident energy and knew they were ready for battle. Nothing small-town about this prosecution team.

Recently elected Judge James Brantley stated the charges: murder (Kentucky doesn't classify murder as first and second degree) and first degree robbery. Russell pleaded not guilty.

To ensure that an impartial jury could be seated successfully, Muhlenberg County had called 175 jurors for Tuesday, with an additional 175 on call for Wednesday if necessary. Though Greenville is a neighbor to Madisonville, most residents subscribe to the Owensboro *Messenger-Inquirer* instead of the Madisonville *Messenger*. Most potential jurors knew little or nothing about the murder case.

We scanned the room, realizing that these randomly chosen citizens would soon decide Russell's fate. Russell must have felt this same vulnerability. Jack and I nudged each other when young women were called to the jury box, remembering Russell's apparent skill at charming the opposite sex. When the final selection was made, we breathed easier. Several young women were excused for various reasons. The handful of jurors who seemed disinterested or who obviously wanted to go home were struck. What remained was a solid group of impartial, hard-working and honest people who appeared to want to find the truth and fulfill their civic duty. Ten female and four male jurors (including two alternates) were seated by the end of the first day. They ranged in age from twenty-eight to sixty. They were a healthy mixture of professionals, industrial/clerical workers and homemakers.

As the jurors filed out when the first day of the trial ended, Russell made eye contact with several as they walked by. Three women jurors smiled at him. I assumed the smiles were simply reflex responses from ladies who'd been taught to be polite.

Immediately after the jurors were selected and sent home till the following day, Judge Brantley addressed a motion by the defense to suppress Russell's second wife's testimony. The defense stated that Kentucky law did not allow individuals to testify about what their spouses told them during the course of their marriage, even after the couples were divorced. Their argument sounded reasonable, and my heart sank at the thought of losing Terri's testimony.

Then the judge called on David Massamore to present his rationale. David's response was slightly louder and sterner than usual. He reminded the judge that motions were supposed to be made months ago. When the defense made none, Judge Brantley had remarked that they were "strangely silent." Then, a day before *voir dire*, the defense introduced a major motion.

After his objection, however, David demonstrated his team's skill. With only a day's notice, he cited cases and provided rationales that successfully opposed the motion. The law the defense cited clearly protected communication that was meant to be kept confidential between husband and wife. However, Russell's communication showed his plan for an alibi. The conversation was meant to be shared with others and therefore did not fall under the protection of the law presented by the defense. It was the first major victory for the prosecution, and they gained it with just a day's notice.

Wednesday morning's opening remarks stretched to the lunch hour. Jack and other witnesses were asked to leave the courtroom until after their testimonies, so I sat alone on the row behind the prosecutors, close to the newspaper and radio reporters. Connie Branson was the only family member sitting on the prosecution side, and she sat directly behind me. Earl sat behind Russell until, as a witness for the defense, he was instructed to leave the courtroom. Russell's sister remained to support Russell, along with his new Costa Rican wife—a striking forty-something brunette with longish hair pulled back in a low ponytail, wearing snug, cropped khakis, a white tailored blouse and large white hoop earrings. Russell and his new wife held hands during recesses the first day. When the *Messenger* reported their handholding, it stopped.

As the proceedings began, I wondered how the jurors could grasp so much coming at them so quickly. Even with a strong general background on the crime, I struggled to absorb all the new evidence.

Once, I'd walked into our family room to find our three-year-old grandson, Taylor, holding his eyelids open as he watched a cartoon on television. I asked what he was doing and he said, "I'm keeping my eyes from blinking. This is my favorite part of the cartoon, and I don't want to miss even one second."

That's how I felt as David quietly and methodically presented the prosecution's case. After being information-starved for so many years, I was scooping up every crumb that came my way. I recognized that some of David's remarks were based on information Jack provided when they met nearly two years earlier. I felt Ben had told us everything he knew, but now I was hearing lots that was new information. Witnesses had come forward and evidence had been discovered in the past few months. The sentence fragments and sketchy paragraphs had finally developed into a detailed story, a story with painful information we would rather not have known. As the weeks wore on, I trusted my assessment. The only times I noticed jurors looking at Russell were when they examined autopsy photos and the morning when he arrived late and they heard his shackles being removed in the holding room. At these times, it seemed the jurors stared at Russell as if he were a killer.

I felt an assurance that finally someone understood Ann's murder. David and his team had gathered all the pieces of the puzzle, and David was laying them out for the jury in a way we could all understand. His opening remarks showed that Russell had an alarming gambling addiction, which steadily escalated until the time of the murder. Ann had given him a deadline—Monday, January 13, the day her body was found—to come up with $30,000. Russell and Earl created an alibi. And when Russell was finally captured and jailed, he involved two inmates in an elaborate scheme in which one of the inmates confessed to killing Ann.

David explained the elements of proving guilt, which could be outlined in the acronym MOM: Motive, Opportunity and Means, and he promised solid proof of all three.

He reminded the jury of what has become known as the "CSI effect": We see so many quick solves on television that we've come to expect that every crime scene, if properly secured, produces usable fingerprints and DNA and that without these forensic evidences, we can't find someone guilty. He explained that most convictions are not made as the result of fingerprints and DNA.

The defense team presented its opening statements. The main defense seemed to be: How could a peaceful man like Russell commit such a heinous crime? The attorney asked Russell to come forward and stand beside him. He introduced Russell to the jury, and Russell said in a quiet, almost-shy voice, "It's good to meet you." At that moment, David turned toward his prosecution team with dropped jaw. Veteran reporter Don Perryman, from the *Messenger*, leaned toward me and whispered, "I've never seen that before."

The defense emphasized that it was the Commonwealth of Kentucky's responsibility to prove Russell's guilt and they did not have to make any statements or present any witnesses. And Russell did not have to testify.

During their *voir dire* questioning, the defense had acknowledged that Russell was a gambling addict who lied to hide his addiction. Now his attorney observed, "Everyone has blemishes and faults, and we're not here to try to put make-up on them." Their only strength seemed to be that the coroner listed 10:00 p.m. as the estimated time of death, and even the prosecution agreed that Russell was home by 9:30. Russell's attorney tossed out a few red herrings—the handyman and the crazy renter. And he sat down.

After lunch, the Commonwealth introduced the first of its forty-two witnesses, reduced from the one hundred-plus who were originally identified. For the remainder of that week and most of the next, David Massamore, with help from Kathy Senter, put together the 1000-piece puzzle that was Ann's murder. The courtroom was pin-drop quiet and the jury was attentive as the story began:

When Ann's husband, Carroll, was still living, Ann was confronted by a mugger as she entered her garage one evening. He approached her from behind, knocked her down and stole her purse. After that, Carroll was concerned about Ann's safety, and he had an elaborate security system installed. The system included the regular motion detectors and door alarms. It also included a camera in her garage with a monitor in the den directly beside the garage. The monitor sat on top of the television.

Ann also had a peephole in the door to the garage. When Jack and I visited, he'd tease Ann by knocking and then covering the peephole. Ann refused to answer the door until Jack removed his finger and she saw him.

Ann regularly carried a panic button which, when pressed, connected her immediately with 911 emergency. She kept another panic button on the nightstand beside her bed.

She used her security system regularly, especially after Carroll died. Even when Jack, armed and dangerous, was there, she activated the system at bedtime, reminding us not to go outside to get something from our car after she punched in the code.

Because she used the system regularly, she was known around the police station for triggering numerous false alarms. Most officers had checked on Ms. Ann when she accidentally walked into a room with motion sensors or opened a door without first disabling the system.

Officer Kelley Rager, smiling and holding back emotion, told of the many times she'd answered calls to Ann's home.

"I'd knock on Ms. Branson's door and call out to her that it was Kelley from the police department. She'd ask if I was alone. Even when I assured her I was, she'd say, 'Are you sure? I don't have my wig on, and I don't let men see me without my wig.'"

Ann's wig was on a wig stand in her kitchen when she was murdered. The last time we spent the night with Ann, five months before the murder,

Jack and I each had our picture made with her the morning we left. She wasn't wearing her wig. She would only let family see her that way.

Though the defense tossed in a few comments and testimonies to the contrary, the prosecution established that Ann was security-conscious. They also established that Ann was a generous businesswoman. She gave generous gifts to her family. She allowed renters to catch up on back rent when they received their tax refunds.

But she kept a little red address book that listed loans. And everyone in the family knew the difference between a gift and a loan. At Christmas, Ann had a generous check for everyone, often thousands of dollars each. Once she'd visited us in Indiana and was concerned that our house wasn't air-conditioned. She wrote us a hefty check and told us to have air-conditioning installed right away. She made it clear that the check was a gift.

About a year before her death, Jack and I borrowed $2,000. We wanted to pay for Penny's car before her wedding so we could give her the title. We asked Ann for a loan. We knew it was a loan. And we immediately paid her back $500 a month for four consecutive months.

The little red address book was filled with lists of loans, not gifts. Earl was listed as having borrowed money, and he'd repaid it. Russell was listed many times as borrowing money. Each time he paid back a little, he borrowed even more. And the amounts were escalating. She'd loaned Russell $27,000 less than two weeks before her murder. The total was now slightly more than $74,000. She made a notation in her red book that he would pay her $30,000 by March 1, 2003, but apparently she decided to collect early. Her friend Yvonne said Ann planned to pay the architect for the home she was building. Instead of cashing in CDs to pay the architect, she gave Russell a deadline of Monday, January 13, to pay her.

Or maybe she was worried about Russell, like she'd told Jack the day before the murder. Bob told us that Earl had warned Ann not to loan Russell money.

Whatever the reason, Ann wrote a simple entry in her red address book that laid the framework for Russell's involvement in her murder: "Gave him a check for $9,700. He gave me a check for $12,000." As David laid out the story, we soon learned that what seemed like an unusual episode of check swapping was, in reality, indicative of the lies and schemes that had become Russell's downward spiral. He'd borrowed and repaid many people in the past three years. But this time, he couldn't meet Ann's escalated deadline, and if Ann deposited the check on Monday, January 13, at the bank where Terri worked, his marriage was in trouble.

That cold Sunday night, Ann warmed a bowl of bean soup in the microwave. The time that she ate her simple meal became crucial as Commonwealth and defense struggled to set the time of death. If she ate before church, as the Commonwealth claimed, she would have been killed soon after she returned home from church. If she ate after church, her death could have been as late as 9:30 or 10:00.

Ann's clothing filled in the blanks. Her neighbor had seen her walk home from church on other occasions, and she'd entered through her front door—the door nearest to the church. Ann's shoes were at the bottom of the stairs, in the foyer adjacent to the front door. Her black cape was laid across a chair in the dining room, directly to her right, off the foyer. Her wig was on a wig stand in the kitchen, adjacent to the dining room, and her purse was on a chair by the kitchen table.

But she had not yet removed her jewelry: four bracelets, a gold pendant necklace, and four rings including a $30,000 engagement ring from Bob and a $35,000 diamond cluster. She was still wearing a black ultra-suede pantsuit with print collar and cuffs—not the old stretch pants and sweater Earl had insisted she was wearing.

We believe she ate supper, attended church, returned home and walked through her house, leaving a trail of shoes, cape and wig. She heard the buzzer at the back door.

Ann picked up her panic button and walked into the den. When she glanced at the monitor and saw Russell standing outside her door, she set her panic button on a table a few feet from the monitor. And she opened the door without her wig, something she'd do only for that small inner circle of people she loved and trusted as family.

# Chapter 59

■ ■ ■ ■

# Money
# Motives

The prosecution described how Russell fed his adrenaline need from 1993 to 2000 with stockcar racing. Ann helped him purchase his first race car and attended some of his races. When Russell failed to excel as a racer, he discovered gambling. And close to that same time, he and Terri decided to divorce their spouses and marry each other. Though Terri and Russell's first wife, Denise, had been long-time friends, they now found themselves at odds.

In 2000, Russell began visiting casinos with more than a casual interest. Each year, his gambling increased dramatically, and by the end of 2002, his total transactions were $1,611,600, and his overall loss was $102,285. Russell was plummeting downward. Fast.

Russell had been unfaithful to Denise, and as he frequented casinos in three cities, he found it easy to be unfaithful to Terri, too. A favorite girl-friend worked at a casino nearby. She and a friend accompanied Russell and his gambling friend, Mike, to Harrah's casino in Metropolis, Illinois.

On that occasion, the girlfriend remembered Russell losing a large amount of money, probably $20,000. She described Russell as normally even-tempered and calm. On that occasion, he cussed briefly. Then he regained his Winstead composure and was a little quieter than usual.

Money didn't seem to be a big concern for Russell. Many people saw him pull out wads of $15,000-$20,000. Ann was a primary source of funds, but she wasn't the only one Russell approached for loans and to fund his trumped-up business deals.

Russell borrowed a total of $12,000 from another friend and paid him back with a boat and a little cash. That friend estimated that Russell still owed him $9,500-$10,000. He gave Russell money for a vacation to Disneyworld and to buy some four-wheelers for his kids. On the day Ann's body was found, the friend refinanced his home to pay his own debts. Somehow, even Russell's male friends fell victim to his charm and persuasiveness.

In September 2002, four months before the murder, Russell borrowed $15,000 from a finance company for a tractor he said he would purchase. He never provided the finance company with a photo of the tractor or the registration number. But two months later, he asked the same company for another loan, this time simply for "capital." When they refused, he walked across the street to a bank and received a loan for $9,989.56, just under the minimum to generate a CTR. Terri cosigned this loan, though other loans were signed only by Russell.

In the months leading up to the murder, Russell became more and more desperate. He created schemes in which friends and family would give him money with the promise of quick returns on their investments.

In November 2002, Russell approached his then father-in-law with a business proposition. Russell said he knew of a 1957 Chevy for $16,000, which he could sell to someone for $19,000. He offered to share the deal with his father-in-law, with each putting up $8,000 and each making a $1,500 profit. His father-in-law gave him the money. He never saw the Chevy or proof of ownership. He never saw his $1,500 profit or his $8,000 investment. This wasn't the first time Russell had borrowed money from his father-in-law, but it was the first time Russell did not pay him back.

In December 2002, Russell invited another survey engineer to join him in a similar venture. This time, the car offered for purchase was a 1956

Chevy. It was available for $15,000 and could be sold for $18,000. The engineer declined to participate in the deal, a deal Russell offered to several others at about the same time.

The engineer noted that, in late 2002, Russell routinely wore a gray camouflage jacket with a leaf pattern. He told her Terri had ordered matching camouflage jackets for them to wear when they went four-wheeling. Every time she saw Russell's jacket, she remembered. "I couldn't imagine Terri wearing such a jacket," she said of Russell's petite, feminine wife. She did not remember Russell wearing the jacket long into 2003.

On Thursday, January 2, Russell called Earl's then-girlfriend, Betty. He asked if he could stop by to see her that afternoon. She had known Russell about four years, but he'd never visited her.

Russell arrived about 4:00 p.m. Betty offered him something to drink and asked how she could help him. He appeared desperate as he told her he'd made a bad investment and wanted to borrow $30,000.

"I was taken back, floored, surprised," she said. She told him she'd have to consult her financial advisor, and he could call back on Saturday (Jan. 4) for a final decision. Her advisor warned her that if she loaned money to family or friends, she may as well consider it a gift because such money was rarely repaid. Betty was not in a financial position to lose $30,000, so when Russell called her back on Saturday, she said she couldn't help him.

As Russell sank deeper and deeper, he found Ann to be his most reliable source of large sums of quick cash. And on January 5, 2003—a week before her murder—he borrowed $27,000. On January 10, he borrowed another $9,700.

About 5:00 p.m. on the Wednesday before Ann's murder, Russell approached co-worker Alex River, who worked with him and suggested that they "take a road trip." According to Alex, Russell never directly mentioned the gambling boat.

River wasn't a big gambler, but he'd gone to the boat with Russell on several occasions. That afternoon, Alex said he wasn't interested in gambling. It was right before payday and he had no money. Russell was persistent, promising that they'd return early to accommodate the next day's 6:00 a.m. work schedule. When he added the lure of a limo picking them up, Alex decided he couldn't pass up his first limo ride.

"Meet me in the Kroger parking lot at seven," Russell told him.

Russell and River were the only ones in the limo, which had Tennessee plates. Alex felt that the Metropolis, Illinois, Harrah's casino had made an extraordinary effort to pick them up, but Russell wasn't impressed. He opened the limo's small refrigerator and surveyed its contents.

"This isn't as nice as the limos they usually send," he told Alex. "They're usually better stocked."

As they rode to Metropolis, Russell told him, "I borrowed some money from my aunt, and I have to pay it back on Monday. I also have a $16,000 payment on Saturday." Investigators were unable to determine the nature of Saturday's payment, and the defense questioned why Russell would kill Ann over the $12,000 check and remain nonviolent when faced with a $16,000 payment.

When they reached Metropolis, Russell pulled out a stack of banded bills that Alex estimated at $20,000. He said he'd seen him bet that much at other times.

Around midnight, River stopped by Russell's table. Russell asked why he wasn't gambling, and he said he had no money. Russell reached in his pocket and handed him two one-hundred dollar bills. River used the money to gamble for another one-and-a-half to two hours, actually making a little money.

Though Russell had promised they'd get back early, he was still gambling at 1:30-2:00 a.m. The limo called to see if they were ready to go. Russell said they'd be ready soon. But over the next one to one-and-a-half hours, Russell "went bust." He lost everything.

Russell was, in River's words, "unusually upset." They started to leave. Then Russell remembered the $200 he'd loaned River, and he asked for it. Russell wanted to go back inside the casino, but River refused, reminding him that they had to be at work in a few hours. Russell took the

$200 back into the casino and quickly lost it.

At that point, Russell's demeanor changed.

"What did he say?" asked David Massamore.

"Is it okay to repeat it?" asked Alex. "It's pretty bad."

When no one objected, he repeated expletives I never expected to hear in a courtroom. Alex said he had never heard Russell speak that way. In fact, he had never seen him out of line in the least. "He just gambled and drank water."

In the limo on the way home, Russell was distraught. He told him, "I'm annihilated."

Russell was wearing a leather jacket. He took an automatic pistol from his pocket, wrapped it inside the coat, rested his head on it, and slept.

"It was the first time I'd seen Russell carrying a gun," Alex stated.

"But he was carrying a large sum of money," the defense reminded him.

Alex had the last word: "He'd carried large sums of money before, but he'd never displayed a pistol."

On Friday, Russell visited Ann. Only Ann and Russell know for sure what he told her, but in spite of his already owing her tens of thousands of dollars, Ann wrote him a check for $9,700. While logic would assume he'd asked for this odd amount to avoid generating a CTR with the IRS, he claimed in a videotaped interview immediately after the murder that she was supposed to give him $10,000 and "got confused."

Ann also received check number 2658 from Russell for $12,000. The wise businesswoman entered the transactions in her simple red address book. And she told her friend, Yvonne, about the transaction when they joined their gentlemen friends on Saturday for a night of television, Rook, and dancing.

"She told me she'd given Russell till Monday to pay her back," said Yvonne.

It was Russell's weekend to have his sons, and he told Denise he'd drive their oldest son to a sleepover on Friday. On Saturday, he told her he had something work-related and couldn't keep the boys.

On Saturday morning, he cashed Ann's check at Old National Bank in Madisonville and headed for Caesar's near Louisville. Russell bought in with Ann's $9,700 and $400 of his own. He lost everything, so the casino comped him a room that night. He had three cell phone calls that day to a friend, who later described himself as only a business associate, and another call to him at 1:49 a.m. on Sunday.

That next morning, he wrote the casino a check for nearly every penny he had in his bank account: $500. He quickly lost this last amount and headed home, calling his friend twice that afternoon, at 12:25 and 12:32.

He picked up his oldest son that evening around 2:00 p.m. His younger sons had other plans. He and Terri drove separate vehicles to Olive Branch Baptist Church. This was Russell's usual procedure if he planned to drive his sons home.

Church dismissed for both Ann and Russell a few minutes before 7:00 p.m. While Ann was trudging through the cold to her home and casually removing her shoes and cape, Russell was dropping off his son at Denise's house. Then he drove the few miles to Ann's. He rang her back doorbell a little after 7:15.

Ann could see his face, but she couldn't see the bone-handled knife he wore on a sheath on his belt. And she couldn't see the two-foot long half-inch breaker bar, an extended socket wrench designed to help loosen tight or rusted bolts and nuts, primarily used for auto and all-terrain vehicle repair but also used in coal mines.

She opened the door.

# Chapter 60

# Attack

At some point, Ann realized that Russell planned to take back his $12,000 check by force. Maybe he brandished the breaker bar. Terrified, she ran from him, fleeing to the closest place she thought would be safe: the basement.

He chased her down the basement stairs and struck her from behind with the heavy-duty steel bar. The blows to the head killed her almost immediately, but after bludgeoning her to death, he attacked her repeatedly with the knife. Her upper back alone sustained sixty-three stab wounds. Many wounds went completely through her frail body. They punctured most of her vital organs. He slit her throat, exposing her voice box and epiglottis.

Ann was dead when Russell released the worst of his rage. Then he stepped over Ann's mutilated body and walked across the basement to the shower.

At 8:17, Ann's phone rang. Ann's brother, David, called and asked her to call back as soon as she got his message. He and Janet were sick, and he was concerned about who would take Grace to the doctor the next day.

But no one returned David's call. Instead, Russell cleaned the blood from his body and clothing, possibly showering in his clothes and drying them partially in Ann's dryer.

Frantic to get home, he pulled quickly out of Ann's driveway about 8:50-9:00 p.m., nearly T-boning another vehicle, driven by a university student. She was Alex's girlfriend. He had gambled with Russell the previous Wednesday. The near-accident happened so fast that she wasn't able to see the other driver. But she knew he was driving a full-sized white pickup truck. During cross examination, the defense tried to get her to say that the truck could have been light colored and not necessarily white. She looked confidently at him and said, "It was white." When unable to shake the young woman on the color of the truck, Russell's attorney observed, "You didn't get a license number. You can't identify the model of the truck." The student had already testified that she saw the truck to her right and then behind her. She would never have been in a position to get a license number.

As Russell left Ann's, he made a series of desperate phone calls to his friend, Mike. He called his cell, then his home, then his cell again—a total of five calls. The married friend was watching a Clint Eastwood movie at his girlfriend's house and apparently had his cell phone turned off.

Russell called Terri at 8:50 to tell her he was on his way home. And he called Earl at 8:52. Russell finally reached his friend at 9:01. He returned home, took a shower and changed his clothes. By that time, the friend arrived.

Terri stood at the breakfast bar in the kitchen and helped her daughter with her homework. Her son watched television. Terri went into the bathroom and found the clothes Russell had worn to church draped over the sink. She picked them up to put them in the hamper. It was a cold, dry night, but Russell's clothes were wet.

That night, Terri slept in her daughter's room. She did not know if Russell left the house again.

But a witness testified that he did.

# Chapter 61

# A Witness
# Sees

The prosecution described how Russell returned to Ann's, probably using the key that hung on a holly bush close to the back door. He parked a vehicle somewhere away from Ann's house.

Someone scrubbed the basement walls. Someone walked across floors to turn on all the lights in the house, perhaps looking for the $12,000 check Ann was holding till Monday. And someone vacuumed the carpeted floors so carefully that the next day, the police found no footprints on the carpet, only the perfect parallel lines made by a vacuum cleaner.

He left all the lights on and locked the house. In his haste, he returned the key to the wrong bush. He walked down the driveway toward the street just as a car turned the corner, shining its headlights directly on him.

A young grandmother drove the red car that turned onto Noel Avenue. She knew Ann's house. She'd done yard work for Ann when she was a teenager. She noticed Russell exiting Ann's driveway. He was wearing a camouflage-like jacket with drawstring and dark pants tucked into lace-up boots. She couldn't see his face clearly enough to tell his age.

The grandmother was hurrying home from playing cards and

"drinking lots of Coke" with friends, and she wasn't sure her bladder would endure the last few miles to her home. But she thought, "If this is a young person, I'll give them a ride, even if I end up urinating on the seat. It's bitter cold, and I don't want a young person out here in the cold."

So she slowed down and followed Russell as he turned right out of Ann's driveway and headed west over the railroad tracks. She followed him, about ten to fifteen feet behind him, until he turned as if to cross the street.

When she saw his face, she said to herself, "He's as old as me. He can walk." Then she sped home to use the bathroom. And Russell went home to catch a few hours of sleep before going to work at 6:00 a.m.

The bailiff set up a television monitor facing the jury so they could watch the crime scene video. The defense team moved next to the jurors to get a better view, and Russell moved with them.

Russell sat directly beside the jury box. As the video began, he glanced quickly at the jurors. When he saw that they were all watching the monitor, he turned his focus there, too.

The room was filled with a quietness I'd seldom experienced. The sound was turned off on the video. No one in the courtroom moved or coughed or even seemed to breathe. The faint hum of the air conditioner filled the vacuum and became the only sound in the silence.

The camera took us into Ann's elegant, immaculate home. We were voyeurs into every room, zooming in on collectibles, personal notes, and expensive fabrics. We traveled through every room of the main floor, up the staircase, and into every upstairs room.

Then we went to the basement. The camera took us down the steep wooden stairs. At the bottom, I saw Ann's legs and stifled a gasp. From my vantage point, I could glance to my left and see the monitor. To my right, I could see Russell's profile. As the detailed, close-up frames of Ann's battered body flashed across the screen, Russell showed no emotion. He sat unflinching. At one point, his posture indicated boredom as he rested his left elbow on the rail of the jury box and his head in his cupped left hand.

# Chapter 62

# Signs of Struggle

The morning after the murder, Ann's fiancé, Bob Fenneman, drove from Evansville, Indiana, to Madisonville to have lunch with Ann before their dance lesson. He had told her to be ready at 11:15, but he was running about five minutes late. He called to tell Ann it would be 11:20, or possibly 11:25, before he arrived. He got her answering machine and left a message.

When he arrived at Ann's house, he was immediately alarmed when he rang the backdoor buzzer and no one answered. Ann's car was in the garage, so Bob assumed Ann had had a stroke or heart attack and needed immediate assistance. He hurried across the street to First Baptist Church and asked the ladies in the office to call the police. Remembering that Ann told him Earl had a key to her house, he asked that they call Earl, too.

When Earl and the police arrived, Earl said he didn't have a key but Ann kept one hanging in the holly bush in the backyard. They searched for what Earl later described as fifteen to twenty minutes. Just as they were turning to leave, an officer located the key hanging on another bush.

They opened the back door. The police went to other parts of the house, and Earl headed for the basement. By the time Bob got in the house,

Earl had already found the body. Bob descended a few stairs and saw part of Ann's body lying on the floor. The police told Bob and Earl to go upstairs.

And rightfully so. Ann was lying face down on the basement floor. Her black ultra-suede top was ripped with knife wounds. Her head was misshapen and her skull splintered and exposed. Small red ants had begun attacking the body, clustering in the blood and brain matter in her hair. It was not a sight a loved one would want as a memory.

As they walked outside together, Bob was sobbing. Earl was unemotional.

The first officers on the scene notified the detective division. They sealed off the crime scene and began what would become a four- and a-half year investigation, initially led by Captain Randy Hargis, who had been a longtime friend of Russell. The two had played softball together and ridden four-wheelers. Their families had rented a houseboat at the lake.

Hargis testified that his primary reason for inviting Ben Wolcott to join the investigation was to give the Madisonville Police Department access to the Kentucky State Police crime lab and other resources.

The only signs of struggle in the basement were a flowerpot and a waste can lying on their sides, Ann's glasses lying on the floor a few feet away, a dent in the bottom of the small freezer and minimal blood. In the kitchen, the trashcan liner was removed from the trashcan inside the cabinet. The sanitation department had already picked up the outside trash by the time the body was discovered.

A silver tea service sat untouched in the dining room, and Ann's armoire was comfortably open, exposing plenty of jewelry. The house was a burglar's dream, yet nothing was missing except a $12,000 check from Russell, which Ann listed in her financial journals as having been received on January 10. The check never surfaced.

The doors had been locked, and all windows were locked or painted shut. The door had no pry marks and no footprints indicating someone had tried to kick it in. The security system was powered, but it was turned off when police first arrived. Each morning, at exactly 6:55 a.m., the security system performed a self-check and placed an automated call to confirm that it was functioning properly. The system made the call to the security company the morning the body was discovered. Unfortunately, the system does not note whether the system is activated at the time of the call.

Ann's monitor was functioning, but it was not the type that provided a tape. Jack had tried on several occasions to persuade Ann to upgrade her monitor to the version that provided a videotape. She never got around to doing it.

Judy Harvey, Ann's housekeeper, quickly appeared on the scene. She said she had spoken with Ann after 9:00 the night before. They'd talked briefly about Ann's plans for the week and Judy was there to do the work Ann had mapped out for Monday. If Ann had lived, she was planning to spend the day with Bob.

Judy suggested Wayne Shelton, the handyman, as a suspect. Judy told Jack and me a few days after the murder that Wayne showed no emotion when she told him about Ann's death. Officer Kelley Rager testified that she was instructed to inform Shelton of Ann's death. Rager said Shelton was so distraught that she was afraid she would have to call for medical help. Shelton was also weak and sick at the time of Ann's death. He died of heart disease about three months later.

Judy told police, as she had told us, that Shelton wanted Ann to sign a paper he needed for child support and was angry that she wouldn't state that he worked full-time. Detective Rager checked with the Hopkins County Child Support Unit, who said they had never asked Shelton to sign such a paper. During cross examination, the defense asked Officer Rager, "Much of what Ms. Harvey told you was correct, wasn't it?" "No sir," replied Officer Rager. The defense then listed broad, general statements such as "She said she was Ann's housekeeper" in an attempt to prove that Judy had given correct information.

Judy had also suggested Ann's renter, Joseph Knight, as a suspect. When detectives visited him, they decided that, like Shelton, Knight was physically unable to inflict the degree of damage Ann's body experienced. The left-handed Knight had had surgery on his left arm three days before the murder. His surgical staples had not yet been removed when police interviewed him. And when Knight was interviewed, he seemed confused that the police didn't solve the crime quickly by simply looking at the tape on Ann's surveillance camera. He assumed her camera provided a record of everyone who entered her garage.

Both Shelton and Knight had police records, but they voluntarily let officers search their houses, and they were open about their past crimes.

Judy led detectives through the house, looking for items that might be stolen. She told the police that Ann kept her rent money in a cookie jar below the sink. The officers found the cookie jar and attempted to photograph it. Judy grabbed for the cookie jar and the police shouted to her not to touch it. Before they could stop her, Judy picked up the cookie jar, possibly damaging fingerprint evidence. She moved so quickly that the police ended up snapping a photo of her picking up the cookie jar. The cookie jar contained only a small amount of loose change.

Judy said Ann made rent deposits on the first and fifteenth of each month and money should have been in the jar. However, when police checked Ann's bank records they found that she'd made deposits on January 2, 3, 6, and 10. Knight's rent payment was deposited on the tenth.

Ann's failure to answer a phone message from her brother David, which he testified was uncharacteristic, led officers to assume that Ann was killed some time before David's 8:17 call. But Judy told them she talked to Ann around 9:00 or 9:30. She claimed her daughter's call to a friend was interrupted by Ann's call. After she talked briefly to Ann, her daughter and friend resumed their call. All three parties—Judy, her daughter and her daughter's friend—testified that Ann had called. But the friend had told police immediately after the murder that the call had not been interrupted, and that Judy and her daughter did not have call-waiting.

An AT&T employee examined Judy's and Ann's phone records and stated that neither record showed the call Judy claimed took place. Judy's phone showed a 154-minute call with no interruption. Ann's line showed no call. He stated that, in his thirty-two years with the phone company, he had not seen a computer glitch that would have caused a phone call not to be recorded on either line. He stated that if there were a glitch, no calls would have gone through at that moment on the entire Madisonville exchange.

Officers Scott Troutman, Shawn Bean, Kelley Rager, Ben Wolcott, Randy Hargis, and Commonwealth Attorney David Massamore stayed at Ann's house past midnight the day the body was discovered and returned early the next morning. David didn't like crime scenes, but he made it a habit to visit them, to make each crime personal enough to give him the anger and edge he needed to find the killer. A former Army colonel with thirty-two years of experience in criminal law, David said he had never before seen a crime scene of the brutality he witnessed that night.

The investigating team felt they were looking for someone close to Ann because they found no signs of forced entry and the degree of damage to the body showed a rage that was most likely personal.

As officers sifted through bloodstained evidence, many grieved personally for Ms. Ann, recalling the times she'd warned them not to squeal their tires at the Dairy Queen and how, since Carroll's death, they'd all answered calls when she accidentally set off the security system she trusted for protection. As the officers pushed their sadness to the backs of their minds and pressed forward with the investigation, Russell pushed forward, too. Casino records showed that he gambled the day after the murder.

# Chapter 63

# Witnesses
# Speak

Russell's name first surfaced when Ann's friend, Yvonne, told police that Ann was holding a check from Russell and planned to cash it the day her body was found. She told police that Ann kept a financial journal that listed all the loans she made. The police went back to the house and searched again. Detective Rager found the list written inside the red address book. Russell's loans were numerous: $8,000 in July 2002, $2,500 in August, another $2,000 in August, $1,000 in September. His total indebtedness to Ann was more than $74,000. Ann was closer to Jack, and he was the only person other than her siblings that she listed as a beneficiary of a life insurance policy. But on a day-to-day basis, Russell obviously held her under a unique charm.

On the day Ann's body was discovered, Alex River, one of Russell's friends and fellow employees heard the news but didn't realize Ann and Russell were related. His shift was temporarily changed to nights, and about midnight, he overheard two supervisors saying that Russell's aunt had been murdered. He remembered Russell's behavior and comments in the limousine and wondered if he was the only person who knew Russell owed his aunt money.

When he got home, Alex slept with his shotgun propped in the corner of his bedroom. The next day, he called Madisonville Police Department detective Marc Boggs. He told him what he knew. Marc put him in touch with Captain Hargis.

On Tuesday, the day after Ann's body was discovered, the MPD sent an unmarked car to Alex's house. They drove him to the police station, pulled inside the parking garage, and took him up a private elevator to a conference room. They videotaped his interview.

That same day, Russell went by the house of another friend. Russell asked him to loan him $8,000. The friend had loaned Russell money four or five times, but only $1,000 or $1,200. Russell had always paid him back, but the larger amount caused him to hesitate.

He asked Russell why he needed the money, and Russell wouldn't say. When his friend continued to hesitate, Russell persisted, asking him four to six times if he had the money. Finally, he gave Russell $1,000-$1,200.

The friend asked Russell if he had a problem. The friend said that, if he did, he would go with him to get help. Russell said he didn't feel that he needed help. Russell never repaid his final loan to his friend.

The following day, Wednesday, January 15, Alex River expressed condolences to Russell. Russell barely responded. Later that day, Russell pulled him aside at a managers meeting at the mines. "This is really something about my aunt," said Russell. "I'm through. I'm through gambling. I'll get you the money I owe you."

Then Russell asked Alex what he'd said to the police. "Did you tell them I was going to commit suicide?" asked Russell. Alex explained that he had simply expressed concern that Russell seemed depressed.

"If you ever hear of *me* being dead," Russell told him, "somebody else did it."

Captain Marc Boggs wasn't directly involved in the case, but one of his duties was taking calls from the public. On January 15, he received a call from a woman. The call came in on the Crime Stopper line, and calls are not traced on that line.

The woman would not identify herself but told Boggs, "You know me." Her voice sounded familiar but he couldn't identify her.

She stated that she'd seen a white male with dark hair step out of Ann's driveway. He was wearing camouflage-type clothing. She had no doubt she'd recognize him if she saw him again.

Boggs tried to persuade her to come forward, but she refused.

The police asked all local family members to come to the police station to provide DNA, fingerprint and hair samples. And Russell was ready.

After a visit to Earl's, Russell told Terri his father thought they all needed to be together on what happened that night. She asked Russell where he'd actually been the night of Ann's murder. He said he was in a parking lot talking to Mike, but he didn't want him to be his alibi. Mike's girlfriend testified that he was with her that evening.

On the Wednesday and Thursday after the murder, Russell discussed his alibi with his wife. He told her that if she was asked about the phone call from his cell to his home at 8:50, she should say he was in the basement and teased Terri by calling her and asking her to bring him a glass of water. He told Terri to say that he arrived home about 7:30 and played video games with her son until his friend arrived to borrow a cordless drill. Though Terri and her children had already eaten when Russell got home, he planned the alibi meal, right down to which of them had crackers with their chili.

Terri and Russell were called to the station on January 23 and interviewed in separate rooms. Terri left the station and began to worry. She talked to her pastor and her father. She told them that Russell was insisting she tell the story he'd concocted. Her dad put her in touch with an attorney, and she accompanied her attorney back to the police station. This time she told them exactly what had happened, as far as she knew. Russell had not been home until a little after 9:00. Police told her the extent of Russell's gambling, and Terri cried.

Russell didn't know that Terri had talked with the police, but he was getting nervous about a lot of people and a lot of details. He knew he had loose ends to tie up, and he'd started doing so soon after the murder.

On the Thursday after the murder, Russell asked to borrow $9,500 from Terri's father. He said he wanted to put money back into Ann's estate. Terri's dad told him that when someone died, their bank accounts were frozen. Russell assured him that Earl was the executor of the will and he could get the money back into Ann's account. Terri's dad refused to loan the money.

The police ascertained that Russell and Mike spoke more than seventy times by cell phone in the thirty days after the murder.

The police obtained a search warrant for Russell's house and truck. They impounded his truck at the MPD. Two forensic scientists processed the truck. They sprayed it with Luminol and found areas that luminesced (reacted with a fluorescent-like glow when viewed under a special light): the gas pedal, the driver's floor mat, the steering wheel, the steering column, the console and the driver's arm rest. Luminol can react to many things, including cleaning solvents and alcohol, so it can only be used as an investigative tool and not as evidence. But the truck had apparently contained blood or been carefully cleaned. The entire truck had been sprayed with a fine mist that reacted to the Luminol.

The forensic scientists also tested the knife recovered from Russell. They found no evidence of blood. They tested various blood-stained items from the crime scene and found only female blood that was all Ann's with a one in eighty-three trillion possibility that it was anyone else's.

As evidence mounted against Russell, his attempts at an alibi became more elaborate. At a family function in May or June, Russell approached Earl's girlfriend, Betty. He pulled her aside and said, "I lied. That money I wanted to borrow [in January] was to pay a gambling debt."

Three or four weeks after the murder, Russell called another friend whom he'd known since high school. The friend's parents lived near Terri's house.

"Did you happen to see my truck at home when you had supper with your parents?" Russell asked him, referring to the Sunday of the murder.

The friend ate supper with his parents at 4:30 or 5:00 Monday through Thursday, but rarely ate there on Sunday evening. He reminded Russell of that.

"I don't need an alibi," Russell told him, "but if you *did* see me, it would help."

A couple of months later, Russell went to a cookout at his friend's house. "Man, I didn't do this. But if they catch me, they'll catch me running," Russell told him.

The friend told Russell if he were innocent, he should "stand and fight."

"Eddyville is filled with innocent men," responded Russell, referring to Kentucky's maximum security prison.

At this point, Terri began feeling pressured and annoyed by his constant calls. Police encouraged her to take out an Emergency Protective Order (EPO). Hopkins County deputy sheriff Richard Hicks served Russell with the papers at 11:58 one evening in March. Russell was allowed to take some of his clothes with him. Russell was quiet and agreeable but, according to Hicks, he "seemed like he was stalling somewhat."

Hicks reminded Russell that he could not re-enter the house, which belonged to Terri. He left the house about 12:25 a.m.

The night the EPO was served, canine officer Jeff Jewell, who knew Russell since high school days, was patrolling in the area. He was aware that the EPO had been served, so when he saw Russell's truck returning to Terri's house, he radioed the MPD. A police cruiser responded quickly and stopped the truck. When the driver exited the truck, they forced him to the ground.

The man driving the truck was the boyfriend of Russell's niece. Russell told the boyfriend he'd been kicked out of his house and needed him to go back to his house and pick up some things. The boyfriend took a knife from between Russell's mattresses, and he took a safe. The knife was later presented to Dr. Becham, who performed Ann's autopsy. Dr. Becham stated that the knife was consistent with Ann's wounds.

Terri continued to see Russell after the EPO, stating that, at the time, she still "loved Russell very much." She pleaded with him to tell the truth. But eventually Terri realized that love couldn't conquer Russell's problems, and she divorced him in June 2003.

Soon thereafter, Russell moved in with a girlfriend. Sometime in the spring of 2003, Russell asked her to drive him to Chicago "for a deposition." She did not. Russell found other transportation to the city where he quietly applied for a passport.

When he came to Evansville, he was driving a white full-sized Chevy Silverado extended-cab truck. He told his girlfriend he was going to trade it in because of "something to do with his dad." In April or May, he started driving a Ford Explorer, and she never saw the white truck again.

The girlfriend was aware that Russell and some friends took a brief gambling trip to Costa Rica in the spring of 2003. Some time after that, he called her from Tunica, Mississippi. He said he'd gone there to sell a car that belonged to his father. He'd lost everything in Tunica's casinos, and all he had left was the check for his father.

When the girlfriend arrived in Tunica, Russell asked her to try to borrow money from her father, but she refused. She saw an unused airline ticket to Costa Rica, but she asked nothing about it.

Before going back to Costa Rica, Russell stopped to say goodbye to another friend. The man had become friends with Russell when his child and Russell's stepson played ball together. He'd gone gambling with Russell ten to twelve times, once watching him calmly lose $15,000-$20,000.

Russell didn't tell the friend where he was going, but he said "they" were trying to pin his aunt's murder on him, that he didn't do it, and he was leaving. (The defense implied during the trial that Russell had not fled the country to avoid prosecution. He had simply taken a gambling trip to Costa Rica, come back to the states, then was indicted while on a return trip.)

Russell made his second flight to Costa Rica June 16. He was indicted a month later. At that time, Captain Boggs received a second call from the woman who'd seen Russell the night of the murder: "You got him! You got him!" She had seen the indictment story and Russell's photo in the *Messenger* and recognized him as the man she'd seen outside Ann's house the night of the murder.

The woman was still reluctant to come forward. "If I saw him, he probably saw me, too," she told Boggs.

But the woman wanted to do the right thing, and she didn't want to be guilty of obstructing justice. Eventually she told Boggs her name was Denise Gilmore. She later made a videotaped statement to the police and testified at the trial.

Russell called his girlfriend from Costa Rica, but it wasn't long before he was looking for new feminine company.

Soon, Russell met a petite, attractive brunette and became romantically involved. Russell told her his real name, though he used at least four aliases in the time he knew her. He had illegal documentation for two names; the others he chose from the Internet.

Russell moved often, trying to stay ahead of the police. He considered moving to Brazil or Cuba because these countries had the same appeal as Costa Rica: no death penalty, no extradition if the death penalty was an option.

His new girlfriend apparently fell under what Commonwealth attorney David Massamore would later refer to as a "Russell-induced stupor," something we saw continually at the trial, as a parade of attractive women confessed their love and past-love for him. Even after Terri filed her EPO, she continued to secretly see Russell. His first wife, Denise, sat on the row behind him at the trial, the same row where his current wife sat.

Even men seemed to fall for Russell's appeal. As witness after witness told of giving him money, with one friend even refinancing his house to do so, I had trouble understanding Russell's appeal. Pheromones are chemicals that attract us to the opposite sex, and a synthetic version is even sold on the Internet. Some bodies apparently produce more pheromone than others, and some researchers believe that pheromones are the reason some average people seem to have above-average sex appeal. Pheromones, charisma, extraordinary confidence—whatever Russell and Earl possessed, these average men certainly seemed to have an unusual number of attentive women.

And, in Russell's case, even men were willing to loan money they couldn't afford so Russell could enjoy luxuries.

But Russell's U.S. luxuries couldn't compare with his Costa Rican lifestyle—a lifestyle we could only assume was financed with Ann's money. His Costa Rican friend testified that Russell never worked while he was in Costa Rica. "He just gambled. He was always gambling. He gambled every day, sometimes all day and night." Earl apparently provided his lifestyle by wiring money to him via Western Union. The girlfriend sometimes picked up the money Earl sent. An informant agreed to help police in a sting operation to catch Earl sending money to Russell. The Kentucky man wired money to a variety of names. Always in $900 increments, though he sometimes made several transactions at a time. Earl paid him $300 for each transaction.

When Kentucky State Police detective Ben Wolcott, by now the primary investigator for Ann's murder, had enough evidence, he obtained a search warrant for Earl's house and Cadillac. In the map pocket on the seats of Earl's Cadillac, police found Western Union forms filled out to various names, each in the amount of $900. In his house, they found one hundred dollar bills, separated into increments of $900. Earl was arrested, pleaded guilty and was put on probation.

Russell's former wives and American girlfriend considered Russell to be peaceful, but the Costa Rican girlfriend labeled him as violent. They argued often and once he hit her repeatedly on her arm. She was afraid of him, but like the other women in his life, she seemed too mesmerized to leave. In spite of his threats to kill her, she continued their relationship until he was arrested.

But their arguments were volatile and frequent. She often threatened to go to the police. He'd respond by telling her, "My father will send somebody to kill you," "I'll burn your house with your family in it."

In March 2005, when she and Russell were staying in a hotel, they had an unusually intense argument. Russell grabbed her arm and asked, "If I killed my aunt, why wouldn't I kill you?"

Still, the girlfriend remained silent. When the FBI at the American Embassy in Costa Rica located her, she initially refused to talk. Russell was finally arrested in San Jose, Costa Rica, in the early morning hours of May

3, 2005. He was carrying a passport that identified him under a false name, and he denied he was Russell Winstead. Ben initially identified Russell's photo, and he was later identified through fingerprints.

Russell owed the girlfriend money, and she contacted him at the Costa Rican jail. He offered her money to "disappear and not to testify." He said his father could pay her a million dollars to disappear. She told him that, if he'd killed his aunt, there was not enough money to buy her off.

While in jail in Costa Rica, Russell married the woman whose hand he held in the courtroom. At that point, the former girlfriend decided to talk to the FBI.

The defense raised the question of whether the ex-girlfriend was simply a woman scorned. She said she knew about his wife and that Russell had "a lot of women always." They asked if she had called Earl, Earl's daughter and Earl's granddaughter. She acknowledged that she had. She said Russell owed her money, and she wanted to be paid back. When she didn't receive the amount of money she felt the family owed her, she talked.

Russell returned to the states February 23, 2006. During the year and a half his attorneys made motions and delayed the trial, Russell stayed in an eight-cell block in the Hopkins County Jail. Each cell had two beds, and most inmates in the block were charged with murder.

At one time, Russell's cellmate was confessed murderer Fred Roulette. His case was the one Jack had forewarned me would become an issue at Russell's trial. In many ways, Russell's and Roulette's crimes paralleled each other. Within fifteen minutes of being picked up by the police, Roulette confessed to the stabbing death of an elderly woman who lived alone. But Roulette had cut the lady's phone lines, kicked in her door and stabbed her outside.

The parallel was close enough for Russell. He persuaded Roulette to take responsibility for both murders. Roulette asked him who would take care of his kids if he were sentenced to twenty-five years in prison. Russell promised him $20,000 trust funds for two of Roulette's sons, $5,000 for his girlfriend, and regular money for Roulette's prison commissary account. Prisoners were required to purchase all but the basics at the commissary, and

Roulette had no one on the outside to put money in his account. It was late December and Roulette was wearing jail-issued flip-flops. Russell sealed the deal by purchasing a generous amount of food and snacks for Roulette and charging a pair of tennis shoes, size ten, to his commissary account. Russell wears a size eleven and a half shoe.

For a week and a half, Russell coached Roulette on the details of the murder of a woman he'd never met. He drew diagrams of Ann's house, describing the furniture and even the color of the carpet. They created a story, based on Russell's actual knowledge of the crime.

In the scenario, Roulette was visiting his mother the weekend of the murder. When David pointed out that his mother did not move to the area until eight months after the murder, the defense implied that Roulette was camping out on property owned by the family, though temperatures that night dipped to eighteen degrees.

Roulette supposedly stopped by the Dairy Queen the afternoon of January 12. As he looked at the classifieds in the *Messenger*, he struck up a conversation with a woman. He told her he was looking for a house to rent, and the woman told him that Ann had a number of rent houses. He called her and arranged to meet her at her house around 8:30 or 9:00.

While waiting for the meeting, Roulette got drunk. When Ann willingly opened the door to a drunken stranger, he chased her down the basement stairs and bludgeoned her with a half-inch breaker bar before stabbing her.

On January 1, Russell helped Roulette write six letters ("conjured up by me and Winstead together"), confessing to Ann's murder. They sent them to Judge Brantley, Commonwealth attorney David Massamore, Russell's attorney, the *Messenger*, Earl and Earl's daughter. After talking to his attorney and realizing he could get the death penalty for an additional murder, Roulette shared those fears with Russell. Russell patted Roulette in a distant manner and said, "That's okay. I'll be there for you."

Roulette had assumed his punishment would be the same for two crimes as for one, and with the additional confession he'd be able to provide for his children and be assured of a few luxuries in prison. "I needed somebody like Russell on the outside. My family won't visit me," admitted Roulette.

But when Roulette realized that Russell didn't care that he could get the death penalty, he recounted his confession to the lieutenant over security at Hopkins County Detention Center. He talked to her on December 23 and she "forgot about it" over the holidays.

On January 5, Roulette asked to speak to her again. He told her Russell had persuaded him to write letters confessing to Ann's murder. He was wearing the tennis shoes Russell purchased for him when he talked to her. She checked Russell's commissary receipts and saw the tennis shoes in Roulette's size, as well as an increase in food purchases. She checked Roulette's commissary purchases and saw that he had not purchased shoes himself. His account was actually in the red.

The lieutenant over security encouraged Roulette to act as though the deal with Russell was still on, and she'd arrange for him to talk to authorities. Roulette asked to be transferred to a jail where he would be allowed to smoke. She told him she'd see what she could do.

Soon Russell also asked to speak to the lieutenant. He told her that he'd become aware that Roulette killed his aunt. She said Russell was calm when he told her there were things he'd like to do to Roulette, but he was keeping his composure. Roulette pointed out under oath that Russell purchased his tennis shoes after he supposedly told Russell he'd killed Ann.

KSP detective Ben Wolcott interviewed Roulette on January 8 and then arranged for him to be transferred to the jail in neighboring Christian County. Ben encouraged Roulette to write a letter to Russell, which he mailed on January 30. In a code-like letter, Roulette reminded Russell that he'd gone out on a limb for him and asked Russell for assurance that he would follow through on his promises of trust funds and commissary supplies.

When Russell received the letter, he was careful not to answer it himself. He paid his new cellmate in commissary supplies to write his reply. As the new cellmate walked into the courtroom in an orange jump suit, belly chains and shackles, sporting a shaved head and long bushy beard, it was hard to imagine him coming up with the letter sent to Roulette under his name:

"I hope you are doing okay. I want you to know nobody here has forgot about you. We just found out last week you were in Christian County Jail.

"We were told you were at K.C.P.C. I want you to know you still have friends here that are true to their word. Sometimes a little patience is necessary. One of the guards said you were moved on the request of Messamore for some reason."

He explained how the letter was written. "Winstead wrote the letter and I copied it."

What happened to Winstead's copy of this and other documentation? "He wrote the letters, chewed them up, and flushed them," said the cellmate. "Russell ate a lot of paper." He explained that Russell was afraid the chewed paper would float up in another toilet, so he put paper in the other toilets and flushed them all.

# Chapter 64

# For the Defense

After assembling the story in convincing, powerful detail, the Commonwealth rested at 12:55 p.m. Friday, August 24, 2007. The defense attorneys used the remainder of Friday and most of the following Tuesday to present their case.

As we left the courthouse on Friday, we were encouraged that the defense seemed to have very little, and what they had, they packaged in innuendos that attempted to shift blame. They referenced Russell's second wife's relationship with him prior to their marriage. They asked Fred Roulette why a man as "experienced" and "savvy" as he was hadn't gotten his  agreement with Russell in writing. Roulette stood his ground and answered with such confidence that the strategy seemed to backfire. (When the defense stated that Roulette had lied about the murder he committed, Roulette stated that he'd confessed within fifteen minutes of being caught, adding, "I lied for fifteen minutes. This lie has been going on for four and a half years." When defense continued to imply that Roulette was lying, he turned the tables, declaring, "*I* took an oath to tell the truth when *I* walked in here.")

That evening, Jack and I watched a true-crime trial on television in our motel room. We were reminded that only what the Muhlenberg County jurors understood and believed about Russell would determine whether he walked free or spent the majority of his remaining years in prison.

As we watched the program about twelve men and women on an Iowa jury, we were both struck by the incredible power of the jury and the equally incredible helplessness of the prosecution and defense. After months of preparation, it all boiled down to what twelve everyday people believed. Though I genuinely respected the Muhlenberg County jurors, I was terrified.

We began to hear rumors that the people in Madisonville thought Russell was guilty, but they thought he'd be acquitted anyway. As we mentally noted the evidence, including the polygraphs, which were not admitted, we wondered if the jury had enough information to make the right decision.

Defense motions had kept Jack from testifying about his parallel investigation and from stating that Ann told him, the day before her murder, that she was worried about Russell. We knew of other information the jury knew nothing about. If they didn't "get it" with the information they'd been allowed to hear, if they didn't see through the defense team's smoke and mirrors, Russell would get away with murder.

Muhlenberg County needed their courtroom on Mondays, so Russell's trial was held Tuesdays through Fridays. We spent a restless long weekend. As we agonized, we knew Russell's and Earl's deeply buried emotions must be even more intense than ours. Each day, the circles beneath Russell's eyes seemed darker and his face appeared thinner. He didn't seem to be getting an adrenaline high from this final courtroom gamble.

The defense team called a handful of witnesses who reiterated forensic evidence. They called Earl; Russell's niece; Russell's gambling friend Mike; Ben Wolcott; convicted felons Pierre McNary and Russell Allinder; Allinder's public defender; Judy Harvey, her daughter and her daughter's friend; and Costa Rican attorney Alejandra Araya Chaverri.

The defense seemed intent on presenting Earl as a frail, kindly and compassionate brother to Ann and grandfather to as many children as they could pack into the courtroom. After explaining that Earl suffered from bruised vocal cords that made it difficult for him to speak, they asked him about the morning of the murder.

"Where did you and Ann eat lunch?" asked the defense.

"A buffet," said Earl.

"And what did you have to eat?"

Earl paused slightly and answered, "Well, you know how it is. You always eat too much at a buffet." The jurors laughed as the defense had hoped.

As Earl described being called to Ann's house the day of the murder, his usually stoic demeanor changed only slightly. "This is kind of difficult talking about this situation. It brings up some bad memories." The defense attorneys scurried to get Earl a bottle of water, and I saw him take only one tiny sip.

When Earl's granddaughter testified, she referred to Earl as Peepaw, then demurely corrected herself and referred to him as her grandfather.

Earl said Ann was generous and didn't care when people paid her back. He said he knew Russell owed Ann about $30,000 because Ann approached him about a month before her death and told him.

"I asked her if there was a problem, and she said, 'No problem at all. I just wanted you to know.'"

He said her surveillance camera never worked so she didn't use it.

Earl and Judy both said Ann kept money stashed around her house. Earl said she liked to keep "operating cash" at home because she grew up in the Depression. In reality, Ann's family was well off during the Depression. Her father owned a coal mine, and Ann had her own car while still in high school.

Earl said Russell had a co-worker who had a business in Costa Rica, and Russell went down to visit and find out about the working conditions.

When Russell was indicted while on his second trip to Costa Rica, Earl sent him money to "buy time" until the real killer was discovered. "I'd seen in Madisonville that in about two years, the truth would come out about a murder," Earl testified.

Earl said that they'd found the bubble wrap with the suspected blood in March when they were getting ready for Ann's auction.

When David Massamore questioned Earl, he asked if Russell had benefited from the will. Earl denied that he had. David asked about the $74,000 Russell owed Ann's estate. Earl stated that he paid the estate and Russell would someday pay him back. David produced a copy of the final calculations for the will. Russell's indebtedness had been reduced to $30,000 and he'd been exonerated because he was indigent. The calculations also noted that Russell was believed to be out of the country. David reminded Earl that when the calculations were completed, he was already wiring money to Costa Rica so there was no reason to simply "believe" that Russell had left the country.

Earl stepped down from the witness stand, carrying the almost-full bottle of water. I searched the jurors' faces to see if they'd believed him. They were expressionless.

The defense called Pierre McNary to discredit Denise Gilmore, the lady who'd seen Russell walking out of Ann's driveway about midnight the night of the murder. McNary said Gilmore told him several conflicting stories, including that the man she saw walking down the street was a black man, that she'd actually given him a ride and that Gilmore could not see well to drive at night.

Instantly, David was on his feet, pointing a finger at McNary as he approached the witness stand.

"I know you, don't I?" pummeled David. "I've put you away a couple of times, and now you're up on cocaine charges." McNary nodded.

David stated that McNary had recently sent him a letter offering to "get lost" and not testify for the defense if David would help with his current drug charges. Then McNary visited David and acknowledged that

Gilmore had not said she'd seen a black man. McNary was now out on bond, because Denise Gilmore, his occasional employer, had posted bond for him and recently she attempted to withdraw the bond.

Then, as close as an ex-Army colonel could get to performing a *pirouette*, David spun around and headed to his seat, his words lingering in the air: "No further questions."

The defense called Russell's niece, who stated that Russell's Costa Rican girlfriend had called her, angry that Russell had married a new wife and wanting money from Earl.

Russell's gambling friend, Mike, a husky man with short dark hair and glasses, now described a relationship where Russell called him two or three times the day before the murder, "basically shooting the breeze." He said there was nothing different about Russell's demeanor or attitude in the weeks before the murder. He confirmed that he'd gone to Russell's house at 9:10 the night of the murder. He went to the basement, just "hanging out, seeing how everything was going."

The defense called Ben Wolcott. They asked why Ben had not put a wire on Roulette when he and Russell made their plans for a false confession. He asked Ben to confirm that, in Russell's lengthy videotaped interview, he denied fifty or more times that he had anything to do with Ann's death. The defense quoted Russell: "I didn't have nothing to do with it. I wouldn't harm her for nothing in the world...I loved her more than anybody...The only sins I've carried into this room are my gambling sins... My defense is innocence. I wouldn't harm this woman for nothing."

Each time the defense quoted Russell, Ben replied, "That's what Russell said, yes sir." I glanced at the jury. They looked bored and maybe a little annoyed. They'd already listened to the defense team's item-by-item account of nearly all 112 pieces of evidence submitted to the Kentucky State Police, though the Commonwealth earlier established that all blood found at the crime scene was female, with a one in eighty-three trillion chance of its being anyone's blood but Ann's. Now it looked as if the defense was sentencing them to hear each of Russell's fifty-plus denials of his involvement.

Now David asked a few powerful and concise questions. Taking the jury back to Russell's numerous claims that he was innocent, David asked Ben, "During the same interview the defense read from, did Russell also deny multiple times that he'd written a $12,000 check to Ann?"

"Yes, sir. He did," responded Ben.

David then asked if Russell had, in the same interview, given them an alibi that later proved false. Then he asked Ben if, in his lengthy experience as a police officer, he'd ever had a suspect deny his guilt.

# Chapter 65

# On the Stand

Judy Harvey, Ann's housekeeper, was called to the stand. She testified that she had a close relationship with Ann, and at one point the defense referred to Ann as "your friend Ms. Branson." Judy stated that Ann was "like a second mother" to her. She said, "I was kind of her confidante, and she was mine." Then, though Russell stated in his videotaped interview that he saw Ann often, Judy stated that she'd only met Russell one time before the funeral.

Judy claimed Ann let renters "come into the house and talk." She claimed Ann kept money hidden in various places in the house.

The Commonwealth had already established that Judy lived in one of Earl's houses and that she'd borrowed money from Ann. Judy now acknowledged that she'd borrowed money but that Ann "didn't pressure or nag" her to pay it back. Both Judy and Earl implied that Ann would loan money with virtually no guidelines for repaying.

Judy testified that she'd talked to Ann at 9:00 or 9:30 the evening she was murdered. Judy described her Sunday evening phone call with Ann in detail. Her daughter and her daughter's friend did the same. Everything matched except the phone records. No call was recorded on either Ann's or Judy's records.

Judy insisted, as she had with us years before, that Wayne Shelton, the handyman, was physically able to carry out the crime. I glanced at the jury, wishing someone could tell them that Wayne Shelton's polygraph showed total honesty.

I waited for David's tough and grueling questioning. He had no questions, and his refusal to nitpick was more powerful than any contradictions he could have pointed out.

Alejandra Araya Chaverri, a Costa Rican woman, took the stand. She told the jurors that she was Russell's attorney in Costa Rica, hired by Earl.

She insisted that Russell had asked to apply for voluntary extradition but, as his attorney, she had persuaded him to use a standard extradition to maintain his protection against the death penalty. The mood in the courtroom seemed to soften a little toward Russell.

But as Alejandra continued her testimony, I sensed that the jury and spectators weren't buying what she was saying. I felt she painted Russell as a potpourri of Mother Theresa, Billy Graham and Emily Post—and the girlfriend as a rival for Glenn Close in *Fatal Attraction*.

Though the girlfriend supposedly told Alejandra that she'd never been with someone as kind and gentle as Russell, she also told her that she would do anything in her power to destroy Russell.

Alejandra stated that the girlfriend was barred, by court order, from visiting Russell in the Costa Rican jail, but she produced no documentation to substantiate her claim.

The defense rested, and David called three quick rebuttal witnesses who closed the trial with the subtle but powerful suggestion that the defense presentation, in their opinions, wasn't accurate.

Jack was called to testify that the substance on the bubble wrap appeared to be a brownish orange paint, but he and Earl had called the police anyway. An officer picked up the bubble wrap immediately.

Officer Sean Bean testified that he had interviewed the young girl, who talked to Judy Harvey's daughter the evening of the murder. She told him that to her knowledge, the Harveys did not have call waiting.

The final witness was Russell's second wife, Terri. She entered the courtroom looking confident and, as she testified, believable. She finished her story: Russell's gambling friend, Mike, had left the house on January 12, but returned the following Sunday night. He and Russell chatted lightheartedly.

298

# Chapter 66

# The Verdict

Closing arguments began Wednesday morning, August 29. I searched the jurors' faces as the defense attempted to present mistakes in the investigation and toss out other possible suspects. Were they seeing what we saw? Did they, like Jack and I, see the defense case as merely an attempt to get the focus off Russell? This jury seemed to be a sharp, hard-working group of men and women who didn't lie, cheat, steal or kill for what they had. I thought they saw the truth.

But if they didn't, a killer was going to walk away a free man.

When David rose for his closing arguments, I took my first deep breath in three weeks. He nailed it. I prayed that the jury heard him validating the points of truth as clearly as Jack and I heard him. I do not believe the little town of Madisonville, Kentucky, and the Commonwealth of Kentucky could have gotten to the truth any better or more elegantly if they had hired Vincent Bugliosi to represent them. On the night of January 13, 2003, when David Massamore visited the crime scene, I believe Ann's death became personal to him. And it was obvious that he was fighting a passionate battle to bring her killer to justice.

"For four years, seven months and sixteen days, Ann Branson has been waiting for justice," David told the jury. "It's a tough job we've given you, but not an impossible one."

David skillfully explained the strategy of all defense attorneys: They're dealt a hand and they have to make due with what they get. Most represent their clients to the best of their abilities. They don't work for the police, and they don't represent the people. Under American law, every accused person brought to trial, guilty or innocent, must be represented by counsel, which presents the accused side of the case. "Let the crime scene speak to you," urged David. Then he reviewed the case, hovering briefly over any aspect he felt the jurors could be confused about.

The time of death? The coroner had set 10:00 p.m. because Judy said she'd last talked to Ann about 9:30, even though we had nothing to document that such a call occurred.

The key placed on the wrong bush? How many random killers would replace the key? Few people knew there was a key, but according to the Commonwealth Attorney's theory: "Earl knew. And if Earl knew, then Russell knew."

When Russell's stepson was asked if he was playing video games with his stepfather, however, he told them the truth: Russell did not arrive home until 9:00.

Fingerprints? Only one usable fingerprint was found in Ann's house and it wasn't Russell's. The defense implied that this made Russell innocent. The problem with this assumption was that the fingerprint was run through AFIS (Automated Fingerprint Identification System). All the people the defense had indicated as alternate suspects were all listed in AFIS. The single fingerprint eliminated them as well. And only one fingerprint in the house? Not even Ann's fingerprints? Or her housekeeper's? It appeared that someone had worked hard to eliminate fingerprints.

David observed: "The absence of evidence is not evidence of absence." In other words, just because there's no evidence of someone being there doesn't mean a person wasn't there.

The unsubstantiated phone call from Ann to Judy? David said simply, "If you believe Judy Harvey, turn him loose."

The weapons? The only knife Russell asked his niece's boyfriend to pick up was the one that fit the wounds. And police were unable to find a weapon that fit Ann's head wounds until Russell told Roulette to say he used a half-inch breaker bar.

Evidence of Russell's deal with Roulette? Other than the tennis shoes and some commissary snacks, the defense had asked Roulette what proof he had of a deal. "The trust funds weren't set up, any more than there was a '56 Chevy," explained David.

David concluded his closing arguments by reminding the jury of the "Where's Waldo" drawings that were popular several years ago. That was the issue now.

"Russell said he was with his gambling friend, but his friend was with his honey.

"Russell said he was with his wife and her children, but they've testified that he wasn't home till 9:00. So the question you have to answer is, 'Where's Russell?'"

# Chapter 67

# Emotional
# Rollercoaster

The jury began deliberating at 12: 26 p.m. We found ourselves on an emotional rollercoaster. We knew a drop was ahead of us, good news or bad. With each minute, we sensed the steady clicking as we climbed another height. And the excitement/panic/anticipation increased as we inched toward the verdict.

Jack had been subject to recall for additional testimony, so he was not allowed to sit in the courtroom until the closing arguments. As we waited for the jury to return a verdict, Jack and I were finally able to discuss the trial in depth.

We used all our new information to fill in the blanks of the story we'd been trying to piece together for years. We weren't sure who should have told us all this information earlier, but we knew someone should have. Family should not hear so much new information at the actual trial, and we realized we would have known even less if it hadn't been for Jack's law enforcement resources.

But there was one thing we knew: for nearly five years, the police, the prosecution team, family, friends and an entire town refused to give up on finding Ann's killer. Many times, 350 miles away, we'd felt alone, discouraged and hopeless. But in that Muhlenberg County courthouse, we came to know and understand and appreciate the little town that never stopped caring.

We initially thought the jury would bring back an immediate verdict, but by early evening, they sent word that they were finished for the night and would return the following day. Our confidence plummeted. If they were gridlocked, we would start the entire process over. If they found Russell not guilty, well... a hung jury was starting to sound okay.

We slept fitfully all night, but still sprung effortlessly out of bed the next morning, skipping breakfast and surviving on adrenaline. The judge repeated the jury's instructions to a courtroom sprinkled with children. Earl's daughter held an infant grandchild and sat next to a preschooler. Alejandra had her infant son in a large stroller and her daughter sat with Russell's wife. Russell's oldest son was there with Russell's first wife, Denise. I wondered if the jury would be influenced by the family-man picture.

We made small talk. We paced. We stared forward. We watched the clock hands creep forward. Then, a little more than two hours after resuming deliberations, the message came back: The jury had a verdict.

Russell's family, Costa Rican girlfriend and children of all sizes slipped into the rows behind Russell. The remainder of spectators sat behind the Commonwealth. The jurors filed in, avoiding eye contact with everyone. The foreperson gave the verdict to the bailiff, and the bailiff passed it to Judge Brantley. He read the verdict silently. Then he instructed Russell and his attorneys to stand.

I wanted to freeze time. My fear of hearing a not-guilty verdict overshadowed my hope for a guilty one. I grabbed Jack's arm, tight. I closed my eyes and stopped breathing until I heard the verdict: Guilty of murder. Guilty of robbery.

If it hadn't been for the *Messenger's* description of Russell's reaction, I wouldn't have known what happened in those next minutes after the verdict was read. I put my face in Jack's shoulder to smother a cry and then sobbed quietly as Jack and I embraced. According to Don Perryman's *Messenger* story, "Russell Winstead dropped his head and then slumped his shoulders. He placed his hands on the table in front of him. Winstead slowly shook his head from side to side—either an expression of disbelief at what he'd just heard, or that the decision just made was wrong."

When I regained my composure, I glanced toward the other side of the courtroom. Russell was expressionless and Earl was characteristically stoic. The courtroom was virtually silent, though I later learned from court security that the women in Russell's family had gone to a downstairs room to cry.

The judge called a recess, and Jack and I slipped outside to call family and friends.

Thirty miles away in Madisonville, the verdict was announced on the radio a little before 11:30 a.m. Someone who'd just heard the verdict stepped inside a local bank and called out: "Guilty!" Everyone knew immediately what he meant. Customers and employees applauded.

After the brief recess, the judge dismissed for lunch. As jurors walked past Russell, he glared at them with such hate that they sent a message to the bailiff that, from then on, they wanted to enter and leave the courtroom by another door so they wouldn't have to see Russell.

# Chapter 68

# The Sentence

Kentucky law assigns sentencing to the jury, so immediately after lunch Judge Brantley began the sentencing portion of the trial. He explained that the jurors could choose ten to twenty years for robbery. Since the death penalty and life without parole were not options because of extradition treaties with Costa Rica, they could now choose a murder sentence from twenty years to life (with the opportunity for parole). They could choose for the sentences to run concurrently or consecutively. However, because Russell had to be eligible for parole, the maximum amount of time he could serve without having an opportunity for parole was twenty-five years.

David Massamore called on Jack to share the impact Ann's murder had on our family. Unlike the formal victim impact statements often read or spoken by family members, this Kentucky court swore Jack in for the third time and he sat in the witness box and answered questions from David. David asked about Ann's life, her marriage to Carroll, her interests, and what she meant to the family. Since the jury had seen only autopsy photos, David asked Jack to show photos of Ann as she was in life. One of the photos he showed was Ann as a bridesmaid at our daughter Penny's wedding, ten months before the murder.

The defense called on Russell's family and friends to tell what kind of person he was. Through tears, they sketched a picture that, to them, seemed admirable. Russell, the perfect brother who, after early childhood, never argued with his sister. Uncle Russell, the only one who never got annoyed when children were too loud or rambunctious. The perfect son, the all-American boy. Russell, the only race car driver to never lose his cool.

To me, each tribute seemed to describe the type of personality that suppressed anger and allowed rage to build. Laid-back Russell, cool and calm. Stoic. A pressure cooker building up steam every time a teacher chastised him, a friend hurt his feelings or a boss criticized his work. The wounds to Ann's head may have been inflicted to silence her, but the stabs to her dead body were for every hurt Russell had experienced since he decided, by sheer will, to become stoic.

Attorneys from both sides closed with pleas for wise sentencing. The defense reiterated that Russell was a good father. David asked how he could be a good father while on the run in Costa Rica.

The defense asked for mercy, but David reminded the jury that Russell showed no mercy to Ann. He reminded them that, regardless of the sentence, Russell would someday be eligible for parole. "There's no parole for death," he added.

When the jury broke, Jack and I drove with Tom Branson for a hurried supper. Then we climbed the courthouse steps, went through the magnetometer and walked up to the second floor courtroom. We were met in the hall by a member of the security team. "They're already back," he whispered as he led us to the courtroom, "and they maxed him out. They gave him the longest sentences possible, for both counts. And they want them to run consecutively."

We slipped into the back of the courtroom for the final details of the sentence, and then walked out arm in arm, euphoric with victory and overcome with grief for Russell's family. About 9:00 p.m., we stopped by the Madisonville Dairy Queen once owned by Ann and Carroll, sitting in a corner booth. Jack went to the counter to order two hot fudge sundaes in a meager attempt to celebrate. I sat with my head down, no longer able to fight back the exhaustion.

After a moment, I raised my head and squinted into the glare of the fluorescent lights. Just before my eyes focused, I thought I saw a dim figure up near the counter—a woman wearing a black cape with a leopard skin collar. The sparkle of diamonds obscured the details of her face, but I could see that she had thick dark hair and she was beautiful. No scars or injuries. No trauma to her body. No bloodstains or torn clothing. She smiled slightly at Jack and gave him a slow, subtle wink. Then moving so gracefully she seemed to glide, Ann left in peace.

# Epilogue

# Changed Forever

We have occasional days now when we don't relive the horror of Ann's murder, but those days are still rare. Even as these times increase, we realize that we can never go back to the way we were. When Ann was murdered, we stepped into another world, the world of "somebody else," those people we always assumed were victims of violent crimes. Now when we read and hear about victims, we realize that they were once people who watched the news and assumed that crimes happened to others. And they felt safe.

We hoped that the verdict would erase memories and images, but we're now resigned to carrying them with us.

Closure has a new definition. It's remembering Ann without our *first* thoughts centering on her death. It's regaining the happy, funny, loving, intense memories of someone we love. Clean and unblemished by horror and regret. Even if only for a few seconds before images of the murder flood our consciousness.

Before January 12, 2003, closure for us was a word tossed around on television crime shows and the 11:00 news. But now, Jack and I understand the depths of its meaning. Until a door can be closed completely, we see just enough to keep us focused on what's on the other side. Justice can close the door and redirect our focus, but it doesn't remove the memories beyond the door.

Knowing exactly what happened to Ann would have brought us abrupt and powerful closure, but the conviction was healing, as well. Whether a door is slammed shut or quietly pulled to, closing it makes all the difference.

Finally, we can think of Ann without thinking first of the murder, even though for now, those unblemished memories are short. These brief respites are like the tiny buds of spring that signal new life.

# Acknowledgements

Most literary works are like the classic children's tale *Stone Soup*. It tells of three soldiers who come to a village, asking for food. The villagers declare that they have absolutely nothing in their pantries, with which the soldiers counter, "Then we'll make stone soup." The soldiers toss some stones into a giant kettle, add water, and kindle a fire. The hungry villagers observe the proceedings, eager to see and taste the magical meal.

After a while, the soldiers observe, "If only we had a potato or two, this stone soup would taste even better."

"I may have some potatoes," a villager offers. After the potatoes are added and the hearty fragrance wafts through the village, the soldiers make the same observation about carrots. Again a villager responds. And on and on until the plain, tasteless water becomes a delicious soup that feeds the entire village.

An author comes with a big pot and some stones. Others fill the pot with their stories, research, observations and insights. The author cooks, stirs and presents the story as his or her own. But it's the others who add the richness.

Following are those who brought nourishment to this book:

My husband, Jack. He was my fellow navigator through a world of murder, disillusionment and deceit. A world we never dreamed we'd enter. But once that gruesome door opened, we walked through it together and steadied each other with every step. Jack willingly, though sometimes painfully, shared the memories and insights that make this book honest. He shared his expertise as a federal law enforcement officer and private investigator to make it accurate. He shared the encouragement and support that completed it.

Our children, Penny LeBaron and Dave Branson (known to his friends as Adam). Throughout the murder, the investigation, and the trial, our children never stopped praying and prodding. They would not have allowed us to give up, if we had been so inclined.

And our grandsons, Taylor and Elliott LeBaron. Their sweet recollections of Aunt Ann helped keep her in the forefront of all we did. Knowing what was taken from them made us diligent in seeking justice.

My mom, Catherine Kinney. She taught me the joy of reading and the therapy of writing. Because she'd raised me to do so, I began journaling my thoughts the day after Ann's murder. When I eventually began this book, I relied on endless written pages instead of memory.

My prayer partners Linda Haas and Jen Rosania. Their prayers made it easier to rewrite painful pages, to face the awful portions of the story, and to wait more than four years for justice.

Sonia McGowen. She used her knowledge of and connections to her native Costa Rica to help us many times.

Kentucky State Police detective Ben Wolcott. He kept the investigation alive and shared information when no one else would. He's truly one of the good guys.

Scott Troutman, Kelley Rager, Shawn Bean, and some others at the Madisonville Police Deparment. Though we worked parallel and unaware of each others' dedication, we know now that they, too, cared deeply about Ann and worked tirelessly to bring about justice.

Ed Williamson and Jimmy Bryan. They took criticism for their good work and helped bring us the closure that for so long seemed elusive.

FBI Special Agent Bill Frank. He provided information on several occasions and kept his part of the investigation moving.

*America's Most Wanted.* Their involvement piqued the interest of others. Until *AMW* agreed to profile the case, it was growing cold despite our efforts.

Kentucky Commonwealth attorney David Massamore and his extraordinary prosecution team: Kathy Senter, Bryan Hart, Amy Jones, Lisa Harris, and Charlie Weatherford. They made Ann's murder personal.

The Madisonville *Messenger*, Don Perryman and other reporters, and photographers Jim Pearson and Lowell Mendyk. They faithfully kept the story before the people of Madisonville.

Our daughter, Penny, and our good friends Bob and Ruth Hall. They proofed and edited and offered invaluable suggestions. They were true partners in the process.

Our agent, Maryann Karinch. Agents find publishers for books. Good agents give literary advice that makes books better. Great agents become partners through the entire process. Maryann, you're great.

Dr. Joan S. Dunphy and New Horizon Press. They shared our excitement for this project and moved it quickly and smoothly through the production process.

Madisonville, Kentucky. They were small, and they were inexperienced in violent crime. But they were the town that never stopped caring.

To Jack, Penny, Dave, Taylor, Elliott, Mom, Jen, Linda, Sonia, Ben, Scott, Kelley, Shawn, Ed, Jimmy, Bill, *AMW*, David, Kathy, Bryan, Amy, Lisa, Charlie, Don, Jim, Lowell, Bob, Ruth, Randy, Maryann, Joan, Madisonville: You wrote it. I just put it together.